Christian Schools

How to Get a School Going and Keep It Growing

Dennis M. Demuth
Carol M. Demuth

PUBLISHED BY:
DEL Publications
5747 South Utica, Suite 101
Tulsa OK 74105-8038

All scriptures contained herein, unless otherwise noted, are from the *King James Version* of the Bible.

Library of Congress Catalog Card Number: 94-94547
Demuth, Dennis M.
   Christian Schools: How to Get a School Going and Keep It Growing/
Dennis M. Demuth, Carol M. Demuth
   p. cm.
   Includes Index.
   1. Private schools–United States. 2. School management and
organization
LB
371.020973—dc20   94–94547
ISBN 1-880705-05-2

Printed and bound in the United States of America.

For more information about other Christian School Publications, write or call:

DEL Publications
5747 South Utica, Suite 101
Tulsa, OK 74105-8038
(918) 749-2157

Table of Contents

About the Authors

Dennis M. Demuth, Ph.D., has been involved in Christian education since 1972. Over the past 23 years Dr. Demuth has served in a number of different positions including teacher, school psychologist, principal, Superintendent of Schools, educational consultant, Minister of Education, Director of Christian Education, and Director of Development and Information Services. He has taught at several institutions of higher education and currently serves as adjunct associate professor in Christian School Administration at Oral Roberts University, Tulsa, OK. His book, *Legal Requirements for Christian Schools*, is being used by Christian schools in all 50 states. *Recruiting Strategies for Christian Schools: How To Recruit and Retain Students* and *Microcomputer Applications for Christian Educators* are among his most recent works. Since 1985, Dr. Demuth has been actively involved in the International Christian Accrediting Association (ICAA), serving as member of the Board, Commissioner and Accreditation Site Team Chairman.

Carol M. Demuth, Ed.D., received her degree in higher education administration from Oklahoma State University. She has been active in Christian education for many years, serving as teacher and administrator. She serves as adjunct assistant professor in Christian School Administration at Oral Roberts University. She has co-authored several books with her husband, Dennis. Her most recent works include, *GranDees: A School-Based Volunteer Program* and *Legal Requirements for Christian Schools*.

The authors have written this book from the perspective of Christian school educators. The book is distributed with the understanding that the publisher and the authors are not rendering legal, accounting, or other professional service. When legal advice or other expert assistance is required, the services of a qualified professional should be sought.

Dedication

This book is dedicated to the first staff members of Abundant Life Christian School (ALCS)—Donna Balfanz, Linda Turner, Faye Alexander and Carol Beckmann, co-laborers in the first Christian school in which we were privileged to serve.

"Now he that planteth and he that watereth are one: and every man shall receive his own reward according to his own labour.

"For we are labourers together with God: ye are God's husbandry, ye are God's building" (1 Cor. 3:8,9).

Abundant Life Christian School (ALCS) is the result of the vision of Rev. Warren Heckman, Pastor of Lake City Church in Madison, Wisconsin. ALCS began in 1978 with an enrollment of 45 students in grades kindergarten through sixth. Over the years, ALCS has grown in quantity and quality. Enrollment is topping 400 students in kindergarten through twelfth grade and 340 students in its daycare and preschool programs.

"Though thy beginning was small, yet thy latter end should greatly increase" (Job 8:7).

How To Use This Book

This book contains ten chapters. Each chapter relates to an important step in starting a Christian school ministry. There are numerous checklists throughout the book. The authors encourage schools to use these checklists to assess their own program. Schools starting for the first time can use these same checklists to identify important ingredients for building a solid Christian school foundation. Established schools can profit from these checklists by pinpointing areas to strengthen.

It is our goal to make this book a working text for pastors, school board members, administrators and other school leaders. Use the new school checklist found in Appendix B to identify tasks to accomplish. Transfer those tasks needing completion to the School Action Plan found in Appendix C. This plan provides for a task objective, the person responsible for completing the task, strategies to follow and timelines for completion. We are confident that as you follow this plan you will accomplish your goal of establishing a Christian school or strengthening one that is already in existence.

Since it is nearly impossible to place in a single volume all the information essential to establishing a successful Christian school ministry, we have created a special Christian School Resource Kit containing sample documents referred to in each chapter. Brackets identify these items, for example, [CSRK 6.1]. The reference number in each set of brackets identifies the document located in the Christian School Resource Kit. There are over 150 such references. Realizing the need for more information, the authors have written two companion books—*Legal Requirements for Christian Schools*, and *Recruiting Strategies for Christian Schools*, expanding upon the information contained in Chapters three and five. Another resource tool that has proven very useful is *Christian School Administration: Administrator and Teacher Guide*. This guide contains 186 pages of Christian day school policies and procedures covering over 100 topics.

Found throughout the book are hundreds of recommendations for getting a school going and keeping it growing. These are usually found as numbered items or bullets. Although the authors would like to expound on every item, the goal is to provide as many suggestions as space allows and to encourage administrators, board members, pastors and other school leaders to prayerfully consider those suggestions that would work for their particular school ministry. Also contained at the end of the chapter are administrative pitfalls to avoid. These pitfalls are based on personal experiences. It is the authors' desire that you would be able to avoid each of these pitfalls.

Printed at the end of each chapter is a prayer of agreement. Jesus said,

> **"Again I say unto you, That if two of you shall agree on earth as touching any thing that they shall ask, it shall be done for them of my Father which is in heaven"** (Matt. 18:19).

The authors welcome comments and personal testimonies of how the information in this book helps in getting Christian schools going and strengthening those that exist. Forward all comments and testimonies to DEL Publications.

Preface

God has said by His Spirit,

"In these last days I am raising up an Army that will go out and possess the land. Part of this mighty Army are the children who are being trained within Christian schools. These young people will be for signs and wonders that will cause many to come to acknowledge Christ as Lord. They are the ones who will do mighty exploits for God.

"The students in these schools will go out under the anointing of the Holy Spirit, empowered to do the works of Jesus, knowing their authority in Christ and using the Word with great effectiveness. These students will not boast or glory in their own skill or wisdom; rather, they will glory in the fact that they know and understand Me, and that I am a rewarder of those who diligently seek Me.

"From these schools will come a new generation of students who will move in and take over the schools, churches, universities and corporations and will literally do the ministry of Jesus.

"My Spirit is searching this world over, looking for men and women whose hearts are humbled before Me, who are willing to be obedient to the voice of My Spirit. It will be these men and women whom I will call to give birth to a new generation of Christian schools" (August, 1985).

STEP 1

IDENTIFY YOUR PURPOSE

It was the first week of August. A pastor and three members of his congregation were coming to visit from a nearby community. Like so many before them, their interest was in establishing a Christian school ministry in their community.

After making introductions and seating everyone, I asked the pastor where we might start. He responded, "God said to start a Christian school. We are here to find out how." It was pleasing to hear him say it was God who had spoken to him to begin this ministry. Most Christian educators would agree, "This is the only foundation on which you can build a successful Christian school ministry."[1]

Clarify Your Reasons for Starting a School

Throughout history there have been many reasons given for establishing Christian schools. Two of the most prevalent include the decaying moral standards and the declining academic standards of public schools. Others justify starting a Christian school in fulfillment of scriptural mandates.

Decaying Moral Standards

A major reason given for starting a Christian school is to provide an alternative for the declining moral standards of the secular schools. Parents of school age children place pressure on the local church to start a Christian school to protect their children from drugs, alcohol, sex and violence. Deuink and Herbster in their book, *Effective Christian School Management*, conclude, "Unfortunately...Christian schools have been started and supported by many well-meaning Christian people solely to escape the evils of public education."[2]

Believing children in Christian schools will not be exposed to these influences is a misconception. Worldly influences will be pulling at youngsters from all directions—unstable home situations, peer pressure, television, movies, video, magazines, music, etc. Even those children who are from what seem to be stable Christian homes may have tremendous conflict in their lives. As long as Christian children are in this world, its influences will affect them. It is near impossible to shelter a Christian student from the influences of the world. Even if the Christian school enrolls all Christian children, there is no guarantee the school would be free from worldly influences.

What then is the answer? Establish a school where educators, parents and students realize it is possible to be in this world, yet to live above

1

this world's system of influence. Jesus said in John 16:33, **"These things I have spoken unto you, that in me ye might have peace. In the world ye shall have tribulation: but be of good cheer; I have overcome the world."**

He continues in John 17: 11-16,

"And now I am no more in the world, but these are in the world, and I come to thee. Holy Father, keep through thine own name those whom thou hast given me, that they may be one, as we are.

"While I was with them in the world, I kept them in thy name: those that thou gavest me I have kept, and none of them is lost, but the son of perdition; that the scripture might be fulfilled.

"And now come I to thee; and these things I speak in the world, that they might have my joy fulfilled in themselves.

"I have given them thy word; and the world hath hated them, because they are not of the world, even as I am not of the world.

"I pray not that thou shouldest take them out of the world, but that thou shouldest keep them from the evil.

"They are not of the world, even as I am not of the world."

NOTE: *The excitement of a Christian school is in having the power of God operating through students and the curriculum and staff, resulting in lives changed and homes strengthened. Train Christian students to live above worldly influences.*

Declining Academic Standards

Others start Christian schools as an alternative to decaying academic standards found in secular schools. The National Commission on Excellence in Education stated bluntly, "A tide of mediocrity" has devastated public education. The report notes, "For the first time in the history of our country, the educational skills of one generation will not surpass, will not equal, will not even approach, those of their parents." "At risk," the commission's report concluded, is "our very future as a Nation and a people."[3]

Unfortunately, public schools have not gotten any better. David P. Gardner, former president of the University of California at Berkley and ten years ago the chairperson of the National Commission on Excellence in Education, in an interview with the Associated Press in April, 1993, stated, "We have not made progress of the kind and order we had hoped.

There needs to be renewed commitment to progress, an invigorated determination to make improvements."[4]

Tim LaHaye in his book, *The Battle for the Family*, comments, "The public-school system, once the most successful of its kind in the world (when it was based on traditional moral values), has during the past sixty years, become the third most destructive force in America, at least where the family is concerned."[5] He lists humanistic thought, absence of the Bible and prayer, socialist un-American one-world view, obsession with sex education, anti-moral teachings of values clarification, violence, crime, drugs and pornography as the major parental concerns.

Following the collapse of the Iron Curtain, several countries, such as Russia and Albania, openly welcome the Christian philosophy of education into their schools. Yet, American schools openly reject the basics of Christianity—the Bible and Prayer. The very fact that secular education leaves God out of education tells the student that God is not important, that is, God has no place in science, history, math and language. "Education that leaves out God is counterfeit. An education without God will not spend in the marketplace of life."[6]

Many pastors and Christian parents have the general belief that the purpose of a Christian education is to provide an academically "good" education. The goal is to gain wisdom and knowledge so students might graduate, go to college, find a job, raise a family, be good citizens, contribute something worthwhile to society and be active in church. Often schools with this purpose end up being Christian in name only.

We are not suggesting that academics are less important: a strong academic program is central to building and maintaining a quality Christian school. However, there is more to a Christian school than academics.

Pastors, parents and Christian educators must realize that apart from God there is no lasting wisdom. God through his servant Jeremiah said, **"The wise men are ashamed, they are dismayed and taken: lo, they have rejected the word of the LORD; and what wisdom is in them?"** (Jeremiah 8:9). Furthermore, the Bible says **"For the wisdom of this world is foolishness before God. For it is written, He is the one who catches the wise in their craftiness and again the Lord knows the reasonings of the wise, that they are useless."** (1 Cor. 3:19,20, NASB).

It becomes clear, knowledge apart from God brings no lasting peace for Christian students. A good academic education will bring only temporary happiness but no lasting joy. It will cram and load their minds with facts only to realize 80 percent of the knowledge they accumulate would most likely never be used, and surely, never prepare them for eternity.

Fulfilling the Scriptures

There have been those pastors and parents who have diligently sought the scriptures to justify starting a Christian school, only to conclude, "God does not issue any command for starting Christian schools." However, the Word of God does have much to say about the education of children. For example, God's command on teaching and training is found in Deuteronomy 6:7:

> **"And you shalt teach them diligently unto thy children, and shalt talk of them when thou sittest in thine house, and when thou walkest by the way, and when thou liest down, and when thou risest up."**

Again in Proverbs 22:6, God said, **"(You) train up a (your) child in the way he should go; and when he is old, he will not depart from it."** God did not say "a way"; He said, "The Way." This leaves no alternatives!

Furthermore, God left no options. He said, **"... learn not the way of the heathen..."** (Jeremiah 10:2). The way of the heathen is the way propagated by humanistic progressive education that invades secular schools, retracting the Bible from its midst, rejecting the concrete and personal revelation of God in Jesus Christ, rebelling against the holy and moral standards of the universe as found in the Bible, refusing to accept or recognize the validity of religious knowledge and experience (in some states even removing celebrations of Christmas and Easter), and removing the dignity and worth of a man as a being created by God.[7]

Knowing that all the treasures of wisdom and knowledge are hidden in Jesus Christ (Colossians 2:3), God emphatically tells parents to see that their children **"Cease, my son, to hear the instruction that causeth to err from the words of knowledge"** (Proverbs 19:27). Furthermore, Christian parents are not to allow their children to be taken captive by the world's philosophies and vain deceptions of men; rather, they are to be rooted and built up in Christ Jesus and established in the faith (See Colossians 2:6-8). The responsibility for a Christian education rests squarely upon the shoulders of parents (Psalm 78; Ephesians 6). This responsibility includes more than an academically sound education.

Thus, the Christian school becomes a God, Christ, and Holy Spirit centered institution, imparting the spiritual convictions of the parents. Also, the Christian school must go beyond just providing a Christ-centered environment where learning takes place; all learning and training must be provided in light of God's uncompromised Word where the secular and sacred are not separated but are interwoven into a lifestyle that leads to words, thoughts, and actions that bring glory to the Creator-God.

H. Gene Garrick, Pastor, Tabernacle Church of Norfolk, and Chairman of the Board, Norfolk Christian Schools, points to the purpose of the Christian school,

> "(The Christian school) is to give a completely God-centered orientation of life to the student, to develop a thoroughly Christian and biblical world view, to create, under God, a Christian mind. Other goals subservient to this are: teaching him to read, helping social adjustment, preparation for marriage and work. These very necessary goals must have the over-arching goal of his thinking and living as a genuine Christian. This is the purpose of his existence. It follows that a thoroughly Christian view of the world and all of life is required to accomplish these goals. This view must permeate the life of the school and its students to create that Christian mind and life-style."[8]

H. W. Byrne author of *A Christian Approach to Education* says:

> "Christian education is seeing things as God sees them. It is thinking God's thoughts after Him...It is to show God revealed. The immediate objective of education is to qualify man to reveal God. This is comprehensive because it involves man in his total being—physically, mentally, socially, morally, and spiritually—in his total environment. It includes both information and training. The ultimate objective for education is the Kingdom of God to come."[9]

We would go one step farther by adding, the purpose of a Christian education is to bring students to the realization that the Kingdom of God has come and it is in their earthen vessels. The life of Jesus is made manifest in the body of each Christian young person:

> **"For God, who commanded the light to shine out of dark-ness, hath shined in our hearts, to give the light of the knowledge of the glory of God in the face of Jesus Christ.**

> **"But we have this treasure in earthen vessels, that the excellency of the power may be of God, and not of us"** (2 Cor. 4:6,7).

Adopt God's Plan for Christian Education

Many educators trace the Christian school movement back to the colonial days. However, God's plan for educating Christian young people goes far beyond the views of most Christian educators—a plan starting with Adam, God's first pupil.

God's plan for education begins at the time of creation. God, Who is a spirit, created man as a spirit being in His likeness and after His kind. He breathed into an earthen vessel the **"breath of life"** (Gen. 2:7). Having been created in the image and likeness of God, man was a spirit being who could live as long as God lived; as such, he was a companion of God, created to associate with deity (Psalm 8:5). God made contact with man through man's spirit. He placed man in a position to exercise dominion on the earth, to actually rule nature in the same manner as the Father and the Son later demonstrated. In essence, man was a spirit being in an earthen vessel with senses that could experience the revealed greatness of his Creator-God.

The entrance of sin resulted in corruption of man's position with God. Romans 5:12-14 says,

> **"Therefore, just as through one man sin entered the world, and death through sin, and thus death spread to all men, because all sinned—**

> **"For until the law sin was in the world, but sin is not imputed when there is no law.**

> **"Nevertheless death reigned from Adam to Moses, even over those who had not sinned according to the likeness of the transgression of Adam, who is a type of Him who was to come"** (NKJV).

As a result of sin, man became dulled to God's voice. Not only was man separated from God, spiritual death resulted, and the process of physical death began. Man became subject to the curse and law, and God was no longer able to talk and communicate with man Spirit to spirit (Rom. 8:7,8). While in this condition, man became dominated by his sense-ruled body and mind—much of the humanistic thought prevalent in secular schools is a logical outgrowth of this domination.

Through the plan of redemption, all that God intended for man that was lost, was restored. We read in Romans (5:17,18, NKJV),

> **"For if by one man's offense death reigned through the one, much more those who receive abundance of grace and of the gift of righteousness will reign in life through the One, Jesus Christ.**

> **"Therefore, as through one man's offense judgment came to all men, resulting in condemnation, even so through one**

Man's righteous act the free gift came to all men, resulting in justification of life. "

At the point of salvation, a person is given a new spirit (heart). He is no longer a slave to his senses. At the same time, the Holy Spirit is released to make His home in the physical body. When given the right of way, the Holy Spirit dominates the recreated human spirit. We refer to the work of the Holy Spirit in the educational process as Spirit-Directed Education and is the subject of a book in preparation with the same title.

In God's plan for education, the Holy Spirit plays a major part. Jesus said:

"But the Comforter, which is the Holy Ghost, whom the Father will send in my name, He shall teach all things, and bring all things to your remembrance, whatsoever I have said unto you" (John 14:26).

When the Holy Spirit is free, He facilitates the teaching and makes learning happen (1 John 2:20,27). The moment the human spirit is recreated, the mind begins the renewal process and is brought back into fellowship with the recreated spirit. With the senses being brought back into subjection to the spirit, control is regained over the body and senses, and once again the revelation knowledge of God can be received (1 Cor. 2:1-16). God could once again communicate with His creation.

It is God's desire to reveal Himself and His creation to man. However, revelation knowledge means nothing to the man of sense knowledge, just like a noisy radio means nothing to a deaf person. Without revelation knowledge, natural man only sees things of God as foolishness (1 Cor. 2:14). It is revelation knowledge that is the foundation for understanding of miracles, creative faith, saving faith, righteousness, dominion, and the very wisdom of God, without which, man will not achieve the dominion level that God originally intended. It is the Holy Spirit that reveals God's wisdom to us (1 Cor. 2:6-12).

Claude E. Schindler Jr. and Pacheco Pyle in their book, *Educating for Eternity,* comment:

"In most of what we have been taught and most of what we do today, our minds lead, not our spirit. Most of us have been so brainwashed by the god of reason that we find it very difficult to appreciate that the most important thing we can do for our young people (and in fact, for ourself) is to develop the spirit part of us so that it can lead our lives."[10]

NOTE: *God's plan calls for Christian schools that are willing to train and develop the spirit of their Christian children—*

*placing the student in a position so he/she can receive the full
revelation of God, and like Jesus, be able to do the will of the
Father.*

Hear From God

As a pastor, a parent, or even a seasoned school administrator, you
must hear from God and "know that you know that you know" God said
to start a Christian school. When you know it was God who said to start
the school and not a person, you can have confidence the school will be
a success.

It has been said, "God does not sponsor any flops." As long as you
incorporate God in the planning and development of the school, your
efforts will be successful. When you receive God's plan, you can be
confident it is already blessed [CSRK 1.1].

You might be asking yourself, "How do I know it is God who is
speaking to me to start a Christian school?" We're believing that before
you finish this book the Holy Spirit will minister to you, and you will
know the answer to your question.

As you focus your attention on those items in the upcoming chapters,
allow the Holy Spirit to quicken your understanding about the specific
plans He desires for your school. Job 32:8 declares, "**But there is a
spirit in man: and the inspiration of the Almighty giveth them
understanding.**" Paul says, "**But God hath revealed them** (the plans)
**unto us by his Spirit: for the Spirit searcheth all things, yea, the deep
things of God**" (1 Cor. 2:10). God wants you to know His master plan
for your school. Once you believe God wants you to know His will, you
are well on your way, for God has an avenue of faith through which He
can speak to you.

Psalm 37:23 says, "**The steps of a good man are ordered by the
Lord....**" If God said your steps are ordered, then they are. Accepting
this truth builds confidence in the decisions you are making. We read in
1 John 5:14,15:

> "**And this is the confidence that we have in him, that, if we
> ask any thing according to his will, he heareth us:**
>
> "**And if we know that he hear us, whatsoever we ask, we
> know that we have the petitions that we desired of him.**"

Jeremiah 33:3 exhorts: "**Call unto me,and I will answer thee, and
shew thee great and mighty things....**" God said, you ask, and I'll
show! Do you want to know how to get your school started? God said
He would give you an answer. Right now, let's pause for a point of
agreement. God said if two shall agree as touching anything, it will be

done unto them (Matthew 18:19).

> Father, I purpose in my heart to hear Your voice about giving birth to a new Christian school ministry. The voice of a stranger I will not hear. It is Your voice that directs my pathway. Your Word says if I stray to the left or to the right of Your perfect will, I will hear a voice saying, this is the way, walk in it. I purpose to walk in the direction You lead. Amen.

It was clear from the voice of this pastor and from the smile on his face that he had in fact heard the voice of the Master. A new school was in the making.

Consider God's Timing

In answering his question, "What do I do next?" I asked my own question, "What have you already done up to this point?" He responded, "As much as I know to do, which has been asking these ladies to come with me. I was hoping that together we would find out what to do to have a school like yours." "Yes," I said, "Over time, it is possible to have a quality Christian school" (which then had an enrollment of 600 students).

"When do you plan to open?" I asked. His answer was enough to shake any seasoned administrator, "This September!" (Remember, this is only the first week in August.) My response was, "Surely you must be mistaken. I know of schools that had been set up and operational in as little as four months, but four weeks is pressing it a little too close. Most schools take at least a year to plan. Two years would be even better."

In the minutes that followed, it was evident that the pastor hadn't even presented the idea of starting a Christian school to the church board. For all he knew, the church would have to amend its by-laws to proceed. Knowing how some boards and congregations operate, amending church by-laws might take weeks, especially if the sponsoring church body exhibits a faction opposed to Christian schools.

During the conversation that followed, it was obvious there were no proposed school constitution, by-laws, or an organizational chart. The public interest and interest of the church body had not been stimulated. No recruitment rally had been conducted. The state laws relating to a private school had not been researched: city zoning laws may even prohibit a school on the church site. No thought had been given to facilities. Books had not been selected. No supplies had been ordered, and no teachers were hired. Four weeks to the opening of school—No way!

I spent the next four hours outlining a mountain of tasks needing to be accomplished within the next four weeks in order for the church to open the doors of a new Christian school, hoping to get the pastor to reconsider. He may have heard from God, but surely God did not mean for him to have the doors open in September of the same year. After all, the pastor was only human. There was no humanly way possible that it could be done. It would truly take the supernatural intervention of God.

When it became obvious the pastor was serious about starting a Christian school, I asked him to respond to a survey to see if he really understood what he was getting himself into. If you plan to start a Christian school in the future, we recommend you complete the survey found in Appendix A before proceeding. (This survey is also an excellent tool for newly established schools.) Once you complete the survey, count the number of "Yes" responses. If you have 30 or more "Yes" responses, you are well on your way to seeing your school open on time. If you count between 20 and 29, you should be able to make it as long as you don't faint! However, if you have fewer than 20 "Yes" responses by the end of April of the year you plan to open, you have a mountain before you, as was the case for this pastor.

After completing the new school survey, the Pastor was wondering whether or not there was sufficient time to get everything completed. The long list of items marked "No"was overwhelming. For some, such a list might even discourage them from starting a Christian school. Not this Pastor; even when he saw all the tasks involved in starting a new school, he was convinced it was God's timing, and with His help, they could pull it off.

If you are not 100 percent sure about starting a new Christian school ministry, it is better to postpone the start date. Starting a Christian school is a matter of determining God's perfect timing. When God gives you the timetable for the doors to be opened, you can rest assured there is a way it can be accomplished.

To make an exciting story short, this pastor and three members of his congregation went out of my office determined in their spirits to speak to every mountain and see it removed. **"For assuredly, I say to you, whoever says to this mountain, 'Be removed and be cast into the sea,' and does not doubt in his heart, but believes that those things he says will come to pass, he will have whatever he says"** (Mark 11:23, NKJV).

By end of the first week in September, the doors of the school opened with an enrollment of thirty-two students. In its second year of operation, the school doubled in size and has been growing ever since.

Place Your Trust in God

What we are sharing with you is the birthing of a new Christian school founded upon the direction of the Spirit of God. There is a specific plan for each Christian school. **"'For I know the plans I have for you, declares the Lord, plans to prosper you and not to harm you, plans to give you hope and a future'"** (Jeremiah 29:11, NIV). Furthermore, God says, **"I will instruct you and teach you in the way you should go; I will counsel you and watch over you"** (Psalm 32:8, NIV).

God's plan calls for bringing into existence a new breed of Christian schools, ones to help usher in the return of Christ. In these schools are students training to be mighty men and women used by God for signs and wonders. **"Behold, I and the children whom the Lord hath given me are for signs and for wonders..."** (Isaiah 8:18).

These students are to be examples in word, love, spirit, faith and purity. They will go forth in boldness to do the works of Jesus—healing the brokenhearted, bringing deliverance, recovering sight to the blind, setting at liberty those that are bruised, casting our devils, speaking with new tongues, laying hands on the sick and having power over the enemy (Luke 4:18, 10:19; Mark 16:17; 1 John 5:14).

They will be ten times better than students educated under the world's educational system. Daniel 1:20 says, **"And in all matters of wisdom and understanding, that the king inquired of them, he found them ten times better than all the magicians and astrologers that were in all his realm."**

In Proverbs 16:9 it says, **"A man's heart deviseth his way: but the LORD directeth his steps."** In the Amplified, it says, **"A man's mind plans his way, but the Lord directs his steps and makes them sure."** God's desire is for your steps to be blessed, victorious and triumphant—this includes the steps in getting your school going and keeping it growing.

Proverbs 3:5,6 declares,

"Trust in the LORD with all thine heart; and lean not unto thine own understanding.

"In all thy ways acknowledge him, and he shall direct thy paths."

The remainder of this book contains nine chapters (Steps), presenting information shared with this pastor and many like him. No one book could contain all there is to know about starting and administrating a Christian school. This book provides enough information to point the way to a successful beginning—determining the organizational structure, assessing legal requirements, obtaining adequate facilities, determining the size of the student body, developing an income and spending plan, selecting teachers, planning the curriculum, establishing ancillary programs and making final preparations for opening day.

Pitfalls to Avoid

1. Failing to write down and to communicate the vision of the Christian school. Habakkuk directs,

> "And the LORD answered me, and said, Write the vision, and make it plain upon tables, that he may run that readeth it.

> "For the vision is yet for an appointed time, but at the end it shall speak, and not lie: though it tarry, wait for it; because it will surely come, it will not tarry" (Habakkuk 2:2,3).

The vision gives purpose and meaning for existence. It serves as the base for building a strong Christian school ministry where every aspect of the school becomes an outgrowth of the vision, shaping every thought and decision. Therefore, one of the first tasks is to clearly define the vision in terms that can be easily understood. For example, the vision for Victory Christian School is

> "To provide a place to train, prepare, and equip young people to take the ministry of Jesus to the ends of the earth, whether it be as a preacher, pastor, evangelist, prophet, apostle, teacher, or as a nurse, technician, educator, or businessman.

> "In an environment of quality academics and strong discipline, students will be trained to witness their faith, share Jesus effectively with others, and love hurting people. They will be taught to operate in the gifts of the Spirit, to minister the healing power of God, to minister deliverance to those that are bound by devils and to be trained to walk in standards of holiness.

> "We realize the solemn responsibility under God to carry out this vision. We look for parents and students who are in agreement with this vision, for without this agreement, our vision cannot be fulfilled" (Billy Joe Daugherty, 1979).

The planning guide found in the Christian School Resource Kit will help pastors and administrators translate a vision into a statement of purpose [CSRK 1.2]. This statement of purpose forms the foundation for planning your school.[11]

2. Establishing a Christian school without a clearly defined philosophy of Christian education. In a classical sense, a philosophy is a system of thought and interpretation; it is what you think and believe. These form the basis for action and practice. Proverbs 23:7 says, **"For as he thinketh in his heart, so is he...."** Jesus said behavior and speech were directed by the heart and mind (Luke 6:45).

Your actions within all aspects of the school should be consistent with your philosophy so your "talked about" philosophy is congruent with your "working" philosophy. Educators who do not have a specific philosophy of Christian education, will by default, base their thoughts and pattern their actions after the systems under which they were trained [CSRK 1.3]. Unless trained at a Christian college or university, the philosophy of default will be that which Paul warns about: **"See to it that no one takes you captive through hollow and deceptive philosophy, which depends on human tradition and basic principles of this world rather than on Christ"** (Col. 2:8, NIV). This is the philosophy propagated by progressive education that encompasses humanistic ideology, new-age thought, politically correct thinking and the new world order.

Knowing what God's Word says about teaching and training provides a foundation upon which to build a strong Christian approach to education. It furnishes the platform for developing educational goals and selecting the curriculum. Allowing the entire uncompromised Word of God to be brought to bear on the educational process will truly make it Christian.

Three strong resources useful in helping you formulate your philosophy of Christian education are Paul A. Kienel's book, _The Philosophy of Christian Education_, H.W. Bryne's work, _A Christian Approach to Education_, and A. A. Baker's book, _The Successful Christian School_. Once you have determined your Christian philosophy of education, write it down. _Recruiting Strategies for Christian Schools_ provides several strategies for communicating your philosophy to students, parents, staff and the community.

> Father, Your Word says that I can do all things through Christ Who strengthens me. Therefore, I can accomplish the task that You have set before me. I put my trust in You. I cannot do this task in my own strength, but in Your strength and in Your ability. Your Word says that I am more than a conqueror; therefore, I believe that I am a conqueror over every obstacle, over every adversity and over every mountain the enemy would try to bring against me to see this school not succeed. You have made it possible for me to always triumph

in You no matter how many tasks need to be accomplished. Let my spirit be sensitive to the leading of Your Spirit as Your plans are revealed.

> **It is up to you to allow your spirit to be sensitive to the voice of God. He will bring understanding in all events pertaining to getting a Christian school going and keeping it growing. Allow your spirit to go beyond the information presented in this book. By doing so, you will begin setting the stage for a Spirit-directed Christian school.**

Christian School Resource Kit

1.1   God's Plans Are Blessed
1.2   Statement of Purpose Planning Guide
1.3   Statement of Philosophy

Endnotes

1   A.A. Baker. *The Successful Christian School*. Pensacola, FL: A Beka Book Publications, 1979, p. 16.

2   James W. Deuink and Carl D. Herbster. *Effective Christian School Management*, 2nd Edition. Greenville, SC: Bob Jones University Press, 1986, p. 8.

3   National Commission on Excellence in Education. "A Nation at Risk." Washington, DC: U.S. Government Printing Office, 1983, p. 36.

4   David P. Gardner. Quoted in "Educators Say U.S. Still Nation at Risk." Tulsa, OK: *Tulsa World*, April 25, 1993, p. 14.

5   Tim LaHaye. *The Battle for the Family*. Old Tappan, NJ: Fleming H. Revell Company, 1982, p. 87.

6   Billy Joe Daugherty. "Christian Education Today." Presentation given at the Oral Roberts University Educational Fellowship, 1984.

7   David L. Hocking. "The Theological Basis for the Philosophy of Christian School Education" in Paul A Kienel, *The Philosophy of Christian Education*. Whittier, CA: ACSI, 1971, p. 9.

8   H. Gene Garrick. "The Administrator as Philosophical Leader" in Roy W. Lowrie, Jr., Editor, *Administration of the Christian School*, Whittier, CA: ACSI, 1984, p. 12.

9   H. W. Byrne, *A Christian Approach To Education*. Milford, MI: Mott Media, 1961, p. 48.

10   Claude E. Schindler and Pacheco Pyle. *Educating for Eternity*. Whittier, CA: ACSI, 1979, p. 48.

11   R. Henry Migliore. "The Use of Strategic Planning in Churches and Ministries." Tulsa, OK: Oral Roberts University, 1985.

References

Dennis M. Demuth and Carol M. Demuth, *Recruiting Strategies for Christian Schools*. Tulsa, OK: DEL Publications, 1993.

Kienel, Paul A., Ed. *The Philosophy of Christian School Education*. Whittier, CA: Association of Christian Schools International (ACSI), 1978.

Kienel, Paul A. *Your Questions Answered About Christian Schools*. Whittier, CA: Association of Christian Schools International (ACSI), 1983.

Kienel, Paul A. *Reasons for Christian Schools*. Milford, MI: Mott Media, 1981.

STEP 2

DETERMINE THE ORGANIZATIONAL STRUCTURE

The way a school is organized determines the locus of control and provides structure for carrying out its educational purpose. The school may be a stand-alone unit arranged as a K-6, K-8, K-12 or other combination, or part of a school system with several different schools feeding a common high school. Control of the school may rest with an individual, or a group of individuals (school board, Christian education board, Christian education committee, etc.) and be organized as an integral part of another organization, such as a church. The school also can be organized independent of another controlling or directing institution, such as a church or business group, where the school is considered as a separate legal entity.

Identify the Type of Sponsorship

Sponsorship of a Christian school may be from several different sources. The most common include: a group of parents or the business community, a single church, or a group of churches.

A Parent- or Business-Sponsored School

In this type of organization, parents or members of the business community who are interested in Christian education come together to set up a Christian school. A board is appointed; those serving on the board could be parents, teachers, members of the business community, or other community leaders. The board appoints a school administrator who manages the school.

A typical organizational structure would include school board, administrator, business manager, teachers and secretary. Depending upon the size of the school, additional administrative positions might include, elementary principal, secondary principal, athletic director, development officer, etc.

Church-Sponsored Schools

A church-sponsored school may be directly under church incorporation, or it can be separately incorporated, but closely controlled by the church (See Step 3—"Assess Legal Requirements," for more detail). The school may be housed in the same building, or located in a different building. It may operate under a separate budget, or be integrated as part of a larger church budget.

The complexity of the organizational structure will be related to the size of the school and sponsoring church. A typical small church-sponsored school includes board of trustees, school board, pastor, administrator, teachers and secretary. As the ministry expands, additional levels in the organization may be added.

Organizational Considerations

There are several advantages of organizing your Christian school as a church-sponsored school. Consider the following:

1   A church is the most logical institution besides the home for the parent to fulfill the scriptural command given to parents (Eph. 6:4).

2   The church usually has educational facilities as well as a functional organizational structure already in position.

3   It is the pastor who is in the best position to communicate the need for a Christ-centered education.

4   A bookkeeping system, legal structure and staff are already in place.

5   The church provides an umbrella of legal protection for the school.

6   Stewardship of the church building and furnishings expands since they are used by both entities.

7   The church congregation provides a potential pool of children for enrollment.

8   The members of the congregation can provide a source of expertise to help in the school development.

Select a Governing Board

It is possible to operate a school without a school board; but to operate a school without sound counsel is not good advice. The Word of God makes it plain there is wisdom in counsel, as Proverbs 11:14 states: **"Where no counsel is, the people fall: but in the multitude of counsellors there is safety."**

If you were a pastor, you would probably have a group of people who you look to for direction. It is this group that can provide the counsel you need in establishing a Christian school. It is important that those providing counsel are "tuned in" to your vision and can "hear the voice of the Spirit of God" and are not moved by their own ideas and traditions of men. If you already have an established church board, consider using this board or members of this board to help in formulating the school.

Determine School Board Functions

In many Christian schools, the school board plays a very active role

—exercising spiritual leadership, establishing policies, employing administrative, teaching and support staff, providing adequate facilities and equipment, maintaining fiscal stability and assuring the continual growth and development of the school. Some school boards, without an experienced administrator, literally have to run the school. This is especially true in schools where a new administrator has not had an opportunity to demonstrate his ability to administrate the school.

Active school boards will need to ensure that their focus is on establishing policies. They should leave the implementation of these policies to the school administrator. Once the school board establishes policy, the administrator works with faculty in developing procedures and rules for the day-to-day implementation of board policy. Boards that become involved in the daily management of the school, or in directly supervising teaching staff, only cause confusion. Where boards are not performing their function or are doing things that they should not do, it becomes the duty of the administration of the school to work with the board to bring about desirable change. [1]

Roy W. Lowrie, Jr. in his book, *Serving God on the Christian School Board*, brings into focus basic functions for Christian school board members and administrators. Although written nearly twenty years ago, this book is an absolute must for all Christian schools with school boards. Of special interest is the reporting of the results of a questionnaire sent to Christian school board presidents. If this survey were administered today, we believe the responses would be nearly the same. Figure 2.1 presents these survey results. [2] We encourage new schools to consider each of these challenge areas and to make plans to avoid them.

School Board Checklist

The following checklist can be of value to a new school in helping it formulate the structure and responsibilities of the school board. An established school will find the checklist beneficial in assessing the strength of its own school board. Place a check mark in the box if the item is true of your school board. [3]

☐ Qualifications for school board members are clearly defined. As a minimum, include the following items:

- A strong Christian testimony
- In agreement with the school's Christian philosophy of education
- Supportive of the purposes and objectives of the school
- Able to invest time in attending school board, committee meetings and school functions

Figure 2.1 School Board Problems

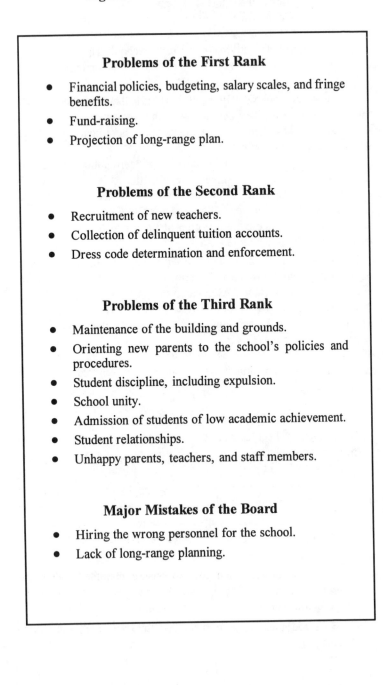

Problems of the First Rank

- Financial policies, budgeting, salary scales, and fringe benefits.
- Fund-raising.
- Projection of long-range plan.

Problems of the Second Rank

- Recruitment of new teachers.
- Collection of delinquent tuition accounts.
- Dress code determination and enforcement.

Problems of the Third Rank

- Maintenance of the building and grounds.
- Orienting new parents to the school's policies and procedures.
- Student discipline, including expulsion.
- School unity.
- Admission of students of low academic achievement.
- Student relationships.
- Unhappy parents, teachers, and staff members.

Major Mistakes of the Board

- Hiring the wrong personnel for the school.
- Lack of long-range planning.

- Willing to accept leadership responsibility
- Support the school program by enrolling his own children

It is advantageous to have board members who have expertise in a certain area of knowledge (for example, financial, legal) or the motivation to do the necessary research about complex situations [CSRK 2.1].

☐ School board members agree with the school's Statement of Faith as evidenced by a signed school Statement of Faith.

☐ Written job descriptions are present for board members, officers and each committee [CSRK 2.2].

☐ New school board members receive a complete orientation before assuming board responsibilities. For example: history, staff, policies, budget, program, long-range plans, school calendar, etc. [CSRK 2.3].

☐ School board by-laws are current. By-laws should include as a minimum:

- Organization structure of the Board
- Lines of authority, power and duties
- Election of officers
- Appointment of committees
- Duties of officers
- Methods of operation

☐ By-laws are enforced. Ensure school board by-laws are strictly enforced, especially those areas providing the greatest legal risk, such as frequency of board meetings, minutes of meetings and required board action [CSRK 2.4].

☐ School board elections provide for continuity over time. For example: members elected for a three- to four-year term. Deuink and Herbster provide the following points of wisdom. "Unrestricted reelection can lead to strong boards, unresponsive to the concerns of others. Simultaneous election of all members risks turnover that could rob the organization of valuable experience. Staggered terms protect the board from single-interest groups."[4]

☐ By-laws are reviewed each year to ensure that they follow the nonprofit code in effect in your state, for example, tax and corporate law, securities laws, etc.

☐ School board meetings are scheduled at least three months in advance.

☐ Attendance records are maintained of all board and committee meetings. Most school boards meet monthly, especially those of new schools. The optimum number of meetings is determined by needs of the school. If school board members are unable to attend school board meetings, they should not become a school board member. When non-attendance falls below an acceptable level (without justification), the school board member should offer his resignation according to the provisions of the by-laws.

☐ School board minutes are maintained at each meeting. Minutes should be sent out to all school board members within ten working days. Give special care to the accuracy of these minutes, seeing that discussions and votes are carefully recorded.

☐ The school board agenda is published well in advance of the meeting. Documents for review should be provided ahead of time. For example, budget reports, staffing plans, etc.

☐ School board agendas focus on policy, not on administrative detail.

☐ The school board approves the annual school budget and receives monthly budget and cash flow reports. School board members should be aware of how the school's money is spent and request clear documentation of financial activity.

☐ The school board arranges for an annual external audit of financial records.

☐ The school's or church's insurance program (Directors and Officers insurance) covers school board members. Some states provide for indemnity of school board members, directors and trustees. Don't assume that this is true of your state.

☐ School board schedules a legal audit/checkup every three to five years to determine the school's legal health and to minimize its exposure to legal risk.

☐ School board policies reflect a system where teachers and parents are notified of important board decisions. Including school board decisions as part of the monthly administrative newsletter is a good way of informing parents. Goldstein suggests,

"Unless there exists a regularly published, periodic summary sheet on board activities, probably the best way to let people know what has happened in regard to critical policies is for an administrator to send a memorandum to the faculty stating: (1) the exact new policy and regulations, (2) the date it becomes effective, and (3) its implications for the school insofar as reasonable interpretation permits. It is wise to remember that while it is vital to communicate with dispatch, it becomes a futile exercise to do so foolishly and in haste."[5]

☐ The school board initiates an annual assessment and evaluation of the chief administrator [CSRK 2.5].

☐ The school administrator maintains a Board Manual for each member. Include the following content: school calendar with school board events, board members, addresses, phone numbers, copy of current by-laws, articles of incorporation along with amendments, copy of long-range plan, school mission statement, committee assignments, job descriptions, insurance provisions, financial statements, conflict of interest policies, to name a few.

☐ The school board receives a monthly or quarterly report from the administrator showing the status of "key school indicators," such as SAT and ACT test scores, student enrollment, achievement test results, physical fitness testing, scholarship awards, college enrollment, etc. [CSRK 2.6].

☐ School board members evaluate their individual and group contributions each year, making appropriate changes [CSRK 2.7].

Count the number of boxes that have checks and compare it to the following standard: 18 to 21 = Outstanding Board, 15 to 17 = Good Board, and 0 to 14 = A lot of work to do.

Appoint a Christian School Steering Committee

Most Christian school administrators will agree that it is not necessary during the formative stages of the school to have a school board; however, you do need to have wise counsel as well as assistance in researching key topics vital to the creation of the school. If you do have an existing school board, consider using members of the church board as chairpersons for various steering committees. A steering committee should be made up of individuals who are supportive of the school vision.

Assign committee members to the following tasks (the items identified below are representative and not a complete listing):

Educational Policies

1 Collect samples of curriculum guides and textbooks from publishers.
2 Obtain student/parent handbooks.
3 Make recommendations for attendance policies based on state statutes.
4 Recommend course of study for each grade level and review and

recommend textbooks.

5   Develop policies to minister discipline.

6   Recommend requirements for admissions, enrollment, promotion and graduation.

7   Recommend an annual school calendar.

8   Recommend extracurricular activities.

9   Review and recommend testing programs.

Facilities

1   Help inspect present site and secure appropriate facilities.

2   Contact local officials for safety and fire inspections.

3   Recommend maintenance and custodial schedule.

4   Collect room usage and space utilization data and make recommendations for most effective use.

5   Formulate ideas for parent volunteer work force.

6   Obtain price quotes for remodeling.

7   Work on obtaining student desks and other furnishings.

8   Evaluate condition of grounds, sport fields and playgrounds.

9   Investigate fire evacuation plans.

Financial

1   Review various financial approaches used by other successful Christian schools.

2   Obtain samples of budgets of other Christian schools.

3   Help set up financial records and reports.

4   Make recommendations on financial policies concerning tuition, fees, wages and salaries.

5   Help establish accounts receivable and payable systems.

6   Review all insurance needs.

7   Evaluate need for capital improvements.

8   Check legal requirements for tax exemption.

9   Investigate potential fund-raising projects.

Personnel

1   Develop job descriptions for all staff positions.

2   Contact teacher placement organizations.

3   Help interview and select staff.

4   Establish a staff record system.

5   Make recommendations for a staff orientation program.

6   Obtain copies of staff handbooks from other Christian schools.

7   Make recommendations for personnel policies.

Public Relations

1   Collect samples of public relations materials from other successful Christian schools.

2   Recommend letterhead and brochures.

3   Help recruit new students and families.

4   Prepare information packets for general and specific distribution.

5   Investigate advertising options, such as newspaper, radio and television.

6   Help plan an Open House.

7   Help write press releases concerning opening of the new school.

8   Assist in setting up an information display table.

9   Provide recommendations for guest speakers to promote the school.

Transportation

1   Conduct a transportation needs assessment.

2   Investigate legal requirements for operation of school buses.

3   Help establish a plan for car pooling.

Consider assigning a committee responsible for each chapter of this book. Make the committee responsible for completing the checklists found in each chapter and developing an action plan to complete every item before school opens. For more suggestions on board committees, see Roy W. Lowrie, Jr., *Serving God on the Christian School Board.*

Select a School Administrator

One of the first questions asked by pastors and church board members is, "Does the school need a principal?" Often, the thought is to have the pastor of the sponsoring church serve as the school principal. It is possible for a pastor to be the school principal; however, as is the case with most churches, the day-to-day operations of the ministry are all-consuming. To carry out the tasks of the school administrator in addition to those of the pastor will result in some other area of the ministry suffering.

Identify Selection Criteria

One of the first tasks the pastor or church board should do is to find a qualified school administrator (principal, headmaster). Bill Kelly spoke of the principal as being an "Administrative Superman":

"In God's chain of command the administrator must serve as a conduit between the policies of the school board, and the needs of the staff and student body. It is the administrator to whom everyone will look for advice and direction. He is responsible to provide the board with accurate interpretive information necessary for their decision making. The staff expects the administrator to be their concerned advocate in professional matters. The student body believes that the administrator should be someone who is approachable and personally concerned about their specific needs. Everyone expects him to maintain spiritual and emotional stability in times of pressurized testing. Certainly this job is for a superman...."[6]

Most administrators would agree that the school will only rise to its level of leadership. J. Lester Brubaker exhorts,

"Because the principal of the Christian school carries the major administrative role (and sometimes the entire load), it is especially important that he (she) be chosen carefully...."[7]

Entry-Level Qualities

The person chosen to lead the school should possess the same entry-level qualities expected of all staff—spiritually, academically, professionally and personally. Some of these qualities include:

- Being born again
- Filled with the Holy Spirit
- Believing and acting upon the Word of God
- Having an active prayer life
- Involved in Christian service
- Prepared professionally
- Experienced.

See Step 7—"Select Teachers," for a discussion of each of these qualities.

In addition to these qualities, the administrator must be an excellent manager of physical, human and financial resources. He must be an effective communicator—orally, and in written form. He must possess skills essential in his role as instructional leader of the school. Furthermore, the administrator is the catalyst for educational quality: he must be able to motivate students, parents and staff. Although these qualities are important, most critical to an effective administrator is being called of God and having a willingness to serve.

A Definite Calling

The administrator must have a definite calling to serve as administrator; it is this calling that will carry him through difficult times, even when he feels like "throwing in the towel." Sometimes, administrators lay aside their calling when events get unpleasant or because of mistakes they make or the mistakes of others. Billy Joe Daugherty, in his book, *You Can Start Over,* says that when someone gives up their calling because of mistakes it is "out of the embarrassment or the predicament that results...they forget about the call or they don't want to go on with it...they are hurt, wounded and rejected...."[8]

Since "...**the gifts and the calling of God are irrevocable**"(Romans 11:29, NKJV), God will never take them back. The best strategy for an administrator who makes a mistake is to own up to the mistake, ask forgiveness, correct the mistake, accept God's grace and then get on with administrating the school. Paul says it this way in Philippians 3:13,14:

> **"Brethren, I count not myself to have apprehended: but this one thing I do, forgetting those things which are behind, and reaching forth unto those things which are before,**

> **"I press toward the mark for the prize of the high calling of God in Christ Jesus."**

Confidence in the call of God is what keeps an administrator from becoming susceptible to "loneliness at the top." In speaking of "The Loneliness of Leadership," Bob M. Wood, Executive Vice-President for Bob Jones University, points to lack of being loved, respected and understood as contributors to this loneliness along with making choices that are personally painful, both physically and mentally.[9] Add to these, lack of confidence and dissatisfaction with job performance. If not checked, loneliness leads to ineffectiveness and eventual resignation.

One of the keys in combating loneliness at the top is to spend time developing a relationship with the Father. Isaiah 58:14 exhorts administrators, **"Then shalt thou delight thyself in the LORD; and I will cause thee to ride upon the high places of the earth, and feed thee with the heritage of Jacob thy father: for the mouth of the LORD hath spoken it."** When discouragement approaches, the administrator must hold on to his call and learn how to gather quality people around him to provide support and assistance to get the job done.

> **NOTE:** *If an administrative candidate cannot voice a definite calling to Christian school administration in general and to your ministry in specific, look for someone else.*

A Willingness To Serve

The Christian school administrator must have a willingness to serve the pastor or school board; he must be committed to fulfilling the vision given to the pastor or to those responsible for establishing the school rather than attempting to carry out his own vision. A willingness to serve brings with it the blessing of God. **"If ye be willing and obedient, ye shall eat the good of the land: But if ye refuse and rebel, ye shall be devoured with the sword: for the mouth of the LORD hath spoken it"** (Isaiah 1:19,20).

It is important for the administrator to be in agreement with the vision of the ministry. Amos 3:3 (NKJV) says, **"Can two walk together, unless they are agreed?"** Being in agreement provides the foundation of faith to believe God for supernatural provision, **"Again I say unto you, That if two of you shall agree on earth as touching any thing that they shall ask, it shall be done for them of my Father which is in heaven"** (Matthew 18:19).

Alternatives

There are times when the pastor or school board cannot find a trained school administrator who agrees with the vision of the school. If this happens, consider using someone in the congregation that has leadership and managerial talents and has been supportive of the vision for the school. Depending upon the size of the school, it is possible to employ an experienced teacher who also would have administrative responsibility. This could easily be the case if the school has an enrollment under 100. However, a well-trained and experienced administrator should be employed whenever the school enrollment exceeds this number of students.

Whether the pastor, pastor's wife, or an experienced teacher becomes the school administrator, the administrative load could be spread out among the faculty by appointing department heads or unit leaders. These should meet with the administrator on a weekly basis. If you are operating an elementary school, consider a unit leader for the kindergarten classes, one for grades first through third and one for grades four through sixth. At the junior high and high school level, combine several subject areas and assign them to a unit leader; for example, math and science. One person could be placed in charge of all the special subjects, such as music, physical education and art.

Determine the Involvement of the Pastor

Even though the pastor chooses not to be principal, his involvement in the school is essential to its success. The pastor should:

1   Be closely involved in the formation of the school.
2   Know of the basics of operation.
3   Give vision to the school.
4   Provide spiritual leadership.
5   Bring unity to the ministry (this is important in order to avoid a "we"–"they" mentality).
6   Assist in resolving conflicts where church and school may be competing for the same resources (human, physical and financial).

Organize the School Office

One of the first organizational units to establish is the school office. Locate the office near the primary entrance to the school and properly furnish it, beginning with a telephone. As the school develops, the office will become the hub of the school, a place of efficient productivity. Careful planning will be necessary to avoid the school office becoming "Grand Central Station." Keller comments,

> "The efficiency of the school office is a valid indication of the quality of the school. The school office staff must be aware of the importance of first appearances. The office is often a new family's first contact with the school. The office needs to be a clean, orderly and pleasant place generating a feeling of efficiency and professionalism."[10]

Foster a Productive Office Climate

As a positive classroom climate has a beneficial effect upon the total development of the student, a positive office climate will influence the entire school. The following suggestions serve as a guide toward fostering a positive office climate.

Businesslike Atmosphere

Since the school office is a central service center, students, staff, parents, and the public will have reason to come to the office. Maintain a businesslike atmosphere always. Make individuals feel welcome and focus conversations on the specific needs being presented rather than on general "chit-chat." Plan for a waiting area next to the main work area.

School Phones

Students need access to a phone to call about their jobs and to contact parents. If the only phone is in the school office, expect a lineup before and after school, and during the noon hour, causing congestion in the office and interference with the flow of operations. The office phone should be used for school business and should not be tied up by students. Consider the following options:

- Place a public pay phone in the hallway for use by students and parents. Locate the phone where it can be easily monitored.

- Publish a clear set of rules with specific times when the phone can be used by students. For example: no one should be released from class to use the phone; the phone can be used before the first bell, during noon hour and after school is dismissed.

- Limit all calls to three minutes or less.

- Provide a phone in a teacher work area for school staff.

It is also important for office staff to remember that the person answering the phone gives the first impression of the school. Marilyn Price has written an excellent minibook offering suggestions for improving telephone techniques in a Christian school office. Every Christian school should make this powerful telephone techniques book a desk resource for anyone answering the school telephone—staff, student aids and parent volunteers. Here are several of her suggestions.

1   Always answer on the first ring if possible. Remember that the caller cannot see how busy you are.

2   Answer the telephone with proper identification. For example: "Thank you for calling Gracemont Christian School."

3   Answer pleasantly. Use a calm, courteous voice. Avoid a curt, impatient, or angry tone of voice. Proverbs 16:24 says, "**Pleasant words are as an honeycomb, sweet to the soul, and health to the bones.**"

4   Give the caller your immediate and undivided attention! Make this your aim no matter how many challenges await you.

5   Smile and put sparkle into your voice! The person on the other end of the telephone line does not have the benefit of your facial expressions to interpret what you are saying. Let the fruit of the Spirit flow through you, which will increase the sparkle in your voice.

6   Be friendly! Make the caller glad he called your school office. Take advantage of opportunities to be helpful and informative.

7   Never engage in gossip or idle talk on the phone. "**But I say unto you, That every idle word that men shall speak, they shall give account thereof in the day of judgment. For by thy words thou shalt be justified, and by thy words thou shalt be condemned**" (Matt. 12: 36,37).

8   Use the person's name which will help to personalize the call. Everyone likes to feel important!

9   Keep paper and pencil (or a telephone message pad) near the phone. As information is being given, write it down. Do not be afraid to ask

the caller to repeat information for clarification, such as the spelling of his name, a number, address, etc. If you will write it down as it is given, however, you will have a head start on getting an accurate message.

10 Speak TO the caller—not AT the telephone.[11]

Staff Accountability

Know the whereabouts of all staff at all times. Accomplish this by maintaining a staff sign in/out log. Use a magnetic locator board for office staff when they leave the office for another part of the building or leave campus. Record where they are and approximate time of returning.

Information Directories

A happy parent is not always the one whose child gets good grades, makes the basketball team, or wins first place in the Science Fair; rather, it is the parent who gets the right answer when they have questions or concerns about student activities, names of class sponsors, dates and times of parent conferences and special events. These parents call the school office looking for answers. Maintaining an up-to-date information and activities log is essential for good public relations. Here are some suggestions.

- Require all staff to submit to the office a copy of an approved activity form in advance of the activity.

- Place the information and activities in a tabbed, three-ring binder. Locate it in a designated area recognized by all office staff.

- Include in the information binder a copy of the parent/student handbook, daily announcements, class sponsors, athletic schedules, school lunch menu, school calendar, copies of teacher schedules, and other information important in the life of the school.

Staff Mailboxes

Locate teacher mailboxes in an area away from the office. Since teachers check their mailboxes throughout the day, locating these boxes away from the office will cut down on the number of office interruptions.

Public Relations

Students, parents and staff coming to the office with grievances, negative perceptions and poor attitudes need to be confronted in love and a spirit of reconciliation. Keller cautions, "Tactful handling of unhappy office visitors takes a great skill cultivated through thoughtful effort."[12]

Train office staff to be calm, not to become defensive, justify the school's position, cut the person off or classify him as a maverick. Hear their complaint. Listen with interest and understanding and either correct the issue or explain the school's position.[13] Foster a spirit of reconciliation at all times.

Train Office Aides and Volunteers

A cadre of well-trained office aides (students or parents) can make life much easier for office staff. They can be trained to answer the phone, deliver forgotten lunches and clothes, manage the lost but found, make coffee, make copies, file, stuff envelopes and distribute supplies.

Set Up a School Records System

Central to the school office is an effective and efficient record-keeping system. There are three main categories of records—staff records, student records and general records.

Organize Staff Records

The U.S. Department of Education recommends nine dimensions for professional records. These include:

1   **Personal Identification.** Provides data to identify the staff member uniquely and provide information on his health, marital status and dependents.

2   **Education and Prior Employment.** Includes data on the staff member's general educational background and qualifications, as well as his experience or employment.

3   **Job Classification and Activity Assignment.** Groups into general categories the kinds of work that staff members perform and divides these categories (or classifications) into activity assignments describing the major activities of each position.

4   **Function and Program Assignment.** Provides data on the nature of the function and program or support service to which the staff member is assigned.

5   **Subject Matter Area.** Identifies the subject matter areas in which the staff members with teaching assignments function.

6   **Scope of Current Assignment.** Relates each current assignment of the staff member with other organizational elements such as the scope of timing of the assignment and its location and schedule.

7   **Current Employment.** Includes materials on the staff member's contractual status, as well as personnel data on participation in insurance and retirement programs, current leave status, and salary.

8   **Career Development.** Relates to the staff member's performance

and growth in his current assignment.

9   **Separation**. Involves the severance of the employment relation-ship[14]

Most administrators prefer to classify all records pertaining to staff as confidential, maintaining them in a separate lockable file cabinet in their office. Before placing a document in these files follow the advice of J. Lester Brubaker,

> "Every office needs a rubber date stamp. As each piece of information is received, it should be dated before being placed in the file. Dating papers when received helps answer questions that may arise in the future."[15]

In setting up your staff records, consider the following tips:

- Use ready-made personnel file folders containing blocks of pre-printed information that can be completed by the school. You can find this type of file in most office supply catalogs.

- Create a document log to record the name and date that each document is placed in the file folder. For example: teacher application, transcripts, references, certificates, evaluations, development plan, etc. [CSRK 2.8].

- Keep all staff records current. At the end of each school term, review each file for its completeness and discard any contents that are outdated.

Establish Student Records

One of the major tasks carried on by the school office is creating and maintaining accurate student records. Unless carefully structured from the first day the school opens, retrieving vital student records information at a later date can become an ever-increasing challenge, especially when records are not kept up to date. Most states require all schools to maintain records, such as attendance, immunization and academics.

Checklist for Student Records

Use the following checklist to determine the status of your student records system.

☐ Create a student record file at the time a student is accepted for admission. Once a system has been initiated, divide the files into three groups: currently enrolled students, former students, and students who have graduated. Arrange each group of files in A to Z order.

☐ Facilitate the task of recording information by using a standardized cumulative record card [CSRK 2.9]. Record information that is subject to change, such as demographic data, in pencil, whereas, information, such as grades, is typewritten or written in ink.

☐ Maintain the following documents in each student record (minimum suggestions): admissions application, a copy of the student's birth certificate, health record and immunization record. Use a standardized document log placed in the front of each record [CSRK 2.10].

☐ Establish written procedures of who has access to these files, including parents. Allow parent access to their child's records only under the supervision of the administrator [CSRK 2.11].

☐ Develop a request form to be signed by parents for the release of student records to other schools [CSRK 2.12]. Use this form in requesting student records from other schools.

☐ Maintain a master tracking log of records being requested from or sent to other schools [CSRK 2.13].

☐ Establish a secured area to maintain these permanent records. Store records in fire-proof files. Using image scanners, permanent files can be electronically stored and retrieved. Equally important is the capability of making a backup copy of the student record information and storing it off campus on computer disks or tape cartridges.

☐ Provide a process whereby parents have an opportunity to request a hearing to challenge the contents of their child's records [CSRK 2.14].

☐ Do not allow records to be removed from the file drawer without signing them out. Require all student records to be viewed in the school office. Under no circumstances should files be removed from the building.

☐ Initiate a policy purging all student records of temporary information no longer essential to the child's school success, such as samples of school work, disciplinary notes, etc.

☐ Plan for a backup copy of all records either in the form of a photocopy, microfilm, or computer image. Begin with graduates. Maintain a second backup copy in a secure location off campus.

Microcomputers add a new dimension to record maintenance. Student records systems, such as *The School System*, take most of the work out of managing student records and provide for efficiency and accuracy. Most computer record systems are capable of producing report cards, progress reports and printing of transcript labels to be affixed to a permanent file (See *Microcomputer Applications for Christian Educators* for more information on student record systems).

Student Transcripts

One of the most important documents in the life of a student is his school transcript. Special care invested in handling transcripts will eliminate future headaches. Consider the following management checklist:

☐ Send photocopies and not the original document when fulfilling transcript requests. Have the administrator or registrar sign the photocopy.

☐ Release records only when the request bears the signature of the parent and school official. Initial any obvious corrections. Better yet, redo the transcript.

☐ Include class ranking and G.P.A. on all high school transcripts [CSRK 2.15].

☐ Designate one person to be responsible for preparing the official transcript. Place a school seal over the signature of the person preparing the transcript. School seals can be obtained from most stationery stores.

☐ Mail transcripts directly to the institutions requesting them. When releasing transcripts to parents or students, stamp the transcripts "Issued to Student" and do not include the school seal.[16] High school transcripts can be sent directly to college admissions offices using a fax. The school can then telephone the college to see whether or not the material was received.

Set up a General Records System

A third category of school records is known as general records and includes substitute teacher files, class schedules, testing reports, accreditation reports, legal and insurance documents, to name a few. Everyone has their own favorite way of setting up these records. Several key strategies contribute to an effective general records file system. Consider the following:

1   File records and documents promptly so they do not get lost. If you must postpone your filing, keep a special file folder stored in the top file marked, "For Filing."

2   Code each item in pencil at the top right-hand corner before filing. This speeds up the filing process and helps relocate a document should it become misplaced.

3   File the most current documents at the front of the file folder where they will be more readily accessible.

4   When filing small notes or clippings, attach them to a standard size sheet of paper, so that they will not get lost.

5   Leave about one-fourth or one-fifth of each file drawer empty to allow for rapid retrieval and rearrangement. [17]

Create a School Forms System

Every Christian school, large and small, in its function as a service center will generate a variety of forms. Office forms are as important to the office's efficiency as furniture and equipment. [18]

Developing and tracking school forms in a systematic way will help avoid unnecessary work and confusion. Consider the following:

1   Organize a centralized filing system for maintaining the original copy of all forms as well as enough for daily use.

2   Organize a master tracking system for all forms. Record the title of the form and date created or revised. For example, form number SA100 2-94 represents Student Activities form 100 developed in February of 1994 [CSRK 2.16].

3   Use a numbering system based on functional categories, such as the 100 series for administration, 200 series for financial, 300 series for athletics, 400 series for ancillary services, 500 series for pupil personal, etc.

4   Use standard size paper for forms that contain information that will be filed as a permanent record. Forms containing data that will be transferred to computer should have the information arranged so it lends itself to easy data entry.

5   Review forms annually to determine their continued usefulness.

6   Where possible, use a computer form generating program. This will save production time, facilitate revisions and provide a professional appearance.

Create Handbooks

Handbooks are valuable tools in formulating the structure of the Christian day school. The employee and parent/student handbooks play a critical role in communicating the organizational structure of the school, its policies, rules and expectations.

Employee Handbook

Knowledge of school policies helps employees work more effectively and contributes to the development of smooth, professional and predictable relationships among staff.

Since courts in some states view the employee handbook as an implied employment contract, employment lawyers suggest adding a disclaimer in the front of the handbook. The intent of the disclaimer is to "clearly notify the employees that the handbook is not intended to create a binding contract and that the employer is not required to follow its provisions in all circumstances."[19] For example,

"This employee handbook is intended to acquaint the employees of [Name of School] with the current policies and personnel practices; however, it is not a contract of employment. [Name of School] reserves the right to make changes in the handbook at any time without notice."

Other lawyers recommend including a disclaimer as part of an employee handbook receipt [CSRK 2.17]. This action precludes an employee from arguing that he was unaware of the requirements to read the policies and to comply with them.

When drafting your employee handbook, consider the following actions:

1   State each policy is simple terms so they are easily understood.
2   Avoid using individual names—use generic terms, such as employee, part-time staff, full-time staff, secretary, teacher, etc.
3   Create a general employee handbook and a detailed teacher policy manual.
4   Don't re-invent the wheel; contact several Christian day schools, obtaining copies of employee handbooks, supervisor manuals and teacher handbooks. (See DEL Publications for copies of these documents on computer disk that can easily be modified to meet the needs of your specific ministry.)
5   Schools that are part of a church should consider incorporating existing church employee policies and school employee policies into one staff handbook. This helps unify the entire ministry and avoid the "we"–"they" syndrome.

Parent/Student Handbook

The parent/student handbook is the main information tool of the school. A well-designed handbook communicates a message of confidence, efficiency and foresight; it establishes an organized, substantial academic and social environment.

Consider the following topics for inclusion in your parent/student handbook. Items are arranged in eight key areas.

1   Philosophy
   •   History

- Vision of the school
- Philosophy of Christian Education
- Goals and objectives

2   Personnel

- Faculty: names, positions, education
- Other staff members: custodial, clerical, bus drivers
- Officers of the parent-teacher fellowship and other parent groups

3   Facilities

- Floor plan, important locations, restricted areas
- Safety precautions, care of grounds and buildings
- Use of telephone and school equipment
- Student and staff parking
- Student vehicles

4   Program

- Opportunities for each grade in ministry, missions
- Program of studies for each grade, electives, exploratory experiences
- Services: health, guidance, food, library
- Extracurricular class activities: homeroom, assembly, clubs, sports
- Schedules: starting times, closing times, school calendar, special events, reporting periods
- Accreditation

5   Policies

- Non-discrimination, admission, enrollment, transfer
- Grading, placement, promotion, graduation, homework
- Excuses, exemptions, eligibility, medicine
- Honors, prizes, awards, scholarships
- Attendance, discipline, suspension, expulsion, sportsmanship, transportation
- Parties, use of facilities, leaving grounds, school visitors, security
- Payment of tuition and fees
- Conduct, dress code, hair code, lifestyle
- Smoking, drinking, drugs, weapons, pregnancy

6   Procedures
  - In classrooms, corridors, assemblies, cafeteria, locker areas, lavatories
  - Getting materials: textbooks, school store, library, gym supplies
  - Obtaining permissions: re-entrance, changing groups, passes, work permits
  - In emergencies: fire drills, accidents, civil defense, school cancellation
  - Studying, lost and found, obtaining information and advice

7   Pupil Participation
  - School government: structure, activities, leaders
  - Organizations: qualifications, activities, leaders
  - School service: traffic squads, committees
  - School spirit: songs, yells, colors, motto, code, symbols, traditions, history
  - Competitions: athletics, contests, intramural events
  - Special events: homecoming, spirit week

8   Parent Participation
  - Parent-teacher conferences, special visits
  - Parent- teacher fellowship
  - Volunteerism: offices, classroom, boosters clubs, fund raising, field trips

Pitfalls to Avoid

1. Failing to properly educate the school board of its role in the Christian school. Resolve this pitfall with the following strategies:

  - Provide every school board member with reading materials, such as *A Guide for Principals and Board Members on Christian School Growth*, *Serving God on the Christian School Board*, *Guidebook for Directors of Nonprofit Corporations*, and *Board Member Manual*. Take a portion of each board meeting to discuss the contents of these books.

  - Provide for periodic board retreats to review the mission of the school, discuss long-range plans, deal with problems that cannot be resolved in a regular board meeting.

  - Recommend workshops at state, regional and national Christian school conferences.

- Purchase and circulate among board members audio tapes purchased from Christian school and management organizations.

- Use simulated situational exercises, such as those presented in *Situational Leadership For Principals*. For example, Dealing with Divided or Misguided Board Members, Coping with Board Members Who Try to Administer a Principal's Building, etc.

- Use professionally produced school board training videos such as *The 1994 Board Member Video Manual*. This video deals with Board problems and personal dynamics presented in different scenarios, such as Dealing with Board Conflict at the Board Meeting, Micro Managing Finances, Meddling with Staff, and The Poorly Run Board Meeting.

- Provide outlets for board member expression. For example, invite school board members to participate in open houses, staff and teacher orientations and to see the school in action.

- Obtain other resource materials from the National School Board Association.

2. Failing to adequately train students and volunteers who serve in the office. Ensure that students and volunteers working in the office give a professional impression. They also should be capable of providing accurate information to those going to the office or when handling incoming calls. Students and volunteers should not be given access to school records, for example, staff and student files, counseling and guidance records, financial records, etc.

3. Viewing administration mainly as a vocation and not as a ministry. Administration as a ministry is different from administration as a vocation. As a vocation, administration requires professional skill, whereas administration as a ministry refers to a divinely given gift to manage the programs approved of God. **"And God hath set some in the church, first apostles, secondarily prophets, thirdly teachers, after that miracles, then gifts of healing, helps, governments** (administration)**, diversities of tongues"** (1 Cor. 12:28).

The administrator can plan and produce a smooth-functioning school, yet, if not gifted, the school will not achieve the purposes of God. Individuals with the gift of administration, regardless of the vocational aspects of administration, can be greatly used by God. Administration as a gift cannot be earned, inherited or acquired through ability. Rather, it is a supernatural impartation from the Holy Spirit. Keep in mind, if a person has a natural ability to lead and manage, he will probably be used of God as an administrator. However, the Holy Spirit is not limited to natural abilities. In other words, the Holy Spirit can bypass a person who has natural leadership and training, but will not yield completely to Him. Paul said of himself, I was "**...not meet to be called an apostle...**" (1 Cor. 15:9). But he concluded, "**And I thank Christ Jesus our Lord, who hath enabled me, for that he counted me faithful, putting me into the ministry; who was before a blasphemer, and a persecutor, and injurious....**" (1 Tim. 1:12,13).

Likewise, David was selected by God to be the commander and leader of His people and to be the administrative head of the government. His background was not one of academic and professional preparation. Still, God called him and he obeyed. Second Timothy 1:9 says, "**Who hath saved us, and called us with an holy calling, not according to our works, but according to his own purpose and grace, which was given us in Christ Jesus before the world began.**"

4. Failing to clearly define the organizational structure. A clearly defined organizational structure helps those working in the school and those being served by the school to know the functions performed by different individuals and groups and their corresponding lines of authority. Having this information published helps identify channels to voice problems when they occur. Not knowing the channels to follow to resolve conflict leads to frustration and resistance to authority.

Knowing the boundaries of authority helps individuals and groups (for example, parent-teacher fellowship, booster clubs, student government, etc.) know the limitations of their authority to make decisions. As Lovell and Wiles point out, "No one can share decisions beyond the authority that he or she has. Frustration is created within groups if the group is led to think it can make a decision that it doesn't have the authority to make."[20]

Frustration can be lessened by having well-documented job descriptions for every position in the school. Each group within the school should have a clearly defined set of guidelines for operation, including responsibilities and lines of authority.

5. Failing to clearly define the responsibilities of the administrator. One of the best tools for defining responsibilities is a clearly written job description. Louise Samson warns,

"Too often, job descriptions are completed, cataloged, put in nice binders, and displayed on a remote shelf to gather dust. It is even worse to lock them up in a confidential information drawer. They should be kept available for all employees."[21]

When constructed properly, the job description helps remove frustration, confusion and uncertainty about role expectations. Include in the administrator's job description clearly stated performance standards. These standards act as the foundation for future performance evaluations [CSRK 2.18].

Father, we believe that You are able to send the right person to serve as administrator of this school. We bind any force that is hindering them from hearing the voice of the Master. We release them to do the will of God. Thank You for guiding them to this school. Amen.

> The way a school is organized determines the locus of control and provides structure for carrying out its purpose.

Christian School Resource Kit

2.1   School Board Application

2.2   School Board Member Job Descriptions

2.3   School Board Tracking and Orientation Checklist

2.4   School Board By-laws

2.5   Administrative Assessment/Evaluation Document

2.6   School Board Key School Indicators

2.7   School Board Assessment

2.8   Staff Record Log

2.9   Cumulative Student Record

2.10   Student Record Log

2.11   Student Record Release Policy

2.12   Records Request

2.13   Student Records Release Log

2.14   Parent Request to Review Records

2.15   High School Transcript

2.16   Master School Forms System

2.17   Employee Handbook Receipt

2.18   Administrative Job Description

Endnotes

1   Bryon W. Hansford. *Guidebook for School Principals*. New York, NY: The Ronald Press Company, 1961, p. 20.

2   Roy W. Lowrie, Jr. *Serving God on the Christian School Board.* Whittier, CA: Association of Christian Schools International, 1976, p. 107.

3   Adapted from Robert C. Andringa. "A Quiz on Your Boardmanship." Christian Management Report, April/May, 1991.

4   James W. Deuink and Carl D. Herbster. *Effective Christian School Management.* 2nd Edition. Greenville, SC: Bob Jones University Press, 1986, p. 33.

5   William Goldstein. *Successful School Communication.* West Nyack, NY: Parker Publishing Company, Inc., 1977, p. 105.

6   Bill Kelly. *A Guide for Principals and Board Members on Christian School Growth.* Whittier, CA: Association of Christian Schools International, 1976, p. 57.

7   J. Lester Brubaker. *Personnel Administration in the Christian School.* Winona Lake, IN: BMH Books, 1980, p. 17.

8   Billy Joe Daugherty. *You Can Start Over.* Tulsa, OK: Victory Christian Center, 1991, p. 16.

9   Bob M. Wood. "The Loneliness of Leadership" in James W. Deuink, ed., *Some Light on Christian Education.* Greenville, SC: Bob Jones University Press, 1984, p. 184.

10 Virginia R. Keller. "Good Public Relations Start in the Office." *Christian School,* Dec./Jan. 1990, p. 2.

11 Marilyn L. Price. *Improving My Telephone Techniques.* Tulsa, OK: DEL Publications, 1994, pp. 3-6.

12 Keller, *op. cit.,* p. 15.

13 Dennis Demuth and Carol Demuth. *Recruiting Strategies for Christian Schools.* Tulsa, OK: DEL Publications, 1992, p. 75.

14 U.S. Department of Education, 400 Maryland Avenue, S.W., Washington, DC, 20202; (800) 572-5580.

15 Brubaker, *op. cit.,* p.140.

16 James W. Deuink. *The Christian School Guidance Counselor.* Greenville, SC: Bob Jones University Press, 1985.

17 Adapted from Cherie Fehrman. *The Complete School Secretary's Desk Book.* Englewood Cliffs, NJ: Prentice-Hall, Inc., 1982, p. 194.

18 K. Forbis Jordan, Mary P. McKeown, Richard G. Salmon and L. Dean Webb. *School Business Administration.* Beverly Hills, CA: Sage Publications, Inc., 1985, p. 69.

19 Nancy Asquith. *WG&L Human Resources.* Boston, MA: Warren, Gorham and Lamont, Inc., 1990, p. 103.

20 John T. Lovell and Kimball Wiles. *Supervision for Better Schools.* 5th Edition. Englewood Cliffs, NJ: Prentice-Hall, Inc. 1983, p. 88.

21   Louise Samson. *Hiring Handbook*. New York, NY: Panel Publishers, 1994, p. 3.

References

Demuth, Dennis M. and Carol M. Demuth. *Microcomputer Applications for Christian Educators*. Tulsa, OK: DEL Publications, 1992.

Dunn, Kenneth and Rita Dunn. *Situational Leadership for Principals*. Englewood Cliffs, NJ: Prentice-Hall, Inc., 1983.

Elliot, Chuck. *The 1994 Board Member Video Manual*. Frederick, MD: Aspen Publishers, Inc., 1994.

National School Boards Association, 1055 Thomas Jefferson St., N.W., Washington, DC 20007; (202) 337-7666.

Overton, George W., ed. *Guidebook for Directors of Nonprofit Corporations*. Chicago, IL: American Bar Association, 1993.

Personnel Policy Service, Inc. 4350 Drownsboro Road, Louisville, KY 40207; (800) 437-3735.

The School System. McGraw-Hill School Systems, 20 Ryan Ranch Road, Monterey, CA 93940; (800) 663-0544.

STEP 3

ASSESS LEGAL REQUIREMENTS

Knowing the legal requirements of educating children under an established religious purpose is critical to getting a new school going and keeping it growing. Taking the time to prepare a proper legal foundation is less costly then repairing a bad testimony of a school that opens its doors, then closes them because of a legal oversight.

There are hundreds of local, state and federal requirements facing Christian schools. Presenting a detailed discussion of each of these requirements is beyond the scope of this chapter. The purpose of this chapter is to point out several key legal concerns associated with establishing a Christian school. The authors have written a special book titled, *Legal Requirements for Christian Schools,* that presents a more complete discussion of legal issues facing Christian school ministries.

The information contained in this chapter is presented with the understanding that the publisher and authors are not engaged in rendering legal, accounting, or other professional service. When legal advice or other expert assistance is required, the services of a qualified professional should be sought, specifically those specializing in Christian school ministries.

Establish the School as a Legal Entity

One of the first tasks is to establish the school as a lawful entity. This involves a decision about the school's legal structure. Most schools are legally established under one of the following structures: incorporated under the church, separately incorporated, or unincorporated.

Any school, whether it be public or nonpublic, is not free of government regulations. Although federal and state governments demonstrate a compelling interest in educating its citizens, those nonpublic schools operating for religious purposes experience fewer governmental restrictions. It is for this reason the authors advocate a close linkage between a Christian school and sponsoring church or churches.

Incorporate the School

Should a Christian school incorporate? Should it seek exemption from federal taxes? The relationship a school has with a church helps determine the answer to these questions.

Incorporated Under the Church

Incorporating a Christian school under the church has it advantages. For example, as long as a church can demonstrate that a school is an integral part of the church ministry, it can share in the church's tax-exempt status. This includes state and federal income tax, local property tax, and unemployment tax.[1] Ensuring a school as an integral relationship to a parent church requires an effort "to intertwine the leadership, funds, property and philosophy of the school with the supporting church. It is urgent that a Christian school never be represented as a separate entity from the church."[2] Accomplish this through regular entries in the church corporate minutes. These should include the following minimum entries:

1   The purchase of land or rental of facilities for common use (whenever possible, house church and school offices in the same building).

2   Specific mention of the school in the church's long-range plan.

3   Any activity fostering a strong relationship with the sponsoring church or churches, such as a ministry-wide master calendar.

It is important to make provision for a Christian school ministry as part of the purpose statement of the organization. For example,

"This congregation is organized as a church exclusively for charitable, religious, and educational purposes within the meaning of Section 501 (c) (3) of the Internal Revenue Code of 1986 (or the corresponding provision of any future United States Revenue Law), including, but not limited to, for such purposes, the establishing and maintaining of religious worship, the building, maintaining and operating of churches, parsonages, schools, chapels, radio stations, television stations, rescue missions, print shops, day care centers, camps, nursing homes and cemeteries, and any other ministries that the Church may be led of God to establish."

Within the organization's constitution should be a separate article with provisions for the ministry of education.[3] As a minimum include: purpose, church participation, staff membership, statement of faith, unity, teaching and Christian walk. The Christian School Resource Kit contains a sample constitutional article for establishing a Christian school [CSRK 3.1]. Churches with existing Christian schools need to review their articles of incorporation to make certain that the articles provide for a day school.

Separate Corporation

A church may choose to organize a school as a separate legal entity.

When a school is separately incorporated, it must apply for and obtain tax-exempt status. Furthermore, separate incorporation might suggest that a school is not in fact an integral part of the church. As such, the school is subject to greater regulation and receives less protection by the courts.

Deuink and Herbster conclude:

"There is usually little practical advantage in separately incorporating a church school. It is often done to separate the financial aspects of the operation of the school from those of the church."[4]

A church can manage its financial affairs and those of the school as a single entity. This can be accomplished using a fund accounting approach, without having to set up a separate legal entity. We will have more to share on this topic in Step 6–"Develop an Income and Spending Plan."

Some churches have chosen to incorporate their schools separately to put some legal distance between the school and church. However, as long as the school operates under the ownership and control of the church, the church will continue to shoulder liability. Furthermore, when a school is incorporated under a church, the Church Audit Procedures Act of 1984 places limits on IRS audits. Unfortunately, this is not true of church schools separately incorporated—one more reason to be under the umbrella of a sponsoring church.

Unincorporated

The government considers a school that is not a corporation as unincorporated. If a school is to be independent of any other organization, or if it is privately owned and operated, the school should request from the District IRS office, Publication #557, "How to Apply for Recognition of Exemption for an Organization."

Each state has different requirements for incorporation. It is well to review the advantages and disadvantages with an attorney. It would be helpful for a school to obtain and review samples of constitutions and incorporation documents from other established Christian schools. The authors agree with Richard Hammer's recommendation,

"As a rule of thumb, it would be more advantageous for a religious school operating independently of any control or supervision of a church or other religious organizations to be incorporated."[5]

Seek Tax-Exempt Status

Under existing law, churches are exempt from income taxation. Therefore, a church-operated school benefits from the sponsoring church's exemption. This includes exemption from taxes, both state and federal, local property taxes and unemployment taxes.

It is not a requirement to obtain tax-exempt status. There are those who are strongly opposed to acquiring tax-exempt status since it constitutes a federal subsidy from the government. There is also the concern that obtaining tax-exempt status may open the door for future control by the government.

Maintaining exempt status requires an exempt organization to report all organizational or operational changes in status to the Internal Revenue Service. This is true of a church adding a Christian school as part of its ministry, especially when the church does not mention educational ministries in its constitution.

Notify State and Local Officials

Some Christian educators take the position that since a school is part of the church, state and local school regulations do not apply. Usually, the courts have not agreed with this position.

It is the responsibility of state and local officials to see that children have a safe school environment. Establishing a good working relationship with all city and school officials is an absolute must; after all, when the safety and health of your students is a concern, everyone should be on the same side.

Paul Kienel, Executive Director of ACSI, offers these suggestions:

"Christian school administrators would do well to take the time and effort to cultivate a cordial relationship with city, county, state and federal officials. Whenever possible, shake their hands and make yourself known to them. Write them letters of appreciation when it is appropriate to do so. Place key government officials on your school's mailing list. Invite them to major school events. Let them know you respect their office and that you are a responsible leader in the community."[6]

Begin building this relationship shortly after deciding to open a Christian day school. Write a letter of intent to open a Christian day school. Send copies from the church board or pastor to the public school superintendent and to the fire, safety and health departments [CSRK 3.2].

Comply with Federal Laws

Once a school establishes itself as a lawful entity, attention should focus on federal, state and local statutory requirements important in preparing for the opening day. Knowing these legal standards facilitates proper formulation of school policies and procedures.

There are numerous federal laws that apply to Christian day schools. Which laws affect your school will depend in part on whether or not your school plans to participate in federal-funded programs.

Compliance by all Schools

The following laws apply to all Christian schools: (For greater detail on each law and recommended action, see *Legal Requirements for Christian Schools*, 2nd Edition.)

1   **Age Discrimination in Employment Act of 1967** (ADEA). This law prohibits discrimination in hiring, discharge, classification, or wage rate of employees based on age (within the 40-70 age range). A school may be at risk when hiring only employees who are younger than age 40. The amendment to the Age Discrimination and Employment Act extends the anti-discrimination provisions to any employee over the age of 40 without any upper age limit. A covered employer may no longer mandatorily retire an employee at the age of 70, but the employer must justify all terminations based on performance related criteria. Also, the same group health insurance provided to younger employees must be given to employees 70 and over. These requirements apply to all employers with 20 or more employees. The law requires schools to keep the following records: job applications, promotion, demotion, transfer, discharge, testing results, results of physical examinations and announcements of job openings.

2   **Americans with Disabilities Act of 1990** (ADA). The purpose of the Americans with Disabilities Act (ADA) is to extend to people with disabilities rights similar to those now available on the basis of race, color, national origin, sex and religion based on the Civil Rights Acts of 1964. It prohibits discrimination on the basis of disability in: private sector employment; services rendered by state and local governments; places of public accommodation; transportation and telecommunications relay services.

3   **Asbestos School Hazard Abatement Act of 1984 (ASHAA).** Each state has its own guidelines concerning asbestos control. The asbestos issue becomes more of a concern when buildings being used for schools were built before the 1970's. However, all school buildings are required to be inspected for asbestos. Check with your state agency or call the Toxic hot line at 202-554-1404.

4   **The Budget Reconciliation Act of 1993.** This recent act affects the way your school will process donations. For example, exchanges of goods or services claimed as deductions must be documented appropriately if the donor gives more than a $75 donation and receives

something in value. Also, a receipt, indicating the fair market value, must be issued for contributions over a specified amount (Check with your CPA for guidelines for dealing with donations).

5   **Civil Rights Act of 1964, Sec. 3. Section 702.** This law allows a religious corporation to discriminate in the hiring of personnel on the basis of religious beliefs. It is important that the application form describes exactly what qualities a school is seeking. Highlight any religious qualifications that a school wishes the employee to possess.

6   **Commercial Motor Vehicle Safety Act of 1986.** This law requires Christian schools to meet minimum standards for commercial driver licensing. Contact your state Department of Transportation for more information. Most communities offer special classes to help individuals pass the written and driving test. In an attempt to reduce the number of vehicle accidents caused by drivers under the influence of drugs and alcohol, the Federal Highway Administration has stated a series of new regulations. Presently, these regulations affect only schools and churches employing 50 or more drivers. However, by January 1996, small employers (schools and churches) will have to comply. Contact your state Department of Transportation for more information on these regulations.

7   **Consolidated Omnibus Budget Reconciliation Act (COBRA).** This act requires employers with 20 or more employees to furnish written notice of the continuation rights to all new employees of health care benefits afforded to existing employees [CSRK 3.3].

8   **Employee Polygraph Protection Act of 1988 (EPPA).** As enacted, the Polygraph Protection Act of 1988 prohibits church-operated schools from using a polygraph test for screening job applicants.

9   **Equal Pay Act of 1963 (EPA).** This act prohibits discrimination on the basis of gender for paying wages, for equal work on jobs where equal skill, effort and responsibility are determined. The courts have found "Head of Household" pay schedules based on religious doctrine to be in violation of the Equal Pay Act. This law also influences the decisions schools make when compensating coaches of boys and girls sports.

10 **Fair Labor Standards Act (FLSA).** The law requires schools to pay at least $4.25 as a minimum wage and time and one-half for work over a standard 40 hour workweek. It also establishes a lower age limit of 14 years old for employment of minors.

11 **Family and Medical Leave Act of 1993.** This law applies to organizations engaged in a business or activity affecting commerce—one that has fifty or more employees. Most churches and schools will be exempt and not required to provide up to twelve weeks of unpaid leave to eligible employees as a result of the birth or adoption of a child or because of a serious health condition. However, each school

and church needs to review its leave policies to see that they are in compliance.

12 **Federal Insurance Contribution Act (FICA)**. Although a church-sponsored school ministry may choose not to participate in social security, employees must unless exempt. For example: ordained ministers. Ministers must file for exemption [CSRK 3.4].

13 **Immigration Reform and Control Act of 1986.** The Immigration and Control Act of 1986 (IRCA) requires Christian schools to check the documentation of all workers when they begin working. This task is to be accomplished within three business days of the date the employee is officially hired. Schools need to complete an Employment Eligibility I-9 form on all employees [CSRK 3.5].

14 **Lead Contamination Control Act (LCCA) 1988.** All water coolers must be on the EPA approved list and drinking water must meet federal standards. This will be a more critical issue in older buildings being used as a day school.

15 **National Labor Relations Act**. The NLRA gives employees a federally protected right to join labor organizations and engage in collective bargaining so employees have input in the terms and conditions of their employment. Providing a just compensation for all employees, especially non-teaching support staff, and a safe work environment will reduce the possibility of the NLRA's effect in your school.

16 **Nondiscrimination (Title VI of the Civil Rights Act of 1964).** Schools need to include a nondiscrimination policy statement in the school's charter, by-laws, or other governing instruments, such as student handbooks. Unless your school can prove to IRS that it does not have a racially nondiscriminatory policy toward students, the IRS considers your school not charitable [CSRK 3.6].

17 **Occupational Safety and Health Act of 1970 (OSHA).** Church-sponsored schools are not exempt from OSHA. It is the school's responsibility to provide a safe work environment. As of March, 1992, OSHA requires schools to develop a written plan dealing with exposure to the HBV virus which causes hepatitis B. For more information write: U.S. Department of Labor, OSHA 2203, 200 Constitution Avenue, N.W., Washington, DC 20210; (202) 219-8151.

18 **Older Workers Benefit Protection Act (OWBPA)**. The Age Discrimination in Employment Act of 1975 (ADEA) has been amended by the Older Workers Benefit Protection Act (OWBPA). The underlying provision of OWBPA prohibits discrimination of employment benefits based on age. Although older workers can still sign away ADEA rights using a waiver, such waivers must be in writing, address the specific benefits waved and exchanges provided. When benefits are waived, the employee must be given at least 21 days to

consider the benefit waiver. The employee has seven days after signing to revoke the agreement.

19 **Radon Measures in Schools.** Currently, there are no existing laws requiring schools to deal with Radon-222. However, the U.S. Environmental Protection Agency has identified an increased risk of lung cancer associated with exposure to elevated levels of radon. The EPA issued an interim report in March, 1989, on how to measure radon in schools and what to do if elevated levels are found. Check with your state EPA for current requirements.

20 **Self-Employment.** The law (as of January 1, 1984) requires all religious organizations and religious workers (except ordained, commissioned or licensed ministers of a church who have chosen not to be covered) to participate in social security. A church-sponsored school may choose whether or not it wants to participate in contributing to social security. If a school does not participate, each employee is considered self-employed and must contribute the entire amount to the social security fund. Coverage by federal and state unemployment tax is not required, although it may be chosen by the church school employer. Schools that are not affiliated with a sponsoring church are not exempt from paying unemployment tax.

Posting of Notices

One of the areas often overlooked by Christian schools is the posting of certain notices required by federal law. These notices should be posted in a "conspicuous place," such as school office, mailbox area, employee break area, etc. You can obtain copies of the official notices from your state Department of Labor. For a special 44-page report outlining the requirements for personnel record retention and notice posting requirements, contact Personnel Policy Services, Inc., Louisville, KY; (800) 437-3735.

Licensing and Commissioning Employees

There has been a growing debate whether or not Christian school administrators and teachers should receive ministerial tax benefits, such as a housing allowance exclusion, and self-employment tax exemption. Various court cases have clarified the position of the IRS as to who is recognized as a "minister" and subject to receive tax benefits.[7]

Eligibility for tax benefits is determined by passing the "five factor test." All five factors do not need to be met to be considered a minister for tax purposes, only condition four. The five factors are 1) administers the "sacraments," 2) conducts worship services, 3) performs services in the religious denomination, 4) be "ordained, commissioned or licensed," and 5) be considered to be a spiritual leader of his or her church or religious denomination. However, ordaining, licensing and commissioning employees solely for tax benefits is not acceptable.[8] Some churches have established an internal policy to require that factor four and two other factors be met to be considered as a minister for tax purposes.[9] (See *Legal Forms for Christian Schools* for a series of housing allowance planning sheets.)

Compliance by Schools Accepting Federal Assistance

Federal assistance programs include such programs as Chapter 2 of the Education Consolidation and Improvement Act, Public Law 97-35, the Drug Free Schools and Communities Act, Public Law 98-377, Title II of the Education for Economic Security Act and Public Law 98-377. Others include: Chapter 1 of the Education Consolidation and Improvement Act, Public Law 97-35, the Developmental Bilingual Education Program, Training Personnel for the Education of the Handicapped, Fund for the Improvement and Reform of Schools and Teaching-Family-School Partnership Program.

Schools accepting federal assistance fall under a number of other federal laws. Some of these laws include the following:

1   **Age Discrimination in Employment Act of 1975**. This legislation prohibits unreasonable discrimination on the basis of age, specifically between ages of 40 and 65, by employers who have at least 20 employees.

2   **Civil Rights Restoration Act (CRRA)**. The provisions of this bill, which include the employment of sexual minorities, and handicapped people (including AIDS patients), apply when an institution directly receives federal funds, such as social security checks, rent subsidies, guaranteed student loans, etc. Schools who receive federal monies should apply for a religious exemption under this existing law.

3   **Family Educational Rights and Privacy Act of 1974.** This law, known as the Buckley Amendment, allows access to student records by the following groups without prior written consent:

    • State and local officials for the purpose of reporting infectious diseases, gunshot wounds and abuse.

    • Accrediting organizations for accomplishing accrediting functions.

    • Educational testing organizations for purposes of test validation and development.

    • Other educational institutions where a student seeks enrollment.

    • Parents, or acting guardians, of students who are dependent for financial support have access to their child's files. Information contained in the student file of an emancipated minor may not be released to his parent or guardian without written consent.

4   **Drug Free Work Place Act of 1988.** The Drug Free Work Place Act of 1988 affects only those schools accepting federal assistance, such as federal grants, title programs and food subsidies.

5   **Rehabilitation Act of 1973 (as amended in 1974).** This act protects against discrimination of handicapped. This includes anyone with physiological disorders or conditions, cosmetic disfigurement, anatomical loss, mental or psychological disorders, and reformed or rehabilitated alcoholics and drug users. Christian schools who receive federal assistance are required to make modifications in their academic programs to accommodate handicapped students. Also, a school would not be able to charge more for providing an appropriate education "when additional charges are justified."

6   **Sex Discrimination in Title IX.** This law simply states that no person in the United States shall, on the basis of sex, be excluded from participation in, be denied the benefits of, or be subjected to discrimination under any education program or activity receiving federal assistance.

7   **Vietnam Era Veteran's Readjustment Assistance Act.** The purpose of the act is to protect disabled veterans and veterans of the Vietnam Era from discriminating employment practices. Schools are required to develop a written affirmative action compliance program.

Check State Statutory Requirements

Standards which private religious schools must meet depend upon the particular jurisdiction in which each school operates. Some state statutes are favorable toward private religious schools, while others are restrictive.

Failure to follow statutory requirements may result in civil disobedience, or in defending constitutional freedoms about parental rights and religious educational liberties. Some of the more recent issues follow.

Accreditation

Although the state may not require a private religious school to be accredited, the question about seeking state accreditation will come up at some time. Accreditation is viewed as a process whereby an outside, impartial, independent agency conducts a realistic and comprehensive review of a school. The accrediting agency (for example, ICAA and ACSI) determines a school's ability to meet standards common to schools and to determine objectively the degree to which a school is accomplishing what it is trying to do.

Compulsory Attendance

All states have compulsory attendance laws. According to William Bentley Ball, foremost Christian school constitutional lawyer, "The compulsory attendance laws of several states are plainly unconstitutional and could not properly be complied with."[10] It is important that a school understands its state's particular position on compulsory attendance.

Curriculum

It is the responsibility of the local school district to present in the classrooms in public schools the curriculum prescribed by the state. Some states may require certain courses be taught in all schools, public as well as private, such as American History and Government. Other states may give only broad guidelines and leave the final selection up to the local school board.

The rule of thumb is to parallel the public school curriculum (subjects) as much as possible. This is important, since some states, such as Arizona, Colorado, North Carolina, Oregon, South Dakota and Utah allow Christian schools to operate free from regulation as long as they agree to participate in standardized testing programs. The testing program generally follows the state adopted curricula.

Employee Taxes

The law (as of January 1, 1984) requires all religious organizations and religious workers (except ordained, commissioned or licensed ministers of a church who have chosen not to be covered) to participate in social security. A church-sponsored school may choose whether or not it wants to participate in contributing to social security. If a school does not participate, each employee is considered self-employed and must contribute the entire amount to the social security fund.

Immunization, Medication, Health and AIDS

In Oklahoma, the law is very specific, "No child shall be admitted to any public or private school unless he has an authorized certification that he has received or is in the process of receiving immunizations against diphtheria, pertussis, tetanus, measles (rubeola, rubella), poliomyelitis and smallpox" (70 O.S. 700,701). Parents should complete a health card as part of the enrollment process.

It is not unusual for some states to provide exemptions from these immunization requirements for those who object on religious grounds. Most states providing these exemptions also furnish schools with a standardized exemption form for parents to complete.

Medication

Unless trained to do so, school personnel are not expected to go beyond administration of first aid. They can be liable for excessive treatment. Only properly licensed personnel should perform medical procedures. Having a medical professional on call is a good course to follow. The school needs to keep a daily medication log, and obtain written permission before dispensing over-the-counter medications.

Length of School Term

Many states do not have any requirements for a standard school term for private religious schools. It is recommended that the number of days established be similar to those for each community.

Registration With the State

A state may have a requirement that private schools be registered with the state and offer an education equivalent to that of the public schools. In some cases, the local school superintendent must evaluate and recommend approval to the local school board.

School Boards

Generally, Christian day schools that are not accredited by the state are not required to have a school board. In fact, it is possible to operate a school without a school board. As mentioned earlier, to operate a school without sound council is not a good policy.

Sex Education

For the most part, the decision to teach sex education rests with the Christian school. Only in cases where the Christian school is accredited by the state, may the state dictate the teaching of sex education. In those states that mandate teaching of sex education and AIDS education, the Christian school is at liberty to select its own curriculum.

Student Testing

Several states are now requiring students to pass competency tests to receive a diploma. In addition, public schools may require the passing of a competency test before students from Christian schools can transfer back to the public school. Check with your State Department of Education and public schools for more information on this topic.

Teacher Certification

Teacher certification requirements vary from state to state. For example, teacher certification in nonaccredited private schools is not required in Oklahoma; teachers are not required to have any particular qualifications (70 O.S. 1981, Section 135). This may not be the case in your state.

Examine Local and Municipal Requirements

Local and municipal requirements placed on private religious schools generally relate to building codes, health, fire and safety codes, traffic codes, and property tax. Some major areas of concern include the following.

Building Codes Compliance

State and local governments require private schools to follow reasonable health, fire, and safety codes. The key word is "reasonable." (See Step 4–Obtain Adequate Facilities.)

Leasing Public School Buildings

Most states permit the use of public school buildings belonging to local school districts for religious purposes. However, some school districts are reluctant to allow churches to use public school buildings for religious day schools.

Zoning Ordinances

One of the first questions to be answered is "does the neighborhood in which the church is located provide zoning for a day school?" If it does not, a change in zoning will be required.

Prepare for Other Legal Issues

There are numbers of other state and federal regulations and IRS rulings that affect Christian schools. This final section presents several that have caused the greatest legal risk in recent years.

Admission of Nonimmigrant (F-1) Students

Only those schools that have been recognized by the U.S. Department of Justice, Immigration and Naturalization Service are authorized to admit nonimmigrant (F-1) students. Check with your state service for specific requirements.

Business Procedures, Records and Documents

The business practices of a school are under the same obligations to abide by the same laws as the general public. In addition, there are hundreds of laws associated with nonprofit organizations. Richard R. Hammer covers these laws in his book, *Pastors, Churches and Law.*

Another very helpful resource is a two-volume work by James E. Guinn *Religious Organizations: IRS and Accounting Issues*.

Church Membership Tuition Discounts

Many Christian schools offer discounts to members of sponsoring churches. However, no stipulations of tithing can be placed on church membership as a condition to receiving a tuition discount. When discounts are awarded to tithing members only and a parent is audited by IRS, a school risks possible legal exposure.

Church Contributions by Parents for Tuition Paid

In a recent IRS ruling (IRS Private Letter Ruling 9004030), the IRS concluded that parents cannot deduct contributions made to a church that pays the tuition of their children at a church-operated school.

Compulsory Church Attendance

Some schools sponsored by churches require all staff to be regular in attendance at sponsoring church services (for example, Sunday and mid-week services). Schools who make this requirement run a risk of legal exposure based on the Fair Labor Standards Act (FLSA). If church attendance is required by the school ministry, the hourly employee is led to believe that his present working conditions or the continuance of his employment would be adversely affected by non-attendance at the worship services, that is, attendance is mandatory rather than voluntary. When this is the case, attendance at worship services must be considered "hours worked"; therefore, this time is subject to minimum wage and overtime requirements under the FLSA.

Compulsory Tithing Requirement for Staff and Faculty

A ministry may require all employees to be tithers, including school staff. Consider the following standards in formulating a compulsory tithing policy:

- The policy is clearly stated prior to employment [CSRK 3.7].
- The policy contains an objective standard by which the ministry can evaluate an employee's tithing performance, for example, ten percent of the gross income received from the school.
- The policy is consistently administered for all employees.
- The ministry allows for due process when violations of the policy are evident.

Tuition Refunds

The courts vary on how they have dealt with refunds on prepaid tuition. As long as the school has established the validity of nonrefundable amounts and has communicated prior to enrollment tuition refund policies, the courts will most likely rule in favor of the school.

Tuition Work Scholarships

In an attempt to make Christian schooling more affordable, schools have devised numerous tuition payment (for example, sliding scale, family plan, shared giving, modified cost) and assistance programs. One plan that is increasing in popularity and at the same time has the greatest legal risk is work-study programs. This is a program where parents or students exchange work (for example, secretarial, custodial, etc.) for tuition. In the sight of IRS, this practice is interpreted as tax-free income and should be subject to income tax [CSRK 3.8].

Statistical Reporting

Many statistical reports requested by states are strictly voluntary, as is the case in Oklahoma, where attendance figures are requested for each grade level. Other states may place strict reporting requirements upon Christian schools. As long as the information provided does not compromise the position of a school or limit its free operation, a school should cooperate with the requests. One of the tasks of administration includes researching state reporting requirements.

School Names and Trademarks

As more and more Christian schools open, the likelihood of a Christian school in the same locality acquiring the same or a similar name is very possible. A school may seek legal protection of its name though the law of unfair competition or under the federal trademark law. A trademark is any word, symbol, or device, or any combination thereof adopted and used by a manufacturer or merchant to identify his goods and distinguish them from those manufactured and sold by others. A school is eligible for a trademark if the mark is used to identify goods or services offered to the public. The Patent and Trademark Office in Washington, DC, determines whether the mark a school proposes conflicts with a currently registered mark. There is a filing fee of around $175.

Teacher Contracts

A private religious school is under no obligation to provide written teacher contracts. Schools providing contracts need to include all the elements of a legal contract, such as name and address of employee and employer, length of time covered by the contractual period, delineation of employee duties, compensation, termination of employment, benefits, extended responsibilities, and the date the signed contract is to be in effect. Reference also should be made to other written and procedural handbooks, manuals, etc. Since employments are governed by each state, schools should check these laws. A sample of a teacher contract is found in the Christian School Resource Kit [CSRK 3.9].

Teacher Tenure

Many states have tenure laws governing public school personnel, a "fringe benefit" granted by state statutes. Unless accredited under a state accreditation system where tenure is required, Christian schools are not subject to state created tenure laws. Christian schools may establish their own tenure system. In so doing, include as a minimum a probationary period of several years, a systematic method of evaluation, a procedure for dismissing an incompetent teacher or when performance drops below satisfaction, and a review and due process procedure.

J. Lester Brubaker comments,

> "Christian schools can rely on something better than tenure for positive relationship—the trust and caring of Christian brother-hood. [11]

Tuition Discounts

The position of IRS has not changed on this issue. Parents are not able to provide a contribution to a church (tithe, love gift, offering, etc.) and at the same time gain a tuition benefit (usually in the form of a reduction). All stipulations that offer a tuition reduction based on tithing should be removed.

Tuition Tax Credit

Parents may be able to claim tuition tax credit for those expenses of sending their children to private schools (for example, Minnesota). Check your particular state. Pay close attention to state-sponsored voucher systems, for example, Wisconsin.

Pitfalls To Avoid

1. Failing to obtain qualified legal counsel. In looking for a lawyer, consider one who specializes in private school law. However, keep in mind that ability, experience, and reputation of the lawyer are more important than whether or not he or she is certified as a specialist. If you are uncertain about a lawyer's qualifications, request a list of private school-related problems the lawyer has handled and a list of references.

Don't take a person's endorsement of a particular lawyer. Check them out yourself.

2. Failing to obtain price quotes before legal services are secured. Lawyers usually charge in one of three ways: a specified hourly rate, an established flat fee for the entire task, or a contingency fee dependent on the amount recovered. In many states, the amount a lawyer can charge is established by law (for example, New York). Usually the amount charged will depend upon the complexity of the problem and the lawyer's ability.

A school may choose to pay a lawyer a fixed fee (retainer) to ensure that the lawyer is available when a legal challenge arises. Some lawyers require a down payment for legal services, and the money is credited toward the legal services rendered.

As soon as the school employs a lawyer, establish a file. Maintain copies of original documents, letters of correspondence, signed agreements, bills, summarized outlines of conversations, phone calls, etc. This helps the school organize responses to legal challenges and provides a ready reference should the school need to change lawyers.

3. Failing to keep good legal records. Consider establishing a separate file drawer for filing all legal documentation relating to establishing the school and its ongoing operation. Consider creating files for the following topics: articles of incorporation, by-laws, I-9's, commercial drivers' licenses, housing allowance eligibility, minutes of school board, nondiscriminatory documents, handbooks, school brochures, scholarship policies, Form 5578, salary schedule, staff handbook, student record access policies, building occupancy permits, fire and safety inspections.

4. Failure to provide for arbitration. Most Christian schools over the course of time will experience conflict. It may be the result of unfair compensation, equal pay issues, breach of duty, discrimination in awarding employee benefits, lack of due process in staff dismissal, and a host of other factors. When a dispute cannot be resolved, there is a high probability it may end up in court. Every attempt should be made to settle disputes out of court through arbitration, mediation and reconciliation. Writing a compulsory arbitration clause into staff contracts will keep staff issues out of court, be less costly and provide an element of privacy, avoiding the potential for negative publicity. A typical arbitration clause follows:

> "In the event of any dispute as to the terms or conditions of employment (including termination), the teacher agrees to follow this procedure: the item of dispute will first be brought to

the attention of the Principal, for resolution. If the matter is not resolved or cannot be resolved within ten (10) days thereafter, the teacher or the aggrieved party may then appeal the matter to the Superintendent. If the matter is not resolved or cannot be resolved within ten (10) days thereafter, the teacher or the aggrieved party (which may include the Principal or another employee of the school) agree to submit the matter to the school board. If the matter is not resolved or cannot be resolved within ten (10) days thereafter, the teacher or the aggrieved party (which may include the Principal or another employee of the school) agree to submit the matter to a panel of three arbitrators, one of which is to be selected by the aggrieved party, one of which is to be selected by the Superintendent, and one of which is to be selected by the school board. The panel of arbitrators shall then schedule a hearing on the matter, and after considering the issues presented to them, shall issue a written decision or award, which shall be final in all respects. The panel of arbitrators shall use as a guide the procedures for conciliation as promulgated by the Christian Conciliation Service, or the rules of arbitration as set forth by the American Arbitration Association. The formal rules of evidence need not be followed in the conduct of the hearing. Any costs of arbitration shall be born equally by the parties, regardless of the award."

5. Not adequately screening volunteers. Most Christian schools greet volunteers with open arms. If schools didn't have volunteers, the cost of education would be much higher. However, very few Christian schools are prepared to deal with financial lost as a result of legal challenges presented from the actions of volunteers, such as violating safety guidelines, failure to report accidents, molestation, sexual harassment, to name a few. Here are four main areas to help prevent liability problems.

- **Establish an effective screening and interviewing process.** Include a background check for criminal records, especially if volunteers will be used in pre-school and elementary grades. During the interview, discuss the volunteer's background, previous experiences in similar work and qualifications for the task. Ask, "Is there anything about your background or experiences that would preclude you from being successful in this volunteer position?" Ask if they have been charged with any convictions? Follow up on all employer and church references.

- **Provide for quality training.** Demonstrate the duties to perform, point out acts that are prohibited (for example, no counseling of students of the opposite gender). Show them the risks involved in performing the duties (for instance, automatic dishwashers). Discuss record-keeping ethics and confidentialities, for example, student records.

- **Present a quality orientation.** Cover rules and policies relating to their duties and establish performance expectations.

- **Assess performance.** Maintain good attendance records. Assign the volunteer to a professional staff person in the area of service.

Father, I thank You for Your wisdom in establishing the legal foundation for this school. Your Word says that You will instruct me and teach me in the way I should go. You will counsel me and watch over this school. You said You would contend with those that contend with me. Furthermore, no weapon formed against me or this school will prosper in Jesus' name.

Building a strong legal foundation for the Christian school reduces future legal risk.

Christian School Resource Kit

3.1   Christian School Constitutional Article

3.2   Letter of Intent to Open a Day School

3.3   COBRA Notification

3.4   Ministerial Exemption Form 4363

3.5   Employment Eligibility Form I-9

3.6   Nondiscriminatory Policy

3.7   Compulsory Tithing Policy

3.8   Work Study Packet

3.9   Teacher Contract

Endnotes

1   Richard R. Hammer. *Pastor, Church and Law.* Springfield, MO: Gospel Publishing House, 1983, p. 301.

2   Freiheit, Lynn A. "Legal Audit." Report submitted to Victory Christian School, Tulsa, OK, 1984, p. 2.

3   David Gibbs, "The Pastor, The Church and Taxes." Conneaut, OH: Gibbs & Craze Co., 1992.

4   James W. Deuink and Carl D. Herbster. *Effective Christian School Management.* 2nd Edition. Greenville, SC: Bob Jones University Press, 1986, p. 28.

5   Hammer, *op. cit.*, p. 300.

6   Paul A. Kienel "The Christian School and Religious Liberty," *Administration of the Christian School*. Roy W. Lowrie, Jr., ed. Whittier, CA: The Association of Christian Schools International, 1984, p. 274.

7   Knight v. Commissioner 92 T.C. 12, 1989.

8   Lawrence v. Commissioner 50 T.C. 494, 1968.

9   Private Letter Ruling 9126048, April, 1991.

10   William Bently Ball. *Constitutional Protection of Christian Schools.* Whittier, CA: Association of Christian Schools International, 1981, p. 6.

11   J. Lester Brubaker. *Personnel Administration in the Christian School*. Winona Lake, IN: BMH Books, 1980, p. 96.

References

ACSI. Association of Christian Schools International. 731 N. Beach Blvd., La Habra, CA 90631; (213) 694-4791.

Demuth, Dennis M. and Demuth, Carol M. *Christian School Legal Forms Packet*. Tulsa, OK: DEL Publications, 1993.

Demuth, Dennis M. and Demuth, Carol M. *Legal Requirements For Christian Schools*, 2nd Edition. Tulsa, OK: DEL Publications, 1993.

Guinn, James E. *Religious Organizations: IRS and Accounting Issues*. Volume 1 & 2, 2nd Edition. Irving, TX: Guinn, Smith and Co., Inc., 1992.

ICAA. International Christian Accreditation Association. 7777 South Lewis Avenue, Tulsa, OK 74171; (918) 495-7054.

STEP 4

OBTAIN ADEQUATE FACILITIES

The community will judge the quality of a school's educational program by the physical condition and general appearance of the facility. Dr. Roy W. Lowrie, Jr. put it this way,

> "Christian school teachers are hard workers, for they view teaching as a ministry not just a job. Having conscientious teachers does not replace the need for proper facilities and equipment. A quality educational program requires good facilities and equipment...When inadequate facilities and equipment are used, the students and the teachers will pay the price. There are no shortcuts, even in the Christian school, to quality education. The buildings should not be luxurious, but they should be big enough and designed well enough to allow a top-quality program."[1]

The effectiveness of teaching and training is directly related to the adequacy of the instructional surroundings—visual, acoustical and thermal environments of the classroom, and to its furnishings. The learning environment should be comfortable, safe, productive and stimulating.[2]

A good physical environment makes itself felt in many ways:

- The student feels happier.
- The student learns more quickly and has a feeling of pride in his school.
- The teacher has more stamina and good morale.
- The teacher is more patient and more relaxed.
- The need for discipline is lessened.
- Vandalism may be negligible.
- Custodial and maintenance costs diminish.
- Recruiting is enhanced.

Investigate Federal and State Requirements

Many existing church buildings, especially those built within the last 15 to 20 years, can be readily used as a day school. Others will need extensive remodeling before obtaining occupancy permits. Most changes will be the result of federal, state and community code requirements that apply to all school buildings. Identifying and meeting these requirements is a task that requires a united effort.

65

Conduct a Facilities Self-Assessment

Conducting an informal self-assessment of the building that you are planning to use as a day school is the first step to determining its adequacy. Consider code requirements, educational requirements, existing conditions, fire and safety concerns and administration requirements.

Complete the following assessment. Place a check mark in the box if the statement is true about the facility you plan to use for a Christian day school. If you are uncertain, leave the box blank. Addressing some items may require research on your part. Don't assume the statement is true. Make sure! Remember, many of these requirements may be different for your particular state and community.

Code Requirements

A major area for assessment is state and local code requirements. Failure to meet these codes will jeopardize the opening of your school.

☐ There at least two means of exit from each floor of the building.

☐ The school site provides for a ground level exit in the lower level. For example, a church wanting to open a Christian day school in a nearby community was unable to do so because it had located the classrooms in the basement of the church. There was no ground level exit. Correcting the situation was no easy task: dirt was removed from one of the basement's walls, and a door and ramp were installed.

☐ The neighborhood in which your school is to be located is zoned for a day school. Careful attention must be given to zoning regulations. "Fair zoning laws are for our protection. Unfair zoning laws should be opposed and changed."[3]

☐ Classrooms, gyms, and specialty rooms have adequate heating and ventilation. Fresh air flows at 15 to 25 cubic feet per minute per student.

☐ There is special venting for science lab odors. A more complete laboratory safety checklist can be found in Christian School Resource Kit [CSRK 4.1].

☐ All ventilating ducts terminate outside the building.

☐ The building meets the city code for smoke detectors.

☐ Fire resistant walls, floors, ceiling and doors separate the heating plant from the main corridors and other parts of the building.

☐ All exit doors open in the direction of exit-travel.

☐ All exterior exit doors are equipped with approved panic locks.

☐ Doors are wide enough to accommodate devices such as wheel-chairs.

☐ There is adequate parking for parents, students, staff and disabled. For example: calculate one space for 20 to 30 percent of the high school students enrolled in the top three grades and one space per staff. Add one-half space for each staff to accommodate visitors. You can fit about 80 to 110 cars per acre. Consult your local code requirements for handicapped parking.

NOTE: *Properly mark all parking spaces, crosswalks and parking zones.*

☐ There is at least one entrance specifically designed to accommodate the disabled—included are curb cuts or other forms of ramping.

☐ Shower facilities have adequate drains.

☐ Major hallway widths meet the code for day schools, usually 6-10 feet. Auxiliary walkways are at least 48" wide. "Internal student traffic can become a disturbingly serious problem unless proper planning has gone into the use of the plant."[4]

☐ Stairways have handrails.

☐ There are adequate commodes and lavatory facilities according to the building code requirements for a day school. The general guidelines for commodes and lavatory facilities are: Boys—Water Closet, 50:1; Lavatory, 50:1; Urinal, 30:1. For Girls—Water Closet, 30:1; Lavatory, 30:1.

NOTE: *There should be a minimum of two fixtures in each rest room.*

☐ Rest room fixtures are at the proper height. For example,

Grades K-3
- Water Closet – 13 to 15 inches
- Lavatory – 24 inches
- Urinal – 15 inches

Grades 4-6
- Water Closet – 15 inches
- Lavatory – 28 inches
- Urinal – 17 inches

Grades 7-9
- Water Closet – 15 inches
- Lavatory – 32 inches
- Urinal – 19 inches

Grades 10-12
- Water Closet – 15 inches
- Lavatory – 32 inches
- Urinal – 21 inches

☐ The school meets all codes established by the Americans with Disabilities Act (ADA).

☐ There is one drinking fountain for each 75 pupils. The drinking fountains are at the proper height for each grade level. For example:

- Grades K – 3 = 24"
- Grades 4 – 6 = 30"

- Grades 7 – 9 = 32"
- Grades 10 – 12 = 36"

Educational Requirements

There are several requirements important to the educational development of students. Consider the following:

☐ There is sufficient lighting in all areas of the school. Light intensities in the school should vary according to the type of usage. Foot-candles range from 25 in corridors to 150 in gymnasiums. It is important to check each room for the amount of light as well as the amount of glare from light sources to the student desks and chalkboards.
Use the following guidelines:

- General Classrooms, 70 foot-candles
- Corridors, 25 foot-candles
- Cafeteria, 100 foot-candles
- Art, 125 foot-candles
- Gymnasiums, 150 foot-candles

You can reduce brightness of desk tops and wall surfaces by using a flat finish with a low reflection ratio. Inspect to ensure that lighting is uniformly distributed through the room with no area that has dark spots. Most older buildings will require additional light fixtures to produce a good visual instructional environment. The use of natural lighting should be maximized.

☐ The lighting can be adequately controlled when using audio-visuals. Use dimmer units in instructional areas. In placing a projector screen, position the screen in the corner of the room, rather than at the front. This increases student visibility.

☐ Wall colors represent neutral tones, such as beige, tans, rather than reds, pinks, oranges and yellows that tend to promote stimulation and excitement. Replace old grays and browns. Light colors will reflect in darker rooms and make small rooms look larger. Select paint with a low shine, preferably a latex enamel. This minimizes glare and makes the walls easier to clean.

☐ Paint rooms having no natural lighting with other colors than blues, greens, grays or lavenders, all of which tend to be repressive and often depressive.

☐ Classrooms are furnished to accommodate the interests of the students occupying the room; for example, kindergarten students verses fourth graders. The equipment needed in various classrooms will depend somewhat upon the general building layout and the type of activities conducted in the room.

☐ In purchasing equipment for the school, keep in mind the needs of other church ministries. Attempt to set up your rooms to match the needs of other groups using the room. For example, you would want to use the elementary classrooms for elementary-aged Sunday school children. Trying to convert a secondary math classroom into a Sunday nursery will have its challenges.

☐ Classrooms housing the same grade levels are located in the same area. For example, lower elementary grade rooms are located in the same area of the building. Likewise, middle school grade rooms are kept at one end of the building, as are high school rooms.

☐ All furniture is in good repair. Many times used furniture is available at a good price. With a little time invested and a few materials, used school desks secured from public school can be refinished and often are much better constructed than some newer furniture. For example, it is not unusual to see school systems discard solid oak chairs in favor of new molded plastic chairs.

If furnishings are beyond repair, institute a yearly replacement plan. Over the course of a few years, it is possible to obtain good looking furnishings. If you need to replace furniture and choose not to do so because of costs, ask yourself this question, "Would replacing this classroom result in at least one more student enrolling?" If the answer is "yes," enrolling one student could very well pay for the new furnishings.

Most companies will work with schools in securing furniture by providing an extended line of credit. In selecting furniture, don't settle for a less than quality product to save a few dollars. The day-to-day wear and tear of hundreds of hands and feet will make quick work of inferior products.

NOTE: *Keep in mind that some parents and students equate quality furniture to a quality program.*

☐ There is a wet sink in the art room or in close proximity.

☐ All ceilings are painted white or near white. Ceilings should be painted white because 80 percent reflection factor is needed to give pupils sufficient light.

☐ Desks and chair units are not all fixed (one piece). Furniture should be able to be moved around to suit the needs of children and the teaching-learning tasks. This will provide opportunity for a rich and varied program of activities.

NOTE: *In purchasing new furniture, specify a prompt delivery date with a penalty for delivery beyond the agreed upon date. If the vendor cannot guarantee a specific delivery date, consider using another vendor.*

☐ Teachers are involved in the selection of classroom furnishings. Since teachers will be directly affected by these furnishings, they should provide input into the selection process.

☐ It is possible to arrange the furniture so orientation for group activities can be toward a given presentation point. Seats or chairs should be able to be oriented to face a display or the focal point of instruction so head turning and neck straining are reduced.

☐ Teacher and student desk arrangements allow easy movement between them. Unobstructed access should be maintained in all areas of the classroom. Maintain a minimum clear aisle of four feet for two-way traffic.

☐ Total acreage is within the suggested standards. Consider the following guidelines:

- Elementary schools = 10 acres plus 1 acre for each 100 students over 300
- Junior High = 20 acres plus 1 acre for each 100 students over 500
- Senior High = 30 acres plus 1 acre for each 100 students over 600
- K-12 School = 20 to 30 acres plus 1 acre for each 100 students over 600

NOTE: *These recommendations are the ideal. The minimum acreage for a school site should be five acres plus one acre for each 100 pupils.*

☐ The school provides an area for common athletic activities, such as basketball, volleyball, badminton, ping pong, tennis, baseball, softball, soccer, etc.

☐ The school has a science lab for junior and senior high school students. Schools that do not have self-contained science labs use portable science tables containing water and gas.

☐ There is a special room designated as the library. Seating capacity is 10 to 15 percent of student enrollment with 20 to 25 square feet per pupil. Thus, a school of 300 students would have a library of about 600 to 1000 square feet. The library contains space for a reading area and an area for small group study.

☐ The school has access to a gymnasium. If not, consider use of the YMCA or other buildings that may be converted to a gymnasium.

☐ There are specialty rooms for art and music.

☐ The classrooms have approximately 16-24 linear feet of chalkboard space and 8-16 linear feet of bulletin board space. Chalkboards are a very important part of the instructional program.

☐ Bulletin boards are at eye level and chalkboards are a comfortable working height. Adhere to the following heights from the floor:
- Kindergarten—First Grade, 24"
- Second—Sixth Grade, 26"
- Seventh—Twelfth, 36" – 42"

☐ Classroom instructional equipment is adequate. For example, recorders, projectors, maps, globes, etc..

☐ The band room is acoustically separated from other classrooms. Allow four square feet of instrument storage for each student enrolled and no less than 35 sq. ft. for individual practice rooms.

☐ The working height of furniture and equipment is at the proper height for the group of students who will be using them. For example:
- Kindergarten = 10 – 11 inches
- Grades one to three = 10 – 13 inches
- Grades four to six = 12 – 16 inches
- Grades seven to twelve = 14 – 18 inches.

☐ All the rooms have trash containers and pencil sharpeners.

☐ Classrooms are not excessively noisy. This may be the case if the school is located near a busy intersection or has an older heating and ventilation system. Excessive noise has an adverse effect on reading comprehension, reduces retention, recall and recognition, and lends itself to a chaotic learning environment. However, a certain amount of background noise is unavoidable and acceptable if not excessive.

Classroom noise can be controlled by the application of

acoustical materials to the ceiling and walls, installation of carpet, lowering ceilings, and increasing the linear footage of bulletin board space. If you have a large noisy gym, multipurpose room, or corridor, you can reduce flutter and echoes by using sound boards and carpet. A carpeted hallway wall makes for a good display area. In carpeting walls, make sure that the carpet meets all building codes; for example, it is made of fire resistant materials.

Existing Conditions

☐ There are no musty smells upon entering any of the classrooms.

☐ The relative humidity in classrooms is between 40 to 60 percent. Thirty to seventy is acceptable.

☐ Wall coverings in rooms where moisture is present, such as shower rooms, dressing rooms and rest rooms, are of moisture-proof or fire-resistant materials.

☐ There are no loose panes of glass.

☐ All playground equipment is free of hazards that could lead to accidents. The type and amount of commercial playground equipment needed will be determined by the grade levels and interests of students. Provide a combination of hard-surfaced areas for outdoor basketball, volleyball, etc. Also, provide a shock-absorbing surface under creative play centers, swings, glides, seesaws, exercise rings, etc. Purchase equipment from reputable dealers who carry product liability insurance.

☐ Ceiling tiles are intact and free of water stains. Failure to check for evidence of a leaky roof could result in major damage, especially if the leak is where you place your library or computer lab.

☐ Floor coverings are in good condition. Ramps and inclines should have a slip-resistant surface. Abrasive strips can be applied to the floor. Careful attention should be given to shower areas.

☐ Carpeted floors are free of unsewn seams, worn holes, etc.

☐ Tile floors are properly adhering to the under-flooring. When considering floor coverings, understand that maintaining carpeted floors compared to tile floors cuts maintenance costs by 75 percent.

☐ Unusual changes in the walking surface are clearly highlighted, for example, ramps.

☐ There is adequate storage in each classroom.

☐ The exterior of the building is in good repair.

Mechanical and Custodial

☐ Temperatures can be consistently controlled, for example, 69 to 76 degrees in classrooms. Check code requirements for heating systems. Some codes require a certified building engineer to be present whenever a school building has a boiler inside the building.

☐ The school is designed to conserve energy. Heating and air-conditioning units that are more than ten years old should be inspected before the building is occupied by school students.

☐ There is provision for regular maintenance and repair of rooms and equipment. One must realize that 100 to 400 students in a building five days a week for six to seven hours daily has a greater effect on facility maintenance than the same number of students on Sunday for two hours.

☐ Provisions are made for housekeeping and custodial duties. The amount of time assigned to these areas depends upon the level or standard of cleanliness desired in your building. Several formulas can be used to determine workloads. However, very few prove to be satisfactory.

Fire/Safety

☐ There is an adequate number of electrical outlets in each room.

☐ Lights are protected from balls and other objects.

☐ Fluorescent lights do not flicker. Flickering bulbs can cause headaches and nausea.

☐ All electrical outlets are properly covered.

☐ Light switches that are susceptible to student tampering are controlled by key switches; for example, hallways, locker rooms, rest rooms.

☐ Waterproof outlets are used in dressing rooms and other moisture prevalent areas.

☐ There are adequate rugs at all entrances to catch dirt and water.

☐ Stairways are in good repair.

☐ There is a proper number of fire extinguishers. For Class A fires, which consist of burning paper, wood, cloth, rubbish, etc., use liquid extinguishers. For class B fires, which consist of burning liquids, gasoline, oil, paint, etc., use CO_2 extinguishers or dry power extinguishers. Class C fires, which include electrical materials, motors, appliances, wiring, etc., use CO_2 or dry-power extinguisher. Areas where computers are located, such as computer labs and school offices, should have halogen extinguishers.

☐ Playground equipment is designed to avoid steep slopes. Ramps, slides and climbing nets should not be installed at angles of more than 35 to 40 degrees.[5]

☐ Preparations are made for a room-by-room emergency evacuation plan [CSRK 4.2]. These plans should include as a minimum:

- The posting of emergency routes in each classroom.
- Planning routes chosen that are unobstructed and the most routine to the nearest outside exit.
- Selection of an unobstructed alternative route.
- An even distribution of the number of students to each of the exits.
- A safe exit for disabled students.

☐ Disaster drills are performed no less than monthly. Keep a record of each evacuation drill—give date, time of day and evacuation time. All personnel exit the building during an alarm. The central ventilation fans are turned off when evacuating the building. Rest room areas are checked for students.

☐ The kitchen has adequate room for cold storage. Use the following guidelines:

- Dry Storage = 5 square feet per meal
- Non-food Storage = 1.5 square feet per meal
- Frozen Storage = 1.5 cubic feet per daily meal

☐ A predetermined signal is used and easily recognized for returning to the building.

☐ All fire exit lamps are lit. Most building codes require battery-powered auxiliary lights in case of a power outage.

☐ Bleacher seats are in good repair.

☐ An outside shut-off valve on the gas supply line is provided and clearly marked.

☐ The following locations are free of accumulations of wastepaper, rubbish, old furniture: furnace room, basement, stage, spaces beneath stairs.

☐ Hazardous material or preparations used for cleaning are safely stored.

☐ The school has an integrated pest management plan in order to minimize exposure to toxic materials.[6]

☐ Corridors are free of dead ends and obstructions that interfere with the flow of student traffic.

☐ Adequate containers are available for disposal of trash—dumpsters with lids.

☐ The city health department has inspected the food preparation area.

☐ The school has been surveyed to determine the existence of lead-based paint on surfaces.

☐ A first-aid equipment storage is provided.

☐ A fireproof file vault is available for storage of student records.

☐ The building can be adequately secured at night. Consider installing motion detectors for nighttime security. The system can sound an alarm outside the building or send a signal to a security station or police headquarters.

☐ Bus loading and unloading traffic patterns are designed so buses will not have to back up. Provide a one-way drive for bus traffic and automobiles.

☐ There is a fire alarm system. Each teacher and student knows exactly where each fire alarm device is located and how the alarm can be activated.

☐ There is a master water cut-off for buildings with a sprinkling system.

☐ Lockers are arranged so doors do not block the hallway traffic.

☐ Solid doors that open into the hallway have a viewing glass to prevent them from being opened into someone on the other side.

☐ Parking lots are adequately lit. Use photoelectric switches and efficient lamps—mercury and sodium vapor.

Administration

☐ There is a room where students can be taken if they became ill. Allow one cot for up to 400 students with 40 square feet per cot.

☐ The health services area is next to the secretary's work area. In the absence of the school nurse, the secretary will be responsible to oversee this area.

☐ There is a master plan for providing optimum use of property and facilities.

☐ There is a room outside of the classroom that has been designated as a teacher area where they can do planning. "A workroom should be considered a necessity rather than a luxury."[7] Unfortunately, many older school buildings and most church buildings used for day schools were designed without areas specifically designed for teacher workrooms.

NOTE: *The work day of a typical teacher is very demanding. Teachers need an area where they can prepare lessons and have access to resource materials and equipment—typewriter, paper cutter, and duplicating equipment and supplies. This workroom should be furnished with a desk and chair. Open and closed shelving should be available as well as a sink and waterproof countertop.*

☐ Adequate office space is provided for staff. Consider the following guidelines for minimum square feet of floor space for a school of 500 students:

- Superintendent's Office 150 – 200
- Principal's Office 100 – 120
- Secretary and Receptionist 120 – 150
- Teachers' Workroom 50 – 100
- Storage of Supplies 100 – 150
- General Storage 90 – 150

☐ There is a place where confidential meetings can be held with parents, teachers and students. It is important for the principal's office to be located in close proximity to the reception room and secretary's work area as well as being accessible to the public. It should be designed to permit private conferences.

Windows should be placed in all doors of offices, especially those rooms used for counseling. Walls can be carpeted or absorbent material placed on the walls. In some offices, foam insulation can be pumped into the walls and insulation placed on top of dropped ceilings. Check local fire codes for use of such materials.

☐ Classrooms and teachers' desks can be adequately secured at the end of the day. This poses a potential area of conflict, especially in buildings that have multiple use. In the elementary level, it is nearly impossible to lock up every student desk, but every student can store his loose items in a school box or other container when desks do not contain storage areas. If you plan to lock teacher desks, purchase desks that are of good quality. Many center desk drawers with locks can easily be broken into.

☐ Provisions are made for the storage of garments, such as coats, boots, etc. Adding a row of simple coat hooks inside the classroom will meet the needs of most elementary children. New or used lockers should be purchased for secondary students.

School lockers are more than places to store books, it is personal space for teenagers. When handles are broken, numbers fallen off, latching mechanisms worn out, locks no longer working, it gives a less than favorable impression on students, parents, visitors, etc. The way the lockers look affects the way your entire school looks.

For a school on a tight budget, replacing lockers may be a luxury your school cannot afford. There is an alternative way of achieving that same new look without the prohibitive cost. Companies such as Dura-Kote can refurbish lockers on site at or about 25 to 40 percent of replacement cost. Dura-Kote uses an electrostatic painting process, durable and scratch-resistant. A refurbished locker will outlast a new one because they are made of a heavier gauge metal.

☐ Rooms used by other groups during the week have a diagram showing how furniture is to be set up [CSRK 4.3].

☐ The school is presentable enough so you would be willing to show it off to the public. Robert J. Krajewski suggests,

"Keep the school looking neat. Too often the quality of the school program is judged by the appearance of the grounds. This is especially true if school is closed for the summer and no one is there to cut the grass. Everyone can see the school grounds."[8]

☐ There are clocks in all classrooms.

☐ The high school has a bell system.

☐ A telephone is available for student use.

☐ There is a public address system.

Estimate Classroom Needs

The space needs for students depend upon a number of factors, such as grade level (for example, elementary, middle and high school), the curriculum and subjects taught (for example, art, science, home economics, music, physical education, etc.), and the type of instructional plan (for instance, self-contained classrooms, traditional scheduling or non-traditional scheduling, such as modules).

Allocate Classroom Space

It is important that enough space be appropriated for each child. A student can be seated in four square feet of floor space; however, few educators would place 25 students in a 100 square feet room. Most schools plan for 20 to 50 square feet per student depending upon the age level and content of the classroom. For example, consider the following square feet:

- Grades K-1 = 40 to 50
- Grades 2-3 = 25 to 30
- Grades 4-6 = 25 to 30
- Grades 7-12 = 20 to 25

- Vocal music = 20
- Band = 25-28
- Computer lab = 20
- Cafeteria = 10 to 12

Determine the Number of Classrooms

The number of classrooms needed depends on the grade level and the type of instructional plan. Consider the differences between elementary grades and junior and senior high school.

Elementary

Planning the number of self-contained classrooms is straight forward. First, decide on the pupil/teacher ratio, such as 25:1. Next, divide the total enrollment by the number of students in the pupil/teacher ratio. For example, 250 students divided by 25 students per teacher equals 10 teachers. Finally, decide whether the classroom occupancy will be by grade level or a combination of grades (See Step 5—Determine Size of the Student Body).

Junior and Senior High School

Determining the number of classrooms needed for junior and senior high school is more complicated, since these levels do not generally utilize self-contained classrooms. Instead, room assignment follows the needs of the master schedules.

When a computer scheduling program is not available, a planning formula will work, especially for traditional scheduling where a subject is scheduled in a classroom for a certain period, usually 45 to 60 minutes. Educators have found the formula presented by Kowalski to be one of the simplest to use.[9] This formula is as follows:

$$NR = [1.15 \text{ x } (ns/cs)] \text{ x } (npw/swp)$$

The formula involves five variables.

1. ns = number of students taking a course
2. cs = desired class size based on pupil/teacher ratio
3. npw = number of periods per week that the class meets
4. swp = number of school week periods

Consider the School Site 79

5. 1.15 = some allowance for variance

When calculated, the result is the number of rooms needed (NR). For example, there are 225 high schoolers who will be taking science (ns = 225). The science lab can accommodate a maximum of 22 students (cs = 22). The classes meet five days per week (npw = 5). The school uses a seven-period day with 55 minutes in each period (swp = 7 x 5 = 35). Therefore, the formula for determining how many labs are needed is as follows:

$$1.15 \times (225/22) \times (5/35)$$
or
$$(1.15 \times 10.23) \times (.143)$$
or
$$11.76 \times .143 = 1.68$$
or
2 science laboratories

Given equal scheduling of students into various science classes, 2 science labs would accommodate 14 sections of science. If enrollment reaches a total of 225 students, each class would have an average of 16 students—well within the projected class size of 22 students. If enrollment increases to 275 students, the average number of students per section would increase from 16 to 20.

Consider the School Site

Careful review of your present facilities may result in a need to rent, lease or build facilities to accommodate your school. Consider the following factors before renting or leasing a facility.

Proximity to Pupils

Since most Christian schools are commuter-based, it is important to consider this when selecting a location. The decision to attend your school is directly related to the driving distance. For example, when Victory Christian School moved to its newly constructed facilities less than five miles from the site it was leasing, enrollment dropped by 65 students. The reason parents gave for not re-enrolling was the additional 20 to 40 extra minutes it took to transport children the extra distance to school and then to pick them up at the end of the school day.

Kind of Neighborhood

Your school will be judged on the type of neighborhood in which it is located, in the same fashion as people judge a city based on the physical appearance leading into the city. Parents want to send their child to a school located in a neighborhood where the buildings and grounds are well-kept and free of evidence of vandalism, such as graffiti on walls, bars over windows and doors. The condition of the streets and parking lot is important, as is the relationship to available highways. For example, will traffic always be a challenge, or does it flow smoothly near the school? Is there a safe route for students walking or riding bicycles?

Leasing Public School Buildings

Most states permit the use of public school buildings belonging to local school districts for religious purposes. However, some school districts are reluctant to allow churches to use public school buildings for religious day schools. Each school district has the freedom to establish fair and reasonable charges to cover the cost of use of property. In leasing or renting a public school facility, consider the following suggestions:

- Check rental costs within the community to determine if the charge is fair and reasonable.

- Conduct a detailed inspection of the building before occupancy. Keep written records of the condition of the building and its furnishings. This will help settle any disputes that may arise when the building is vacated.

- Request the public school district to be responsible for all maintenance of mechanical and electrical equipment. The school district has the responsibility to maintain school buildings in a condition that meets building codes and safety standards. Never agree to lease a building "as is." You may occupy the building and find out that the roof and air-conditioner need replacing, as was the case for one Christian school.

- Since most states only permit a 12-month lease, request a lease whereby, for each month used on the lease, an additional month is added to the end of the lease. This allows for a continual 12-month leasing period.

Renovate or Build New

Conducting a careful inspection of the present facilities available for a day school often leads to a decision between renovating or building new. Luke offers best advice for renovating or building:

> "For which of you, intending to build a tower, sitteth not down first, and counteth the cost, whether he have sufficient to finish it. Lest haply, after he hath laid the foundation, and is not able to finish it, all that behold it begin to mock him, saying, This man began to build, and could not finish" (Luke 14:28-30).

As a rule of thumb, renovation costs one-third to one-half the price of building with an average of $80 per square feet. Unless conditions are favorable, renovation is not recommended when costs exceed 50 to 60 percent of the cost of new construction.

NOTE: *The effective use of professionals, such as architects, engineers and contractors, will expedite the building or renovation process. It is important to hire those who have had previous school building experience.*

Investigate the Use of Portable Classrooms

The use of portable classrooms might be an attractive alternative to constructing a new building. When the Lake City Church (formerly the Madison Gospel Tabernacle) was faced with expanding its school facilities, Abundant Life Christian School, the financial feasibility of entering in a major building project was not possible. Several vendors of portable classrooms were contacted and asked to make a presentation to the board. A final selection was made and construction began. The portable classrooms were attractive and functional. They allowed the school and church to continue to grow until an educational complex could be erected.

It is possible to purchase portable classrooms that can be designed for almost any need, such as office space, rest rooms, cafeteria, shower rooms, etc. Furthermore, given declining enrollments, many public schools have vacant portable buildings available for sale.

Maximize the Use of the Present Building

The key word here is flexibility. The efficiency of the school plant utilization depends to a large degree upon the way in which various rooms can be used during all hours of the day. Any school that does not fully utilize its facilities is running the risk of being criticized for not being good stewards of God's resources. In contrast, when the utilization reaches the range of 90 to 100 percent, the educational program and students will suffer. An average room utilization between 70 and 80 percent is recommended.

Developing a room utilization chart of all available classroom space will provide a bird's-eye view of rooms that are in use and empty rooms for each period of the day. Some computer programs like *The School System* include room utilization as part of the scheduling module.

By constructing a "building utilization chart," the degree of utilization can be determined. The chart lists the rooms by number and kind and gives the following data:

- Number of students in each room

- Type of room (e.g., elementary, art, lab, etc.)
- Class use (e.g., 4th grade, science, etc.)
- Square footage per room
- Daily capacity of each room based on the average of 25 square feet per student
- Number of students occupying each room

Using this data determine the percentage of utilization for each room and the total percentage of utilization for entire building by adding the total student capacity assigned for all classrooms combined [CSRK 4.4].

Develop a Strong Custodial/Maintenance Team

The blessing of increased use of a church building by a Christian day school directly relates to increased custodial and maintenance requirements [CSRK 4.5]. A challenge often confronting church leaders with newly established schools is determining who should be responsible for the overall custodial and maintenance program.

In many churches, these responsibilities are part of the church business manager or church administrator. However, since the day school usually occupies the building for a greater part of the time (except during the summer months), the building principal could be assigned responsibility for the physical condition and cleanliness of the school plant. This will require the principal establishing a strong working relationship with other users of the building.

A first step is to establish a ministry-wide calendar and facilities reservation system that will minimize conflicts [CSRK 4.6]. There are several computer programs available that make the scheduling of church and school resources much easier. For example, the *Automated Church Systems* allows for the scheduling of rooms, furnishings and equipment. A special feature warns of overlapping events to prevent scheduling two events at the same time, even if the events are in two different locations.

The following suggestions will facilitate the transition of a church building into a day school.

- List the building maintenance needs for the first year and work out a systematic plan for addressing those needs.
- Establish a routine schedule for daily custodial work.
- Obtain estimates from other private and public schools about the paper product needs per pupil.
- Establish an inventory control system.
- Identify and label (tag) all equipment.
- Establish an energy conservation plan including exterior and

interior lighting, heating, ventilating and air-conditioning, water heating. Include your plan in a policies handbook and distribute to all staff.

Investigate the Use of Computer Technology

Computers are being used effectively in many areas of Christian school management, including facilities. Areas include: maintenance schedules, safety checklists, equipment inventories and inspections, operating security systems, monitoring of heating and cooling systems, planning new facilities and monitoring construction timetables. For example, low cost shareware programs, such as *Maintenance DBS*, are especially helpful for scheduling custodians. You can create a master schedule showing where everyone is working, what they will be doing and the number of hours for each task. The program allows you to schedule any number of personnel, hours, shifts and tasks. The tasks can be divided into days, hours, shifts and functional areas (for example, cafeteria, classrooms, administrative offices, gym, dressing rooms, etc.). Schedules can be created in increments as small as 15 minutes.

This program is an excellent choice for schools who use teaching staff, students and parents to care for the facilities. Once you have created a master schedule, you can produce an individual schedule for everyone involved in housekeeping, custodial or maintenance tasks. Another excellent program is *Working Hours*. (See *Microcomputer Applications for Christian Educators* for more suggestions on the use of computer technology and available programs for managing facilities and other Christian school departments.)

Pitfalls To Avoid

1. Failing to work with city officials. Shortly after a decision is made to open a Christian day school, send a letter of intent to the public school superintendent as well as the fire, safety and health departments. Sometimes, Christian educators and school boards take the position that since the school is part of the church, school regulations do not apply. In their chapter on physical facilities in Christian schools, Deuink and Herbster comment, "Churches with schools are unwise to resist reasonable standards simply on the basis that the rules do not apply to a church."[10]

Since the city inspectors have as their primary responsibility providing a safe environment for children, it is beneficial to establish a good working relationship with these officials. Very seldom will an inspector go through a building without finding something that does not meet standards. This is their job. They may even make recommendations that are beyond required standards. When this happens, keep in mind the following strategies:

- Request all recommendations be placed in writing.
- Focus on what is right rather than who is right.
- Indicate a willingness to meet all reasonable standards and as soon as possible comply with legitimate demands.
- You have a right to appeal a decision.
- Believe that your school will find favor with your city officials.
- Believe God to reveal to you those hidden things that may be perceived as a problem and give you the wisdom as to how to take care of the situation.

A good example of finding favor is illustrated by Victory Christian School and its move into a remodeled, used car dealership. Although everyone was working hard to get the school completely ready before the students arrived from summer vacation, there were several items where the school did not meet building codes. In particular, the major hallway did not have a dropped ceiling. Because of the positive working relationship with the building inspector and fire marshal, the school was given permission to open the school without the dropped ceiling installed. It wasn't until six months later that the ceiling was complete.

Before you ask the city inspectors to visit your school, consider inviting two or three administrators who are operating successful Christian schools and have been through inspections, to visit your building. Conducting an informal inspection will be very beneficial.

2. Failing to provide for vandalism control. There is nothing the devil would like more than to destroy God's property. Christian schools are not immune from vandalism, sometimes by the very students who attend. As Candoli, et. al., point out, "It (vandalism) is not confined to the inner city, rural, suburban, or other type of educational setting. It is a widespread phenomenon...planning is a major deterrent to vandalism."[11] They further point to the following suggestions to reduce vandalism:

1   Provide a system of emergency telephones at strategic locations.
2   Avoid alcoves and recesses, both in and outside of buildings.
3   Light the premises. Light is a deterrent to criminals and vandals. Provide well-lighted pedestrian paths between major activity centers and parking lots.
4   Avoid large shrubbery masses.
5   Locate bicycle racks near well-traveled pathways.
6   Place play areas in highly visible areas.

7   Use wall coverings that are nonabsorbent and easily cleaned.[12]

Father, we agree for the meeting of every need relating to buildings and grounds. Let every code requirement be met. Provide the financial resources to provide a comfortable, safe, productive and stimulating learning environment. We agree for favor with the city officials and inspectors. Let the angel of the Lord be encamped around this school. Let no evil intention manifest. In the name of Jesus–Amen.

> **Planning for adequate educational facilities is essential to establishing a Christian day school. Once the school is up and going, attention shifts to managing the school plant effectively and efficiently. This requires continual planning and is basic to all operations of the school.**

Christian School Resource Kit

4.1   Laboratory Safety Checklist
4.2   Emergency Evacuation Plan
4.3   Room Usage Constitution and Chart
4.4   Room and Building Utilization Chart
4.5   Maintenance Request
4.6   Facilities Reservation Plan Sheet

Endnotes

1   Roy Lowrie, Jr., Headmaster, Delaware County Christian School, Malin Road, Newtown, PA 19073.

2   James R. Marks, Emery Stoops and Joyce K. Stoops. *Handbook of Educational Supervision: A Guide for the Practitioner*. Boston, MA: Allyn and Bacon, Inc., 1971, p. 728.

3   James W. Deuink and Carl D. Herbster. *Effective Christian School Management*. 2nd Edition. Greenville, SC: Bob Jones University Press, 1986, p. 221.

4   Marks, *op. cit.*, p. 728.

5   Dennis R. Bunklee and Robert J. Shoop. *A Primer for School Risk Management*. Boston, MA: Allyn and Bacon, Inc., 1993, p. 95.

6   *Ibid.*, p. 96.

7   Theodore J. Kowalski. *Planning and Managing School Facilities*.

New York, NY: Praeger Publishers, 1989, p. 57.

8   Robert J. Krajewski, *Elementary School Principalship.* New York, NY: Holt, Rinehart and Winston, 1983, p. 271.

9   Kowalski, *op. cit.*, p. 77.

10   Deuink and Herbster, *op. cit.*, p. 74.

11   I. Carl Candoli, Walter G. Hack and John R. Ray. *School Business Administration: A Planning Approach.* Boston, MA: Allyn and Bacon, 1991, p. 271.

12   *Ibid.*

References

Dura-Kote. 2704 Buell Avenue, Austin, TX 78757; (800) 423-7390).

Demuth, Dennis M. and Demuth, Carol M. *Microcomputer Applications for Christian Educators.* Tulsa, OK: DEL Publications, 1992.

Computer Software

Automated Church Systems. Computer Dimensions, Inc. P.O. Box 3990, Florence, SC 29502; (800) 669-2509.

Maintenance DBS. Harold F. Pfannenschmid, H&P Software, 218 Newman Avenue, Pueblo, CO 81005.

The School System. McGraw-Hill School Systems, 20 Ryan Ranch Road, Monterey, CA 93940; (800) 663-0544.

Working Hours. PowerUp Software, P.O. 7600, San Mateo, CA 94403; (800) 851-1917.

STEP 5

DETERMINE SIZE OF THE STUDENT BODY

Having reviewed the adequacy of your facilities, you are ready to deal with the issue of determining the size of your student body. This involves identifying an enrollment philosophy, establishing grade levels, determining class sizes, projecting school enrollment and recruiting students.

Identify an Enrollment Philosophy

The first step is to formulate an enrollment philosophy. Most Christian schools adhere to one of three philosophies—evangelistic open enrollment, Christian kids only, or Christian kids who meet special requirements. Each philosophy provides varying levels of restriction. The more restrictive the philosophy, the smaller will be the pool of students from which to enroll.

Evangelistic Open Enrollment

This is the least restrictive and has the potential for the most students. Many refer to this philosophy as an "Open" philosophy. It embraces any student as long as the student meets enrollment standards. This approach has the side benefit of reaching the most unchurched families with the Gospel.

Christian Kids Only

This enrollment philosophy is more restrictive, drawing students from Christian families. Acceptance is usually contingent on agreement to a general doctrinal position. By enrolling Christian kids only, schools expect to provide a spiritually healthy atmosphere for shaping values, attitudes, character and spiritual perception.[1] The goal is to provide a climate that is free of the influences of non-Christians.

Schools following this philosophy need to understand that just because students come from Christian homes, this does not mean they are free from the spoiling influences of the world in which they live. Colossians 2:8 says, **"Beware lest any man spoil you through philosophy and vain deceit, after the tradition of men, after the rudiments of the world, and not after Christ."** Most Christian students enrolling in a new Christian school will be coming out of a secular, humanistic, progressive school system. For some, the Christian school placement will contribute to immediate changes in the lives of students. For others, the change will take more time; it may take two to three years of consistent Christian school ministry before parents and teachers see results.

Students With Specific Requirements

The final enrollment philosophy is one where students come from families who agree with a specific doctrinal position propagated by a sponsoring church, group of churches or denomination. This group holds the potential for the greatest academic and spiritual growth because the home, church and school are in agreement, an important biblical success principle found in Amos 3:3, **"Can two walk together, except they be agreed?"** Also, in Ecclesiastes 4:12, it says, **"...and a threefold cord is not quickly broken."** However, the pool of students is the most restrictive. Therefore, more effort must go into recruiting students.

Regardless of the enrollment philosophy, it is important to establish clear admission standards and lifestyle expectations and then to hold students accountable. We will have more to say concerning admissions standards later in this chapter.

Following the selection of an enrollment philosophy, the next step is to establish the grades to offer. Associated with this task is the determination of class size and enrollment projections.

Establish Grade Levels

Is there an effective way to determine how many grades to offer? Unfortunately, there is no established formula to determine the number of grades to offer during the first year of operation; however, there are two major approaches to establishing grade levels: a step approach and a block approach.

Step Approach

Using a step approach, a school starts by offering kindergarten and lower elementary grades, preferably just through third grade. Each year an additional grade is added. The advantages to this approach are summarized by Dr. A.R. Horton, founder and President of Pensacola Christian Schools:

- The children coming into your school in the lower grades are, for the most part, unspoiled by public education.
- The cost involved in offering the lower grades is much less than offering the upper grades.
- There are fewer grades to master the first year.
- It is generally easier to recruit students (as well as staff) for the

lower grades than it is for the upper grades.

- In offering a few lower grades, your opportunity of producing a good academic product the first year is increased. Remember, your academic product is the most successful means of advertising.

- Finally, you can add one or two more grades each year by carrying your students with you and then mastering these new grades as you go along. [2]

The goal is to offer as many lower elementary classes as possible. By broadening the base at the lower elementary level, there will be a larger pool of students at each grade level to feed the next grade level, thus helping to maintain full classes. For example:

First Year
Offer Grades: K 1 2 3
Second Year
Offer Grades: K K 1 2 3 4
Third Year
Offer Grades: K K K 1 1 2 3 4 5

There are two distinct disadvantages of this approach. First, it takes an extended period to provide for a full spectrum of grades. Second, no provisions are made for families who have children in the grades not offered. Some schools attempt to overcome this last drawback by offering a separate instructional program for those students whose grade levels are not included in the initial steps. These programs generally include an individualized instructional approach, such as Alpha-Omega Life Pacs, ACE-Accelerated Christian Education Pace, or A Beka Video School.

Consider offering a half day four-year-old kindergarten program, a five-year-old kindergarten program, as well as an advanced kindergarten program. There will always be those students with younger siblings who would normally attend a pre-school program and could very well be enrolled in a four-year-old kindergarten program. Some schools open pre-school classes for two and three year olds as direct feeder programs to the day school. For example, Abundant Life Christian School of Madison, Wisconsin, provides a day care and preschool with a total enrollment of 350 children. Each year, many of the preschool children enroll in the day school. The school has grown from 45 students to an enrollment of just over 400 students.

Check state requirements; some states may require day care licensure when schools enroll children under the age of four, or the school day for these ages is more than a set length of time; for example, six hours. For more information on accreditation of preschool programs, contact the International Christian Accrediting Association (ICAA).

Block Approach

The second approach is blocking. In this approach, you divide the full range of grades into grade blocks. A decision to open an additional block of grades is contingent on a pre-determined number of students enrolled.

Using a blocking strategy allows the school to offer a full range of grades over a two- to five-year period. An example of this strategy follows.

Year	Plan 1	Plan 2	Plan 3	Plan 4
1	Open K - 2	K - 3	K - 3	K - 6
2	Add 3 - 4	4 - 6	4 - 8	7 - 12
3	Add 5 - 6	7 - 9	9 - 12	
4	Add 7 - 9	10 - 12		
5	Add 10 - 12			

Using Plan 1, it would take five years to set up a K–12 program. In Plan 2, it takes four years, while Plan 3 requires three years. Plan 4 requires only two years. Unless the state mandates specific requirements, kindergarten classes should be a half-day program. One teacher could teach a four-year old morning class and a five-year old class in the afternoon. When you add more than one grade level as a block, base the decision on natural breaks in the curriculum, such as K - 3, 4 - 6, 7 - 8, or 9 - 12.

Victory Christian School first opened its doors in the fall of 1979, offering grades kindergarten through sixth. Initial enrollment was 269 students. At first, the strategy was to employ a step approach, adding one grade each year. However, part way through the first year, while in prayer, the Holy Spirit impressed upon the pastor to plan on adding grades seven through twelve the following year, a block approach. When school opened in the fall of the next year, 422 students were enrolled in grades kindergarten through twelfth. This provided a solid base for continued enrollment resulting in a steady growth to a high of 835 students in nine years.

Whether a school employs a step or block approach or a combination of both, the important task is to monitor the number of students enrolling. Then, adjust your class offering accordingly.

Combined Grades

Often parents ask the question, "Should a school offer combined grades?" There may arise a situation where there are not enough students to offer a single class at each grade level. Therefore, it may be necessary to combine grades. The main reason for combining grades is to help make your school economically possible.

Classrooms ranging from 25 to 30 students are not unusual. Consider the example with an enrollment of 109 students.

Grade	Enrolled	Class	Placed
K4	15	K4	15
K5	23	K5	23
1	15	1-2	15
2	10	Combine with 1st	10
3	13	3-4	13
4	11	Combine with 3rd	11
5	12	5-6	12
6	10	Combine with 5th	10

Given these enrollment figures, there are several possible combination class options.

- Keep K4 and K5 as single grades. Since 38 K4 and K5 students is equivalent to 19 full-time students, a special attempt should be made to enroll more students in these grades with a possible goal of 25 students per grade (depending upon available space within each classroom). Sharing a teacher's aide between the two classrooms may allow the class size to increase to 26 students each.

- Combine grades one and two for a single classroom of 25 students. Allow this classroom to build to 30 students before re-evaluating the need to separate the grades.

- Combine grades three and four for a single classroom of 24 students. Monitor the enrollment in all combined classrooms. If there is an adequate increase in enrollment resulting in at least 20 students in both first and fourth grades, consider offering a single first grade class, a single fourth grade class and a combined second and third grade classroom.

- Combine grades five and six for a single class of 22 students.

The moment you decide to combine grade levels into a single classroom, prepare to address the potential drawbacks of combined classrooms. A.A. Baker provides some positive strategies for answering questions concerning combined classes.[3]

Challenge Situation 1: The teacher will have multiple preparations and must concentrate on teaching the three R's, since there will be little in the schedule for "extras."

Response to Challenge: A dedicated teacher will rise to the challenge and the students will receive a superior basic education.

Challenge Situation 2: There will be adverse feelings from people who think their children will not get the full benefit of the teacher.

Response to Challenge: The children will be helped by being exposed to the interaction of the teacher and students in the higher grades. Children will be exposed continually to both direct and indirect teaching.

Challenge Situation 3: The school will not be able to expand and grow as fast as would be possible with individual classes.

Response to Challenge: The solution is to phase out the combined classes on the lower grades one at a time and as soon as is possible.

Early in the enrollment process it is easy to promise parents that their students will be placed in a single grade classroom. However, having promised this, it is ten times more difficult to notify parents of the need to break your commitment and to place their child in a combined classroom. Avoid this situation by establishing a teacher employment policy based on maximum class size; for example, one teacher hired for every 25 students enrolled.

At first, you may only enroll 12 first graders and 13 second graders. If so, you would have one combined class of 25 students and one teacher. Continue to monitor enrollment, placing students on waiting lists until another 25 students are enrolled. Figure 5.1 illustrates how one school arranges its grades as a result of increasing enrollment.

Determine Class Size

Determining class size and projecting enrollment are important steps to establishing a good foundation. The decision of how many students to assign a particular class needs to be made with the following knowledge.

1   Although some schools offer small classes as proof of "quality" education, research has yet to substantiate a given class size is a guarantee of educational success of all children. While some authors indicate the ideal pupil teacher ratio as 1:20, there will always be credentialed, experienced teachers who have challenges teaching fewer than twenty students. On the other hand, there are teachers who can successfully teach class sizes of thirty to thirty-five students.

NOTE: *The real key for the Christian school is not "how to arrange for smaller classes," but rather, "how to hire teachers*

*to manage larger classes in which they teach more efficiently
and effectively.*"[4]

Figure 5.1   Grades Based On Enrollment

> **Enrollment as of June 15: 75 students.**
>
> | Grade | Enrolled | Classes | Students | Waiting |
> |-------|----------|---------|----------|---------|
> | 1 | 25 | 1 | 25 | 0 |
> | 2 | 30 | 1 | 25 | 5 |
> | 3 | 15 | 0 | 15 | 15 |
>
> **PLAN**: Offer 1 first grade (25), 1 second grade (25) and 1 combined 2nd and 3rd grade (20).
>
> **Enrollment as of July 15: 121 students**
>
> | Grade | Enrolled | Classes | Students | Waiting |
> |-------|----------|---------|----------|---------|
> | 1 | 45 | 2 | 25/20 | 0 |
> | 2 | 48 | 2 | 25/23 | 0 |
> | 3 | 33 | 1 | 25 | 8 |
>
> **PLAN**: Offer 2 first grades, 2 second grades and 1 third grade. Keep 8 students on new class list.
>
> **Enrollment as of July 15: 144 students**
>
> | Grade | Enrolled | Classes | Students | Waiting |
> |-------|----------|---------|----------|---------|
> | 1 | 50 | 2 | 25/25 | 0 |
> | 2 | 48 | 2 | 25/23 | 0 |
> | 3 | 46 | 2 | 23/23 | 0 |
>
> **PLAN**: Offer 2 first grades, 2 second grades and 2 third grades.

2   The Educational Research Service (ERS) found that in the early primary grades, smaller classes had a positive influence on reading and mathematics for students who were low-achieving and from economically or socially disadvantaged backgrounds. The general conclusion is, "unless the teacher changes teaching methods, reducing class size has no demonstrative advantage."[5]

3   Class size may very with the subject taught. It may be more appropriate to deal with 35 students in a secondary English class, but the same number of students in a geometry class may pose a challenge. Smaller classes permit greater student contact and individual attention.

4   Class sizes should be planned in terms of educational instruction. See Figure 5.2 for suggestions.

Figure 5.2 Educational Pupil/Teacher Ratios

Type of Instruction	Pupil/Teacher Ratio
Tutorial	1:5
Group Discussion	1:15
Group Plus Individualization	1:25
One-Way Lecture	No limit

NOTE: *Class size configuration will not eliminate the need for teaching excellence, and for adjusting materials and methods to meet the needs of students.*

5   Larger class sizes mean an increase in accountability for teachers who are already deeply engaged in preparation, curriculum planning, sports, field trips and grading—plus parent evening conferences and meetings. Thus, these teachers have little time for reflection, self-analysis and feedback— important ingredients for successful instruction.

6   Class size relates to staffing patterns that can be converted into real dollar costs. Philip Elve states, "A class size of thirty saves approximately 12 percent of the cost of a class of twenty-five."[6] Four classes of twenty-one could become three of twenty-six to twenty-seven and save one teacher's salary. Furthermore, increasing the average class size by three could save as much as 10 percent.

One answer to the class size question is to keep classes as small as is economically possible, encouraging teachers to vary their instruction, plan for maximum student participation in discussions and accommodate various student learning styles. Furthermore, make every effort to raising a cadre of trained parent volunteers who can ease the load off teachers, freeing them to be more effective educators.[7] For detailed information on how to establish a school-based volunteer program, see the authors' book, *GranDees: A School-Based Volunteer Program.*

Project School Enrollment

How can one determine how many students will attend? There is no easy answer to this question. Public schools compute the average percentage of increase/decrease in enrollment over a sequence of grades for a span of time to determine enrollment. In contrast, schools in the first year of operation have no previous history upon which to base its enrollment projections. These school have to rely on other measures.

Although there are no established formulas to calculate first year enrollment, certain conditions favor a potential for a strong first year enrollment. These include:

- A strong local economy.
- Positive community and local church attitude of Christian schools.
- The past success level of the sponsoring church and strength of its existing programs, such as the children's ministry, youth programs and Sunday school.
- Quality educational facilities available.
- Level of commitment to academic excellence.
- Zealousness of recruiting efforts.

Since there is an absence of real enrollment numbers, new schools can take several actions to estimate enrollment:

1 Collect first year enrollment figures from Christian schools located in communities of comparable size and sponsored by ministries of similar size and vision.

2 Conduct an interest survey, especially when a church or group of churches sponsor the school [CSRK 5.1]. Generally, the amount of interest in the school will be greater than the number of those responding. The advantage in doing the survey is to get a list of names of parents who can later serve on study committees and actively help promote the school.

3 Prayerfully seek the Lord for an enrollment goal. Although some may conclude, "You can never know how many students to expect," it is God's desire to reveal to you this piece of information. How does it come? First Corinthians 2:10 says, "**But God hath revealed them unto us by his Spirit: for the Spirit searcheth all things, yea, even the deep things of God.**" Furthermore, the Bible says, "**But ye have an unction from the Holy One, and ye know all things**" (1 John 2:20). "All things" include the number of students to expect.

4 Once the Spirit impresses upon you the number of students to expect, Romans 4:20,21 says to speak out what you believe. Mix faith with your goal. Begin to call students in from the east, west, north and south. Luke 13:29 says, "**And they shall come from the east, and from the west, and from the north, and from the south, and shall sit down in the kingdom of God.**"

5 Command the principalities and powers that are holding students back from enrolling to be removed: "**For we wrestle not against flesh and blood, but against principalities, against powers, against the rulers of the darkness of this world, against spiritual wickedness in high places**" (Eph. 6:12).

6 And finally, command the blinders to be removed from the eyes of

parents so they would see the value of a Christian education: **"...darkness hath blinded his eyes"** (1 John 2:11).

Once a history of enrollment has been established over a period of two to three years, you can more accurately project future enrollment for each grade level. For example, if a school experiences a 2 percent increase over the past three years, the best estimate for the next year would be an increase of 2 percent (all other factors being equal).

Recruit Students

Immediately following the announcing of the opening of your Christian school, you will begin to receive inquiries from parents and students wanting more information. This is especially true in those cities where there are fewer Christian schools. However, as A.A. Baker points out,

> "Many have the idea that just because they open a Christian school in their community, the people in the community are going to beat a path to their door and enroll their children. The fact of the matter is, it is not so!"[7]

Student recruitment is a continual concern regardless of whether your school is in its first year or fifth year of operation. Unlike public schools, where students come from assigned attendance areas and are obligated to attend based on state law, Christian schools much like colleges, must resort to student recruitment. The authors' book, *Recruiting Strategies for Christian Schools*, contains over 250 pages of ideas for enhancing enrollment.

Every school needs to develop a first response piece, a school brochure, and an enrollment packet before launching an initial student recruitment program. Several suggestions follow.

First Response Piece

Follow up on every contact made with the school, using an attractive first response piece. This may be a school brochure, information packet, or letter from the administrator. Since first impressions are lasting, make it a quality piece. Furthermore, don't stop with just one contact: most schools use several different promotional pieces.

School Brochure

A quality school brochure is an effective marketing tool. A school does not have to spend tens of thousands of dollars on a school brochure; however, the school brochure must be a quality piece. Consider the following elements:

- Use good quality pictures—select photos showing good looking, smiling, fun-loving students rather than photos of students thinking and studying. If you want to picture the building, classrooms, computer lab, etc., show them in carefully planned backgrounds behind pictures of students.

- Present the purpose and vision of the school in simple language.
- Place address and phone number in plain view.
- Provide for variety.
- Accent quality.
- Mention student activities and sports (80 percent of a typical study body will participate in these activities).
- Use two- or four-part color.

Enrollment Packet

Once the parents decide to seek enrollment, place an enrollment packet in their hands. This packet should contain, as a minimum:

- A letter from the administrator to the student/family.
- A letter from the president of the parent-teacher fellowship.
- An application form. We recommend a four panel, 8 1/2" by 11" application. This provides a natural pocket for inserting enrollment materials [CSRK 5.2].
- Fee schedule. Include a list of all fees.
- A listing of the enrollment steps. Keep these steps simple and easy to follow.
- A sheet of questions and answers (See *Recruiting Strategies for Christian Schools* for a listing of common questions and appropriate answers).

Finalize the Application Process

You must let parents know what to do to apply to your school. Don't make the application process so complicated parents and students feel like they are trying to gain admission to Fort Knox. Remember the formula KISS—Keep It Short and Simple. Don't bog parents down with a ton of forms.

The simpler the procedures, the more likely parents will enroll their children. As soon as you receive the name of a prospect, take the following actions:

- Send an information packet containing a letter from the administrator, school brochure, calendar and handbook. The copy of the handbook will help answer questions.
- Make a follow-up telephone call inviting the student and his

family to visit the school.

- Arrange for a tour of the facilities. This is the time to accent all the positive points, such as the gym, swimming pool, modern science lab, typing/computer lab, attractive classrooms, etc. Over the summer, set up one classroom at each division (K-3, 4-6, 7-9, 10-12) as it would look for the first day of school; use this room for visits. Just as a furnished house increases the likelihood of someone making an offer to purchase, a completely furnished classroom with attractive bulletin boards, displays of children's work, etc., help sell the school.

- Display your curricula. Have available for inspection various samples of curricula from each grade level. It is worth the initial investment. Parents and students will be impressed by the high quality of Christian curricula. Viewing the textbooks may be the deciding factor for enrolling in your school. Consider a goal of having on display a complete set of the entire school curricula.

- Provide an opportunity to meet students, teachers and other parents at the time of the tour. Treat each prospective family as V.I.P.'s.

Once the parents decide to complete an application, there should be a standard sequence of events to follow in processing the application. The following sequence will help:

1　Obtain a completed application for each student enrolled [CSRK 5.3].

2　Review the application.

3　Require at least two letters of reference for students grades 7-12 [CSRK 5.4].

4　Have parents submit an official copy of the child's birth certificate.

5　Require a current immunization record. Most state laws require this. This record must be presented before a student starts school. It is much easier to obtain immunization records at the time the application is made or before enrollment, rather than after school starts.

6　Request payment of a non-refundable application fee when the application is submitted. Return this fee only when the school does not accept the applicant for admission. Consider a student officially enrolled only after the student pays this fee.

7　Arrange for an interview. At the time of the interview, ask for a copy of the student's transcripts and report card. Transcripts are important for the selection of course work.

8　Notify parents of the admission decision. Make each admission decision after prayerful consideration from an admissions team. In-

clude the following on this team: administrator (headmaster), principal, teacher, parent leader, pastor, youth worker, counselor or chaplain. Keep the number of team members from three to five. The team
approach is important for it provides a level of safety in a multitude
of counselors (Prov. 11:14). It also provides a more thorough and objective assessment of the applicant; it removes a single person from
making an admissions decision, thereby avoiding the "bad guy" label often attached to the bearer of bad news. Decide as soon as is possible.

9   Communicate a tender, caring concern rather than making judg-
mental statements to those students the team rejects. Though the
team rejects a student, the student must sense that the team cares
about him. When warranted, offer an opportunity for the applicant to
reapply at a later date. Keep this information on hand for future follow up. Remember, God is still in the business of performing miracles.

Determine Admission Standards

Christian schools have various academic, behavioral and spiritual
admission standards. Meeting these standards is essential for admission.
The following suggestions will assist in making quality acceptance and
placement decisions.

Academic Standards

Typically, a student is expected to have progressed one grade level
academically as measured by a standardized achievement test for each
year of schooling. These test results, combined with current academic
records from previous schools, provide information necessary to make
quality acceptance and placement decisions.

Placement Decision. Often, schools admit students only if students
can pass an entrance examination. Although some schools have very
stringent academic admission standards, most schools admit all students,
but maybe not at the expected grade level. For example, a student applies
for seventh grade, but because of academic standards, the school accepts
him at the sixth grade level. This type of placement decision is not easy
to make. Figure 5.3 presents several decision strategies.

Grades K – 8. Base acceptance in the kindergarten, five-year-old
program on age. For example, in Oklahoma a student must be five years
old by September 1. A simple kindergarten screening assessment made
up of knowledge of letters of the alphabet, understanding of numbers,
simple directions, auditory and visual discrimination, listening and
speaking vocabulary, with samples of the completed kindergarten material, will provide the school with information important in making

Figure 5.3 Admission Decision Strategies

Test scores	Class Work	Decision
At or above grade level	Passing all subjects	Accept at enrolled grade level
	Failing some subjects	Accept at enrolled grade level; place on probation
One year or more below grade level in either math or reading	Passing all subjects	Accept at grade level; place on probation; be prepared to offer remedial assistance
Two or more years below grade level	Failure in all subjects	Accept at previous grade level only if remedial assistance is available

placement decisions.

Grades 9 – 12. Classify students in grades nine through twelve by grade based on completion of credit hours; for example, "x" number of credits equals a certain classification, such as freshman, sophomore, junior, or senior (It is best to parallel the public school standard); accept students into classes based on successful completion of the subject requirements as identified by a passing grade and earned credit.

Other Factors. Although standardized achievement scores and present grades are good predictors of future achievement, testimony after testimony relates academic success to several positive factors. These include the positive effects of a well-disciplined classroom, increased involvement by parents with their child's education, a Christ-centered environment and faith in the Word of God.

Once students who were poor achievers begin to accept in faith what God's Word says about them and make it part of their school life, they will begin to be successful. For example, 1 John 5:4,5 says,

"For whatsoever is born of God overcometh the world: and this is the victory that overcometh the world, even our faith.

"Who is he that overcometh the world, but he that believeth that Jesus is the Son of God?"

School work and studying are part of the student's world. Given this thought, students can know that God has given them ability to overcome in these areas. When Christian students fail to realize the "Greater One" resides within them, they become discouraged or even fear receiving a failing grade. By looking at the circumstances, they find themselves speaking words of doubt like, "I can never get the assignment" or, "Brother, I must be stupid" or, "I can't solve this problem. It's too difficult for me." When a student makes statements like these, doubt enters his mind and he fails to realize his potential; finally, he begins to lose his ability to be a success because his faith becomes suppressed.

First John 5:5 says since they believe that Jesus Christ is the Son of God, they will overcome. This belief, coupled with God's promises, gives them God's ability and power to overcome any homework assignment, special project, quiz, nine-week tests, or any other school challenge. Since Jesus is within them, they have the ability of God, wisdom of God and understanding of God, all providing the foundation for school success.

Behavioral and Spiritual Standards

Every school administrator would like to enroll students whose behavior is a strong example of Christ-likeness. However, since only a small percentage of students entering Christian schools for the first time are self-disciplined disciples of Christ, we caution schools not to set their behavioral standards so high they exclude the type of student who could benefit the most from the Christian school.

Spiritual standards are based on the school's enrollment philosophy. As was mentioned earlier, even those students from Christian homes and those who appear to "have it together" behaviorally and spiritually, may have major challenges in their lives.

Success for enrolling students improves under the following conditions:

1   There is an environment charged with the love of God where students are loved no matter what, totally accepted as a creation of God; no matter how bad they have fallen, they will be forgiven.

2   The Holy Spirit is given complete freedom. This will lead to conviction (John 16:8): "**And when he is come, he will reprove the world of sin, and of righteousness, and of judgment,**" and changed lives "**For it is God which worketh in you both to will and to do of his good pleasure**" (Phil. 2:13). When the Holy Spirit is the chief Admissions Officer, you can have confidence He knows what He is doing and will never allow a person to enter your school whom you can-

not reach (Acts 13:2). The Holy Spirit knows what is in a person (1 Cor. 2:9-15); He will reveal it to you (Col. 1:27); and tell you what it takes to see change take place in his/her life (1 John 2:20,27).

3   There is an expression of concern rather than judgment, forgiveness rather than condemnation.

4   There are clear standards of conduct. Don't be under the misconception that acceptance breeds automatic approval of inappropriate behavior. Hold students accountable to a prescribed lifestyle [CSRK 5.5].

Begin to Recruit Students

There are several initial actions to consider in recruiting students. For example:

1   **Recruit sponsoring church families first**. Some of the first students to recruit are from families attending the sponsoring church or churches. These families are the ones who will be the most familiar with your school. Recruit from active church members, leaders and special groups, such as Sunday school classes, men's and women's ministries, children and youth. Focus recruiting efforts on the entire church congregation. Use:

- Bulletin inserts
- Pulpit announcements
- Ministry mailings
- Special letters to all parents of school age children
- Telephone calls
- An information table set up at church services
- Christian school reading materials
- A special Christian school emphasis day

2   **Inform other churches in your community**. Contact pastors of other churches without a Christian school and share your vision, goals and purpose.

- Begin with a special letter of introduction.
- Follow up with a telephone call and then arrange for a personal contact.
- Provide copies of Christian school literature and your school brochure.
- Assure pastors of the desire to provide a quality Christian education program for the community.
- Seek support of the pastors by their willingness to promote your school in their churches, both from the pulpit and by making

promotional fliers available.

- Invite them to visit the school and participate in a special chapel honoring pastors who have students attending from their churches. Welcome their input.

3   **Develop public awareness.** Making the entire community aware of your school requires a commitment of human and financial resources. Awareness activities might include:

- Bulk mailings.
- Mass media advertising.
- Press releases.
- Outdoor advertising.
- Newspaper articles.
- Radio programs.

4   **Contact community institutions and organizations.** Once the public awareness campaign is underway, a special invitational letter and information packet should be sent to the following institutions and organizations:

- Day cares and pre-schools.
- Service organizations, such as "Welcome Wagon" and the Chamber of Commerce.
- Industrial trade groups, professional associations, technical societies and credit unions.

5   **Employ an informed, positive secretary and receptionist.** A.A. Baker offers the following advice.

"You may create much interest in your school through promotions, advertising, brochures, and fliers. All, however, will come to naught if you do not have someone in your office to turn interest into the positive action of enrolling the students. A bright, positive secretary with a pleasant telephone voice and the right answers is a must. It is this person who is the key to follow-up contacts of enrollment in your Christian school. You need to be certain that the person who answers the telephone in your office is helpful, friendly, has right answers, and can satisfy the people who are calling concerning your school. She should take the initiative to give all the advantages of your school as well as answering questions."[8]

Keep Good Records

Establish a follow-up record-keeping system. The key to effective follow up is a systematic tracking system. Whether you use a computer or manual (card) system, include the following as part of your database:

- Name, address, zip, date of contact, phone number, children's names and grades [CSRK 5.6].

- Classify each family in one of three categories: plan to attend, not attending, or undecided.

- Further categorize those who are undecided according to the reason, such as financial, relocation out of the community, transportation or miscellaneous.

- Target these groups for additional follow up.

- Maintain an enrollment processing log to keep track of each student as he completes each stage of the enrollment process [CSRK 5.7].

Conduct an Open House

Broadly defined, an open house is a school-sponsored gathering open to the public. A well-orchestrated open house is the most cost-effective means of recruiting students. It has the potential for recruiting the greatest number of students in a single event, since those who come to an open house already have a genuine interest in Christian education.[9] Consider the following elements of a good open house.

Timing

Schools just starting need to provide for at least three open houses. The first open house should take place the first week in March. This is important since many Christian schools are beginning to announce re-enrollment for the coming year. It is difficult to get a parent to your open house if they have already enrolled at another school and paid an enrollment fee. When parents make a financial commitment to attend a school, they usually attend.

Conduct the second open house the first week in May. This provides the last opportunity for parents to view your school before the school their children are attending closes. Parents will be undecided about enrolling in a Christian school and will have many questions to be answered.

Plan a third open house for the first week in August. There will still be many families who have not decided about enrolling. Many new families will be moving into the city. Since classes will not be in session, it is important to have several classrooms set up for the first day of school. Ask teachers who are available to participate in the open house.

Hold another open house just before the end of the semester. This provides a natural break in the academic year for those parents who are considering mid-term placement.

Exposure

The turnout for an open house is difficult to predict. The secret to a bulging attendance is exposure, exposure and more exposure. Use newspaper ads, TV spots, neighborhood door hangers and other advertising methods to publicize the event.

Be creative in your efforts. Try using an 18-foot advertising balloon; invite a local radio station to broadcast from the open house. Church-sponsored schools will find a personal invitation from the pastor to be very effective.

Building

First impressions are lasting. Clean and neat classrooms, rest rooms and hallways are important. Don't overlook the outside. Get in your car and drive up to the school building and view it through the eyes of parents and students as if it were the very first time they saw it. What do you see? Is the parking lot clean? Are the school grounds free of paper and items that look out of place? Are the windows clean? It is amazing what clean windows will do for a building. Would some fresh paint make a difference? How about some flowers next to the entrance?

Involvement

Involve as many people as possible—administrators, teachers and parents. Make sure they are all well-dressed and well-groomed. Use elementary and high school students and parents as greeters and ushers. Friendly, caring, polite students send a strong message to those who are visiting. Direct communication with students in a discussion group following the main program is a good technique for attracting upper-level students who otherwise may not have been interested in changing schools despite the enthusiastic efforts of parents.

Gifts

Very few items win the hearts of young and old as a helium-filled balloon. Everyone who comes through the door should receive a balloon with the school name. You can add other messages on the balloon as you so desire—"See you in the Fall!" "To our very special guests." Use the school logo and motto.

Information Packets

When putting together information packets, ask yourself this question, "What will be the very first impression visitors get from this packet?" Communicating a central message in a concise, neat fashion is very important. Develop the literature contained in the packet to meet the needs of parents and students who are the target for the literature.

Goodies

No open house is complete without a time of informal fellowship around a tray of cookies, punch and coffee. Put your best "people persons" where the goodies are—people who are full of the life of God and show the most enthusiasm for the school.

Make sure they are well informed about the school. Conduct a preparation meeting before the open house. Assign administrators to this area to greet the visitors individually and answer questions.

Plan Student Registration

Conducting a student registration is an important step in preparing for the school to open. Registration should take place well in advance of the start of school and no less than two weeks before school opens. Every school experiences situations where parents may have enrolled, but between the time of enrollment and registration, a decision may have been made not to attend for one reason or another. Registration provides an opportunity for the school to really find out how many students are actually coming.

Conduct a review of each enrollee before registration to ensure all necessary information is present in their file: authorization for emergency medical treatment; birth certificate; immunization record; health card; transcripts; and any other piece of information to make their file complete. On the day of registration, monitor how long it takes to complete the registration process, and work toward no more than a 30-minute process. Adjust the flow as needed. Have additional staff "on call." Avoid backlogs at all costs.

The extent of your registration process will vary depending upon the size of the school. Most schools prefer to use a station approach. Registration can take place in a gym, classrooms, or even the hallway. When planning your registration, consider the following:

1   **Registration Information**. Send out registration information to all those who received an application but have not enrolled. Provide enough time before school starts to follow up on all students who were enrolled but did not attend registration.

2   **Free Offers**. Make the registration packet attractive on the inside as well as the outside by including special items, such as a school bookmarker, pencil, decal, or even fast food coupons from area vendors.

3   **Signs**. Use plenty of printed signs. Parents and students need to know where to go and what to do. This leaves the impression of a well-organized school.

4   **Stations**. Use a station approach. Place at each station a table and two chairs. A small investment in tablecloths large enough to cover the top and drape over the front and sides will give a professional look to each station. When deciding whether or not to purchase these tablecloths, remember, they can be used several times throughout the school year.

5   **Schedules**. Schedule teachers and parent volunteers to man each station. If possible, make each department (for example, food services, transportation, athletics, etc.) responsible for their own station.

6   **Tracking Form**. Request each parent to proceed from station to station using a tracking form. Those at each station initial the form. Parent will turn in all forms as they exit registration.

7   **Greeters**. During the registration process, it is important for the administrator to be the Ambassador of Goodwill, greeting parents, students and staff. The administrator should remain free to talk with parents and guardians.

One school uses the following station approach. Smaller schools can combine several stations into one.

- **Entrance**. Select a room where you can control both the entrance and exit. At the entrance station, place an A-Z student listing, divided into two to three groups (A-G, H-P, Q-Z), depending upon the number of students expected. Schools over 200 students may consider using two different registration days. All parents will receive a registration packet containing a tracking form and all the necessary information.

- **Finance Records**. The first stop should be to check on payment of tuition and fees. Since this is a confidential area, arrange it as such. Prepare to write receipts for payment. Using a parent sign-up sheet will help any backlog that may arise. Review all financial records before registration so only those parents where there is a question need to attend this station.

- **Admissions**. This station is for those students who are applying for the very first time. A complete admissions packet should be available.

- **Student Records**. Parents stop at this station to check immunization files, complete emergency authorization forms, health cards, transcript requests, etc. This station is extremely important and should be manned by the school registrar (secretary).

- **Class Lists**. At this station the child's grade placement is verified. If possible, tentative class rosters are posted so parents can find out who their child's teacher will be.

- **Schedules**. This station is for high school students to select their course study and to complete schedules.

- **Athletics**. Provide sign-up lists for fall sports, booster club information, game schedules, physical forms for athletes. This is a good station to display athletic and gym uniforms. Selecting a sporting goods vendor in the community and directing students to this vendor for the purchase of P.E. uniforms greatly reduces the amount of hassle. Give students two to three weeks to obtain a gym uniform.

- **Fine Arts**. If your school is planning to offer a fine arts program, this is a good place to sign students up for music, band and private lessons.

- **Special Programs**. A good example of a special program would be after-school enrichment program.

- **School Uniforms**. Schools planning to use a standardized dress code (uniforms) should consider a clothing display. Have available purchase information and location of vendors as well as resale information.

- **Fund-Raising**. Schools participating in special fund-raising programs such as Campbell's soup labels, Homeland Apple Computers, etc., should have information sheets and displays.

- **Parent Ministry**. At this station parents are given an opportunity to sign up for volunteering. Have a list of positions and volunteer tasks and the name a contact person.

- **Transportation**. Provide information on car pooling and bus routes. Students who ride the bus purchase their first week ticket and sign a ridership waiver.

- **Handbook**. Parents who haven't received a handbook should receive one at this station. Use an A to Z listing and check off the names of all who receive a handbook.

- **Exit**. Using an A-Z list, check off the names of all students completing the registration process. Collect registration sheets and answer any questions.

Friendly Environment

Place your strongest staff monitoring areas where traffic is the heaviest. Provide a refreshment area. Treat every person as a V.I.P. Provide a small gift for everyone in attendance. For example: pencils, balloons, buttons, book markers, etc. Consider using students to provide a tour of the building.

Post Registration

Following registration, reduce all materials from each station to one or two tables. Place these in an unoccupied room and use them for late registration. If a room is not available, consider using the end of a hallway or other open area (cafeteria, library, teacher workroom, etc.). Following registration, revise and print schedules for high school students and have them made ready for distribution to teachers. This is a very time-consuming task and will require the full attention of the principal.

Follow Up

Identifying those who were not in attendance at registration is an important task. Weigh the following actions:

- Compare registration attendance records from your A-Z parent list to your enrollment roster.

- Make phone calls the day following registration, letting parents know they were missed and ascertaining whether or not they intend to send their children to your school. Have teachers accomplish this task. Utilize the student enrollment tracking form (See CSRK 5.6).

- Forward this information to the registrar who then updates enrollment figures—removing and adding names to the class lists.

- Make last-minute teacher assignments to accommodate changes in elementary class sizes as well as secondary courses.

Pitfalls To Avoid

1. Failing to consider student attrition when planning for enrollment projections. In establishing class offerings, keep in mind the idea of attrition—losing students during the course of the year, especially within the very first weeks of school. Since student attrition is a factor, do everything possible to enroll the maximum number of students at each grade level.

Do not enroll more than two or three students over the projected class standard; you may find yourself retaining every student and having to cope with classroom overcrowding. Parents may put up with an overcrowded classroom for the first month or so; after that, they may begin to notice the effects upon their children and seek another placement.

2. Confusing pupil/teacher ratio and average class size. There is a significant difference between average class size and pupil/teacher ratio. Some schools fall into the trap of comparing one ratio with the other, when in fact both calculations are different. Average class size is the average number of students in the classrooms of the school, whereas pupil-teacher ratio is the number of students in the school divided by the number of teachers.

The challenge with average class size is that it fails to reveal the diversity of class size. A school may have two classes, one of ten and another of forty; the average class size would be twenty-five.

The challenge with pupil/teacher ratio is that it fails to take into account staff other than teachers who have a significant impact upon the lives of your students, especially in Christian schools; for example, the administrator, guidance counselor, or chaplain. The answer is to use a staff/student ratio. This would take into account all professional staff who are involved in the day-to-day lives of the students.

3. Thinking that reducing class size will automatically improve quality of instruction. Although small class sizes will allow teachers to better manage students, class size configuration will not eliminate the need for teaching excellence and for adjusting materials and methods to meet the needs of students.

Effective school research over the past 20 years indicates factors other than class size as characteristics of high student achievement and morale. These characteristics include:

- Vigorous instructional leadership.
- A principal who makes clear, consistent and fair decisions.
- An emphasis on discipline and a safe and orderly environment.
- Instructional practices that focus on basic skills and academic achievement.
- Collegiality among teachers in support of student achievement.
- Teachers with high expectations that all their students can and will learn.
- Frequent review of student progress.[10]

The U.S. Department of Education concludes: "Effective schools are places where principals, teachers, students, and parents agree on the goals, methods, and content of schooling. They are united in recognizing the importance of a coherent curriculum, public recognition for students who succeed, promoting a sense of school pride, and protecting school time for learning."[11]

Dear Heavenly Father, we release the Holy Spirit to cause those students ordained to be in this school to come forth. Let the blinders be removed from the eyes of parents and guardians so they will follow Your command to teach and train their children in Your ways. Let this, Your school, be filled to capacity.

FL 32523; (800) 874-BEKA.

ACE-Accelerated Christian Education Pace. Accelerated Christian Education, P.O. Box 1438, Garland, TX 75041.

Alpha Omega Life Pacs. Alpha Omega Publishers, P.O. Box 3153, Tempe, AZ 85281; (800) 821-4443.

Demuth, Dennis M. *Student Study and Assignment Guide.* Tulsa, OK: Victory Christian School, 1982.

Demuth, Dennis M., Demuth, Carol M., and Black, Mary Martha. *GranDees: A School-Based Volunteer Program.* Tulsa, OK: Praise, Inc., 1990.

International Christian Accrediting Association (ICAA). 7777 South Lewis Avenue, Tulsa, OK 74171; (918) 495-7054.

Kienel, Paul A. *Reasons for Sending Your Child to A Christian School.* La Habra, CA: P.K. Books, 1978.

> **The size of your student body is dependent upon your enrollment philosophy and the amount of effort directed toward recruiting and enrolling students.**

Christian School Resource Kit

5.1   Interest Survey
5.2   Enrollment Packet
5.3   Student Application
5.4   Letters of Reference
5.5   Honor Code
5.6   Student Enrollment Tracking System
5.7   Enrollment Processing Log

Endnotes

1   Robert M. Miller, "Admissions Policies and Procedures," in Roy W. Lowrie, Jr., ed., *Administration of the Christian School.* Whittier, CA: The Association of Christian School International, 1984, p. 74.

2   A.R. Horton in A. A. Baker's, *The Successful Christian School.* Pensacola, FL: A Beka Book Publications, 1979, p. 64.

3   Adapted from A. A. Baker, *Ibid.*, p. 68.

4   Don Stewart. *Educational Malpractice: The Big Gamble in Our Schools.* Westminster, CA: Slate Services, Publishers, 1971, p. 72.

5   Educational Research Service (ERS). *Class Size: A Summary of Research.* Arlington, VA: Educational Research Service, 1980.

6   Philip Elve. *Financing Christian Schools.* Grand Rapids, MI: Christian Schools International, 1984, p. 168.

7   A. A. Baker, *op. cit.*, p. 143

8   A. A. Baker, *op. cit.*, p. 115.

9   Dennis M. Demuth and Carol M. Demuth. *Recruiting Strategies for Christian Schools.* Tulsa, OK: DEL Publications, 1992.

10   U.S. Department of Education. *What Works: Research About Teaching and Learning.* Washington, DC: U.S. Department of Education, 1986, p. 45.

11   *Ibid.*

References

A Beka Video School. A Beka Book Publications, Box 18000, Pensacola,

STEP 6

DEVELOP INCOME AND SPENDING PLANS

O ver the past ten years scores of Christian schools have been established. During this same period many Christian schools are closing their doors. The main reason is lack of finances. This dilemma is not an issue unique to Christian schools. It is a concern facing every educational institution, public and private, large or small. Philip Elve in his book, *Financing Christian Schools,* comments, "Adequate funding for a Christian school is essential to its well-being. Often, the quality of a school relates directly to its financial base."[1]

Preparing for the financial success of your Christian school ministry is an important task. Luke 14:28-30 admonishes:

"For which of you, intending to build a tower, sitteth not down first, and counteth the cost, whether he have sufficient to finish it.

"Lest haply, after he hath laid the foundation, and is not able to finish it, all that behold it begin to mock him,

"Saying, This man began to build, and was not able to finish."

A well-planned financial program is critical if a school is to continue to grow and develop, even when the financial outlook doesn't look very promising. This chapter presents six key ingredients to establishing a school on a solid financial foundation:

- Operate on God's plan for financial success.
- Identify goals and set priorities.
- Develop a comprehensive budget.
- Institute an accounting system.
- Set up a system for managing the budget.
- Practice sound accountability measures.

Operate on God's Plan for Financial Success

Ensuring sufficient financial resources to fund a quality program begins by operating within God's plan for financial success. This plan involves acknowledging that God owns everything, believing it is God's will to be financially successful and adopting God's plan for financial blessing.

113

Acknowledge that God Owns Everything

Begin by acknowledging God's ownership of your school. Psalm 24:1 says,

> "The earth is the Lord's, and the fulness thereof; the world, and they that dwell therein."

This means transferring everything over to Him—school building, furnishings, equipment, supplies, books and staff. As owner, God gives pastors, administrators and boards the responsibility of overseeing His holdings. Being successful in this role means accepting God's condition for control. You can find this condition in the fifth chapter of Deuteronomy.

> "Ye shall observe to do therefore as the Lord your God hath commanded you: ye shall not turn aside to the right hand or to the left.
>
> "Ye shall walk in all the ways which the Lord your God hath commanded you, that ye may live, and that it may be well with you, and that ye may prolong your days in the land which ye shall possess" (Deut. 5:32,33).

Thus, obedience becomes the catalyst for supernatural provision. Obedience to God's Word and His voice leads to making right financial decisions. Furthermore, receiving God's financial provision directly relates to the level of obedience. "**If ye are willing and obedient, you shall eat the good of the land: But if ye refuse and rebel, ye shall be devoured with the sword: for the mouth of the Lord hath spoken it**" (Isa. 1:19,20).

The more willing and obedient a school is, the more it will see financial provision. It is this trust in God's provision that results in continual financial increase. "**The Lord shall increase you more and more, you and your children**" (Ps. 115:14).

Believe It Is God's Will to be Financially Successful

It is true, God will provide for every need facing your school. "**But my God shall supply all your need according to his riches in glory by Christ Jesus**" (Phil. 4:19). Moreover, God wants to take your school beyond the level of meeting basic needs to a level of abundance. "**The thief cometh not, but for to steal, and to kill, and to destroy: I am come that they might have life, and that they might have it more abundantly**"(John 10:10).

When John penned the words, "**Beloved, I wish above all things that thou mayest prosper...**" (3 John 2), the phrase "Above all things" shows that God puts these blessings as top priority.

Adopt God's Plan for Blessing

God has given a pattern for bringing His financial blessing down to your school. It is found in Mark 11:24,

> "Therefore I say unto to you, What things soever ye desire, when ye pray, believe that ye receive them, and ye shall have them."

In this verse, Jesus was simply saying, "You've got to believe you have it (financial success) before you can receive it." Get your attention off from what you as an individual or a board think the school should have. Instead, concentrate on what the Spirit of God is saying for your school. Allow God's desires to become your desires. This means focusing and believing that financial success will come to pass.

Christ has redeemed your school from the curse of impoverished circumstances. Paul says,

> "Christ hath redeemed us from the curse of the law, being made a curse for us: for it is written, Cursed is every one that hangeth on a tree:

> "That the blessing of Abraham might come on the Gentiles through Jesus Christ; that we might receive the promise of the Spirit through faith" (Gal. 3:13,14).

God may have spoken to you to start a Christian school in the middle of a community where economic circumstances point to lack; remember, you are not subject to these conditions, to the curse of lack. In fact, God's Word says you are to have dominion over these circumstances:

> "For if by one man's offence death reigned by one; much more they which receive abundance of grace and of the gift of righteousness shall reign in life by one, Jesus Christ" (Rom. 5:17).

NOTE: Poverty is not to rule and reign over your school.

Sometimes parents and students have the idea that coming to a Christian school means that they will have to give up or do without. This is not God's plan; it is an attempt of the enemy to keep Christian schools and their sponsoring ministries under the curse. Pastors, administrators, teachers and parents must believe that provision belongs to them and their children.

Begin today to realize that supernatural provision is the plan of

God for your school. Dare to believe God for abundance. God reminds us, **"Keep therefore the words of this covenant, and do them, that ye may prosper in all that ye do"** (Deut. 29:9).

Identify Goals and Set Priorities

One of the greatest challenges facing a new school and many existing schools is spending quality time in planning. For instance, it may not be financially possible the very first year to have a full music program, complete with choirs, stage band, orchestra, individual and group lessons, and so forth. However, it is possible to have a music program; and if planned right, it will blossom into a successful music program. Simply stated, "Unless you take time to figure out where you are going, you will never get there."

Establish Goals Before Costs

During the process of planning, don't place the cart before the horse by asking, "What is it going to cost?" before you ask, "What is God saying we should do?" What are His plans for this school? The danger in asking the cost question first is it produces a tendency to avoid any action to accomplish the goal, since the cost is going to be greater than the capacity to provide. Tapping into the creative provision of God means believing God for wisdom to set priorities, to determine the right timing for each program, to secure adequate facilities, and to obtain financial and human resources to carry out the plan.

Expect God to Reveal Programs and Services

God has a specific plan for your school. God says, **"I will instruct you and teach you in the way which you should go; I will counsel you with My eye upon you"** (Ps. 32:8, NASB). Begin by asking God to reveal His plan for your school and to give you the power to achieve this plan. Believe God to show you the programs and services the school is to offer, evaluation strategies for school-wide improvement, enrollment projections, finances and resource development, faculty and staff requirements, facilities and everything else.[2]

"Many are the plans in a man's heart, but it is the Lord's purpose that prevails" (Prov. 19:21 NIV).

Develop a Comprehensive Budget

Budget is the miracle word for Christian schools. Starting a quality educational program is an expensive task. Furthermore, it takes adequate financial planning and program management for a school to continue to grow. As Jordan points out,

"The basic function of a budget is to serve as an instrument for planning so the educational program will not be interrupted or restricted because of insufficient funds or depleted accounts. Sound budgeting practices do not guarantee a never-ending source of funds for the school, but such practices do provide school officials with information that can be used in financial and educational planning for a given period of time."[3]

Select a Spending Plan

Your budget is nothing more than a planned pattern of revenues and expenditures to achieve the goals you have agreed upon over a specified period. The budget becomes the management control tool that specifies the allocation of financial resources. The goal of every Christian school ministry should be to balance costs and expected revenues.

In developing your comprehensive school budget, consider two spending levels:

- **Base Level Budget**. The design of this budget is to carry on essential services, those that are absolutely necessary in carrying out the educational plan.

- **Enhancement Budget**. This budget establishes spending priorities when additional or unexpected financial resources become available.

Using these two levels of budgeting, a school achieves a balance between what is ideal and what is possible. For example, after developing a base budget of $350,000, you might add $40,000 for additional teachers, to lower your pupil/teacher ratio from 25:1 to 20:1. You can add $9,200 to enhance your science laboratory and $3,000 for improvements to the creative play center. Although it would be a helpful to add these enhancements, your school could function very adequately without them.

The budget expenditure plan should show the spending of school funds to be in direct support of the school's educational goals and needs. Assessing needs is an ongoing function of budgeting. Since resources are limited and because requirements and expectations change, needs are inevitable. Schools will go broke attempting to meet every need that arises. One way to address needs when they arise is to answer the question, "Is meeting this need essential to the current success of the school?" If you answer "yes," then meet the need by including it in the budget. Focusing on current needs does not negate the necessity to plan for the future, such as adding more classrooms to accommodate a steady increase in enrollment.

NOTE: *As you develop your budget, the goal is to balance* *actual expenditures and revenue. Having a balanced budget means adjusting the budget during the operating year to accommodate differences between the initial budget estimates and the actual circumstances. Month-by-month and year-to-date reports are critical to this task.*

Since cutting back during the year is not an easy task, consider spending only 90 to 95 percent of the projected income. This will help your cash flow as well as provide a cushion should revenues fall below projections.

The primary steps in developing a comprehensive spending plan for new schools include developing an educational plan, projecting student enrollment, estimating initial start-up costs and developing an income plan.

Develop an Educational Plan

A major component of the budget process is developing an educational plan. The beginning elements of this plan include school goals, objectives and priorities. Gross cautions,

"The organization must know what its goals are before it can prepare a budget. If it doesn't know where it is going, obviously it is going to be very difficult for the organization to do any meaningful planning. All too often the process is reversed and it is in the process of preparing the budget that the goals are determined."[4]

For example, achieving the goal of developing the total person requires strategies to meet the students' physical needs. This suggests the creation of a school-wide physical education program. Similarly, a goal of developing knowledge and appreciation of the fine arts will require art and music programs. Thus, the educational plan includes goals, programs to meet these goals, staff, supplies, curriculum, equipment and facilities to carry on the program.

Project Student Enrollment

Knowing the number of students who plan to attend your school helps in estimating the need for facilities, equipment, textbooks and personnel. In addition, enrollment estimates relate directly to revenue projections. Chapter 5 provides information on the process of projecting student enrollment.

Estimate Initial Start-up Costs

The initial needs of a new school consist of facilities, equipment, textbooks, supplies, promotional materials, staff compensation, indirect costs and fixed charges.

Facilities

Schools operating out of a church building may already have access to adequate facilities. In this case, very little additional expense is necessary. In other situations, there may be minor aspects of the facilities that need changing to meet local city safety codes, such as the correct number of fire extinguishers, etc. Some schools may require major remodeling. This was the case with Victory Christian School. Moving the school into a building, formerly an auto dealership, was a major project. The front showrooms were remodeled into a chapel, library and computer science room and church bookstore. One of the three service bays was converted into a 1,200 seat auditorium which doubled for a gym. A second service bay was transformed into classrooms while a third bay became the cafeteria, kitchen, art and music rooms. A second-story parts wing was converted into secondary classrooms with science, home economics and business labs. A section of the outside parking lot was covered with dirt, sodded and made into a soccer field, baseball field and recess area.

Include in your facilities cost such items as:

- Mortgage payment
- Rental contracts
- Insurance

- Utilities
- Housekeeping
- Maintenance and repairs

Equipment (Capital Outlay)

Conduct a survey to see exactly what equipment is available. Survey data will determine what you must purchase, lease or borrow. A sample survey is found in Figure 6.1.

Costs for equipment and furnishings will vary with the particular area of the country. Consider the following strategies:

1   **Check on used equipment and furnishings**. Before purchasing equipment, check on the availability of used equipment and furnishings. Many times used furniture is available at a good price.

2   **Consider a joint purchase**. Some vendors will put together an order from several schools thereby reducing the unit cost. For example, your school may only need 10 new student desks. When combined with 40 desks for another school, the unit cost may drop as much as 25 percent.

3   **Investigate purchasing items through a Christian school association**. The combined buying power of 200 to 2,000 schools has a tremendous financial advantage.

4   **Shop around for the best price**. Get price quotes from at least three different vendors.

5   **Use a written bid system.** This is especially useful for all purchases over $500 [CSRK 6.1].

6   **Establish partnerships with a few quality vendors.** Ask for preferred customer rates. This can easily produce a 3 to 5 percent saving and up to 15 percent in some cases. Most companies will work with schools in securing furniture and equipment and will provide an extended line of credit.

Figure 6.1   Equipment Survey

	No	Condition	Unit Replacement Cost
Chalkboards			
Bulletin boards			
Elementary desks			
Secondary desks			
Tables-adjustable			
Tables-standard			
Pencil sharpeners			
Wastepaper baskets			
Flags and holders			
Double pedestal desk			
Single pedestal desk			
Files-two drawer w/l			
Files-four drawer w/l			
Files-fire for records			
Bookshelves			
Slide projector			
Movie projector			
Movie screen			
Tape recorder			

Textbooks

No school is complete without textbooks. Textbooks impose content, methods, sequence, goals and objectives, evaluation measures, and influence the life experience of students. For these reasons, the selection of textbooks is a serious task for a school administrator (See Step 8—Plan the Curriculum). Ordering the correct number of textbooks and accompanying instructional materials relates directly to the number of students

A good rule of thumb is to order two to five more textbooks than you actually need. It is far easier to return unused books than to place a second order and run the risk of books ending up on a back order. Acquire textbook samples from various publishers.

Supplies

There are four major classes of supplies used by Christian schools. These include classroom, office, housekeeping and instructional.

Classroom. Involve teachers in selecting teacher supplies. This will help assure the ordering of supplies they actually need and will use. Also, budget a specified amount for teacher supplies, so teachers do not have to pay for supplies personally without reimbursement. The Oklahoma Department of Education Teacher Expense Poll showed that a teacher spends on the average of $358 per year of her own money on classroom supplies.[5]

The most common way of budgeting for supplies is a lump sum approach. This requires assigning a specific amount per classroom. Project classroom supplies at no less than $200 per classroom, per academic year for new schools, with another lump sum (for example, $500 to $750) in reserve for unanticipated supplies. Figure 6.2 shows a list of basic teacher supplies:

Figure 6.2 Basic Teacher Supplies

• Bulletin board paper (36" rolls)	• Grade book
• Chalk	• Lesson plan book
• Chart stands	• Markers
• Construction paper	• Masking tape
• Dictionary	• Scissors
• Erasers	• Stapler and staples
• Flags (American and Christian)	• Staple extractor
	• Transparent tape

After the first year of operation, calculate the average cost for supplies and budget this as a per student cost. Add a percent to cover the rise in costs and multiply this amount by the projected number of students (for example, 5 to 8 percent—depending upon the economy). The more dollars you budget for classroom supplies, the less money teachers will need to spend out of their own pocket.

Office. Operating any school office requires supplies. Figure 6.3 contains a list of basic office supplies.

Housekeeping. Supplies would not be complete without toilet paper,

Figure 6.3 Basic Office Supplies

• Cumulative folders	• Pens/pencils
• Ditto fluid/toner and copy-paper (1 ream per student)	• Report cards
	• Stamps
• Desk supplies	• Paper clips
• Envelopes	• Staplers and staples
• File folders w/pendeflex	• Stickum pads
• Letterhead	

paper toweling, floorcare products and equipment, cleaning supplies, trash can liners, etc. The amount needed depends upon the number of students enrolled and the number of square feet in your facility. You can secure estimates of these costs by contacting other Christian, private and public schools in your community.

Instructional. These are supplies required for certain subjects, such as art, science, home economics, etc. They are consumable and need restocking each year. For example, acrylic paint, construction paper, test tubes, etc.

Very closely related to instructional supplies are instructional aids: items such as curriculum guides, maps for history class, specimens for science, tumbling mats for physical education, maps and globes. Curriculum guides and teacher textbooks contain listings of suggested and required instructional aids for each subject.

NOTE: *After the initial start-up year, the cost for supplies, materials and equipment (upkeep, repair and replacement) should range from 6 to 7 percent of the total budget.*

Promotional Materials

Our experience has shown that about 80 percent of those students who attend Christian schools come as a result of satisfied parents encouraging other parents to send their children. Since a new school does not have a group of satisfied parents through which to advertise, direct a certain amount of financial resources toward promotion and publicity. A list of promotional expenses is shown in Figure 6.4.

Strive for quality in producing promotional items. New schools without an established history of quality will be judged for quality based on their promotional items. Consider the following:

- Use an experienced desk-top publisher.
- Have a skilled printer do your printing.
- Select designs and layouts that are attractive to the eye.
- Use no less than two-part color.
- Get price quotes from several printers.
- Figure the postage cost for mailing.
- Order a good supply, keeping in mind that the cost of printing is absorbed in the first 500 copies. However, be careful to avoid overprinting.
- Make sure the pieces are not dated so they can be used for an extended period.

Spend quality time designing your school logo. Keep it simple and easily recognizable. Finally, spend a little extra for quality paper on all promotional items.

Figure 6.4 Promotional Expenses

• Attractive brochure	• Church bulletin inserts
• Radio announcement	• Bulk mail flier
• Newspaper advertisement	• Outdoor advertisement

Supply and Equipment Management

Because of the increasing cost of school supplies and equipment, the importance of proper management takes on added significance.[6] Supply and equipment management responsibilities involve six functions: requisitioning, purchasing, receiving, storing, distributing and inventorying. Consider the following guidelines:

1   Use a team approach in selecting and requisitioning supplies. This will avoid costly duplication and help prioritize spending. Use a standardized requisition form [CSRK 6.2].

2   Centralize the purchasing process using a standard purchase order. Appoint one person to be responsible for all purchasing [CSRK 6.3]. Use a three-part purchase order. One copy goes to the vendor, a second to accounting, and a third acts a receiving document. Jordan cautions, "If the purchase order is being issued in response to a quotation, all the elements of the quotation should be included."[7]

3   Inspect all shipments, checking each item against the invoice and

purchase order. Inspect for damages and shortages. Notify vendors immediately and request an adjustment or replacement.

4   Store supplies and equipment in a secure, convenient place. Allow for storage of some supplies in classrooms for easy access.

5   Distribute supplies from a central location and have an assigned staff person responsible.

6   Maintain an accurate inventory of all supplies and equipment. Inventory equipment annually and supplies each quarter [CSRK 6.4].

7   Inventory all instructional materials. Add to this inventory as you receive materials [CSRK 6.5]. Include textbooks, workbooks, reference books, supplementary texts, instructional kits, games, puzzles and audio-visual materials [CSRK 6.6].

8   Computerize your inventory. Inventory systems rely upon a vast amount of information that continues to collect over time. Computerizing the inventory will end tedious and costly paperwork and provide a rapid means of retrieving information. Some computer programs keep track of vendors, location of supplies, vendor quantity, vendor transactions, purchase records and much more.

Staff Compensation

There are two categories of compensation. The first is salaries (for professional staff, such as administrators and teachers) and wages (custodial, secretarial, food services staff). The second is benefits. It should be the goal of every Christian school to provide a fair living wage, with attractive fringe benefits.

The staffing ratio influences the total salary expense. The higher the student to staff ratio, the fewer teachers needed, and the less a school pays in salaries. (Consider projecting benefits as a percentage of gross salaries and wages or as a fixed dollar amount.)

Use the following formula to calculate teacher salaries.

$$Ns \ / \ STr \ x \ ATs = \ SE$$

where Ns = 240 (number of students)
STr = 20:1 (student to teacher ratio)
ATs = $17,000 (average teacher salary)

$$240/20 \ x \ \$17,000 = 12 \ x \ \$17,000 = \ \$204,000$$

Consider the following strategies in minimizing staff costs:

1   Make good use of volunteers, especially for non-instructional tasks.

2   Consider cooperative services with other Christian schools. For example: data processing, pooling use of maintenance specialists, employing a librarian as part of a consortium of Christian schools, etc.

3   Require administrators and counselors to serve as substitutes five to ten days per year.

4   Employ temporary help for periods of peak work loads rather than regular clerical help.

5   Use in-house staff for teacher development rather than consultants.

6   Increase class size.

NOTE: *A simple rule of thumb is to expect personnel costs to range from 78 to 82 percent of the total budget.*

Indirect Costs

Schools operating as part of a church ministry may find the church already provides several services essential to the success of the school. Sharing these services is much more economical than duplicating these services again in the day school. As soon as possible, the school should pay their fair share for these services. Determining this amount is no easy task. One approach is to use cost allocation based on several different factors (See Figure 6.5).

Figure 6.5 Cost Allocations

Item For Allocation	Basis for Estimation
Accounting	Total Dollar Volume or Number of Transactions
Auditing	Direct Audit Hours
Data Processing	Direct Hours of Employees
Disbursing Services	Number of Checks Issued
Insurance	Dollar Value of Insurance Premiums
Mail Service	Number of Documents Processed
Transportation	Miles Driven/Days Used
Equipment Repairs	Direct Hours of Employees
Space Usage	Square Feet of Space Used per Hour
Payroll Services	Number of Employees
Printing/Copy Service	Dollar Value of Documents

Suppose a youth director teaches Bible classes 25 percent of his employed time and carries out pastoral duties the other 75 percent. How much should you charge to the school? In this case, record 25 percent of his pay and benefits under school instruction and 75 percent under the church budget.

In charging for the use of facilities, calculate the amount of gross floor area in use and the length of time the floor area is in use. For example, suppose you want to prorate a $14,000 custodial expense between the church and school. The building is open 60 hours per week, the gross floor area of the facility is 20,000 square feet, and the school program uses 15,000 square feet of floor space 25 hours a week. Based on floor area, charge the school a ratio of 15,000 square feet to 20,000 square feet, or 3/4 of $14,000, or $10,500. However, the school uses the church facilities only 25/60 or 5/12 of the total time. Therefore, assess the school with 5/12 of the $10,500, or $4,375. Eliminate the time cost for the concurrent use of floor space and prorate the expenditures in proportion to the gross floor area used.

Individuals familiar with cost accounting can be good resource people for estimating these and other costs. Include a special chargeback line item on the chart of accounts and post departmental and ministry chargebacks using a standard journal entry at the close of each month.

Fixed Charges

Contributions to the employee's social security program, unemployment compensation, worker's compensations, health, life, and liability insurance, retirement programs, and utilities are examples of fixed charges.

One area of fixed charges that is often overlooked is insurance. Failing to provide for adequate insurance coverage leaves an avenue open that could place a Christian school in jeopardy of closing. Using a church site for a day school may result in significant alterations in the types and amount of insurance. Therefore, churches with schools should conduct a comprehensive evaluation of their insurance needs.

There are two broad categories of insurance: those that are necessary and those that are optional. Necessary insurance includes full property insurance and extra coverage, property damage and comprehensive liability and vehicle insurance. Optional insurance consists of all-risk, vandalism, fidelity and surety bond and student accident insurance.

Full Property Insurance and Extended Coverage. This type of insurance should cover the church and school building and their contents. If financially possible, purchase replacement insurance. The rule of thumb is to have protection against a major loss. Conduct an appraisal to get accurate property valuations. This is important, since valuations form the basis for premium payments. Also, if valuations are too low and a loss occurs, a coinsurance penalty may result.

Property Damage and Comprehensive Liability. Liability insurance relates to any injury to or death of any person and any damage to or loss of property of others caused by negligent acts of school staff, or resulting from the ownership, operation and maintenance of any school facilities, including building, playgrounds, elevators, equipment or vehicles.[8] Since both church and school may be taken to court when negligence contributes to property damage or bodily injury, it is important to have adequate coverage. Most claims will be settled out of court to the degree of the policy coverage.

Liability should cover all staff within the church and school. Malpractice insurance should be available for all administrative staff. If not paid for by the school, staff may purchase this type of insurance through homeowners' or renters' insurance providers.

Vehicle Insurance. It is wise to carry extra insurance on school vehicles, especially those that are driven often. Vehicle property insurance protects the school from physical damage to vehicles resulting from collision, fires, thefts, explosions, hail, tornadoes, windstorms, earthquakes, floods and aircraft damage. The newer the vehicle, the greater the replacement cost.

Vehicles, such as school vans and buses used in the transportation of students, should have adequate liability insurance. Consider purchasing a minimum of $500 deductible. Conduct a periodic audit of vehicles and adjust the premium accordingly. The fiscal year, rather than a school year, is the period for purchasing school insurance. This provides for year-around coverage, whether or not the school is in session.

NOTE: *If possible, avoid the use of private vehicles to transport students to sport games and activities.*

All-Risk Insurance Coverage. This type of optional insurance is extremely important for school equipment, such as musical instruments, audio/video units, computers, typewriters, cameras, etc. In addition, insure any equipment of significant value ($500 or more) that is taken off campus. For example, in one school a secretary took a memory typewriter home to work on a student handbook. Upon carrying the typewriter from the car to the house, it was dropped and damaged beyond repair. The $1,500 paid to replace the typewriter would have more than paid for an all-risk coverage on all equipment in the building. Needless to say, this school now has all-risk coverage. Purchase a floating policy that will cover theft and damage. Also, all-risk insurance covers loss by fire.

Vandalism. Check your policy to see that it covers cases of vandalism. It is not unusual for schools to be broken into and severe damage done in a very short period. Covering the cost of repairing broken windows, paint sprayed on walls, ceiling, and floors, bulletin boards cut up, and smashed desks can be challenging. Usually, vandalism coverage is part of the extended coverage comprehensive portion of the school fire insurance program.

Fidelity and Surety Bond Coverage. Who would think that a staff person would take tuition money, or money from the cafeteria, concession stand, student activities fund, mission trip fund, fund-raisers, athletic and book fees? Embezzlement should never take place in a Christian school, but it does.

Include all employees who handle school funds in a blanket commercial fidelity bond. Also, a broad form money and security policy would cover all losses from within the premises caused by destruction, disappearance, or theft.

Student Accident Insurance. Since many parents do not have accident insurance, schools should offer student insurance for every student enrolled. Allow parents the option of selecting coverage for a twenty-four hour period, as well as obtaining additional insurance for special sports, such as soccer, football, etc.

Some schools prefer carrying a blanket insurance policy on every student, a policy that is secondary to the parents' primary coverage. For example, one Christian school did not have any form of student accident insurance. The school rented physical education facilities off campus. During a physical education class, a high school student tripped on some Astro-turf while playing flag football and suffered a linear skull fracture. The parents did not have any medical insurance. The school had a choice of either doing nothing and opening itself to a possible liability suit, or helping the parents pay the medical costs. The amount the school paid for medical costs was far more than the cost to provide individual insurance for the entire student body. The following year the school chose to include the cost of student accident insurance as part of the student registration fee and has been doing so ever since.

How Much Insurance Is Enough? Almost everyone would agree that today's society is litigious: all it takes is one good-sized lawsuit to close the doors of a Christian school. How much insurance is enough? It is not uncommon for schools to secure an umbrella liability coverage limit of $1,000,000.[9] However, each school must research its own needs. The dollar amount of coverage depends upon a variety of factors.

- The school age served (for example, elementary vs. secondary).

- Total number of students.
- Extent and state of repair of the facilities.
- Nature of high risk activities (football, shop classes, etc.).
- Kind of discipline used (especially corporal punishment).
- The extent of student medical coverage. This does not eliminate the need for liability insurance but does reduce significantly the prospect of being sued.

Christian school administrators must work to avoid all possible risk. Although physical education programs can present a high level of risk, one should not do away with them; rather, everything must be done to avoid the possibility of risk, such as placing padding on the walls at the end of basketball playing courts, placing non-skid paint on locker room floors, training students and staff to avoid accidents, instituting school safety programs, fire prevention programs, safety inspections, and clearing the grounds of unsafe hazards.

NOTE: *Fixed charges should range from 10 to 12 percent of the total budget.*

Self-Funding Programs

There are some programs that should be self-funding, that is, they should break even: total revenues equaling the total cost. These programs include food services, transportation and student activities.

Let's say you want to determine the number of meals you will need to serve in the cafeteria to break even when the cost of a meal ticket is $1.50. You can use the following formula to determine the break-even point.

$$Q = Fc/(Ru - Vc)$$

Q (the quantity of units) = Fc (the fixed costs, e.g., salaries) divided by Ru (revenue per unit) minus Vc (the variable costs, for example, food supplies)

where,

Fc = Fixed costs is $50

Ru = Revenue per unit (Ticket costs e.g., $1.50)

Vc = Variable costs per meal (Food, supplies, e.g., $1.00)

$$Q = Fc/(Ru - Vc)$$
$$50/(1.50 - 1.00)$$
$$50/.50$$
$$Q = 100$$

You will need to serve 100 meals to break even. As you adjust the cost per unit, fixed and variable costs, the number of meals needed to break even will adjust accordingly. Keep in mind that when you increase the cost of a meal, you run the risk of reducing the number of meals served.

Develop an Income Plan

Once you identify the items in your spending plan, the next task is to generate the necessary income to fund your spending plan. There are several primary sources of income. These include tuition, fees, sales, fund-raising and other sources of income, such as interest, gifts and pledges.

Tuition

According to Kotler and Fox, "Research confirms that consumers often use the price of a product or service as an indicator of its quality... In practice, consumers seem wary of schools that charge significantly less than comparable schools. They may wonder what is wrong with the school and presume that the other, more expensive schools offer a better education."[10]

There are two basic tuition options: full cost and adjusted cost. Select the plan that best matches your financial situation.

Full Cost Tuition Plan. In this plan, everyone pays his own way. Having projected the number of students expected, divide this figure into the projected cost for operating the school. For example, $50,000 (Operational Costs) divided by 40 (Number of Students Enrolled) equals $1,250 per student.

Adjusted Cost Tuition Plan—Percent Reduction. These plans may take several forms. Rather than charging parents the full tuition cost, a specified percentage of the total cost, for example, 10 percent will be raised through various fund-raising projects. Divide the remaining 90 percent of the projected costs by the number of students expected. For instance, $50,000 (Operational Costs) minus $5,000 (Fund-raising Income) equals $45,000 divided by 40 (Number of Students Enrolled) equals $1,125 per student.

Adjusted Cost Tuition Plan—Multiple Member Discount. Another adjusted cost tuition plan provides a multiple family member discount; per-pupil tuition cost decreases by a certain percentage or fixed amount for each additional family member enrolled. Exercise caution in accurately projecting the expected number of children as the first, second, third or fourth child.

Calculate the adjusted tuition level using the following formula:[11]

$$F_1B + F_2 (\%B) + F_3 (\%B) = OC$$

where,

F_1 equals the number of students from one child families
F_2 represents the number of students from two children families
F_3 stands for the number of children enrolled from families with three children
B represents the base tuition
%B represents the percentage of base tuition established
OC depicts your operational costs

Let's say your operational costs are still at $50,000, and you have 25 children coming from one child families (F_1). There are 13 children who come from two children families (F_2) and 2 children coming from families with three children (F_3). You establish tuition reductions of 10 percent (or 90 percent of the base tuition) for children from two children families and a 30 percent (or 70 percent of the base tuition) for children from three children families. Using our formula, the following results are evident (B represents the base tuition)

$$F_1B + F_2 (\%B) + F_3(\%B) = OC$$
$$25B + 13 (90B) + 2(70B) = 50,000$$
$$25B + (13 \text{ x } .90)B + (2 \text{ x } .70)B = 50,000$$
$$25B + 11.70 + 1.40 = 50,000$$
$$3\,8.10B = 50,000$$
$$B = \$1,312$$
$$F_1 \text{ tuition is } \$1,312$$
$$F_2 \text{ tuition is } \$1,181$$
$$F_3 \text{ tuition is } \$918$$

Rounding the final figures upward makes them easier to manage.

Adjusted Tuition Plan—Range Adjustment. A third adjusted tuition plan provides a real dollar reduction in tuition based on the earning ability of parents rather than the number of members enrolled in the family. Accomplish this by identifying various ranges of gross family income. Then, set up corresponding tuition rates for families with one child, two children, etc. One school uses the following range adjustment plan:

Range	% Reduction for 1-2 Children	%Reduction for 3-4 Children	% Reduction for 5+ Children
20,000+	0	0	0
15,000-19,999	1	2	3
12,000-14,999	2	3	4
9,000-11,999	5	6	10
Below 9,000	10	15	20

Begin using this plan the second year of operation. This gives the new school one year to establish income ranges for families. Include on your application an opportunity where parents can identify their particular range of income. Parents who want to take advantage of the adjusted tuition plan will need to provide copies of the previous year's income taxes.

Tuition Assistance. Even with adjusted tuition, it may not be possible for some parents to send their children to a Christian school. A tuition assistance or scholarship program will help. Consider the following guidelines:

1   Develop a special brochure to give to people interested in giving to the fund. Make special note that all contributions to a general scholarship fund are tax deductible, while monies given to a particular student are not deductible.

2   Provide written guidelines outlining the conditions for qualification as well as the steps to follow in applying. Qualified recipients might include: children of widows, missionaries, ministers, fatherless and single parents.

3   Design a formal application. Ask for basic demographic information, listing of joint income, listing of assets-savings, cash, checking account, property, insurance, stocks, and major financial setbacks. Request a statement showing the reason they should receive aid, a minimum amount requested and a statement from the parent about the importance of a Christian education [CSRK 6.7].

4   Notify parents in writing of the receipt of the application. Return all incomplete applications to parents for completion before they go before the review committee.

5   Print on the application the cut-off date for receiving applications. Require all applications to be in by 14 days before the time school begins.

6   Appoint a tuition assistance review board of no less than three members.

7   Review each application.

8   Make awards based on priority of need.

9   Communicate awards in writing to parents or guardian.

Tuition Collection

Install an effective collection system. There are five main approaches to tuition collection: payment by cash or check, automatic payment, educational loan, collection agency, and credit cards.

Payment by Cash or Check. Most schools require parents to sign a tuition agreement (See CSRK 5.2). The agreement stipulates how tuition payments are to be made—by cash or check, and how frequently—by month, semester or year. Most schools request tuition payments due on the first of the month. A grace period is given before charging a late payment fee, usually three to five days. Parents may receive monthly statements of their account or use a coupon book similar to those used to repay bank auto loans.

In addition to a monthly payment plan, some schools offer a discount for tuition paid by the year or by the semester. When this is the case, base the discount rate on the prevailing savings interest rates. Monies collected on semester or yearly payment plans provide available cash for "start up" expenditures.

The major challenge with this plan is the tendency for some families to write checks that bounce because of insufficient funds (ISF). Unless you have a very efficient deposit system, it may take two weeks before receiving notification of the ISF checks. By the time, you let parents know about the ISF and ask them to write a new check or send through the old ISF check a second time, two to three additional weeks may have passed. Even when parents submit a second check, you have no assurance that sufficient funds are in the account unless you call the bank. All of this adds to the uncertainty of just how much cash you have to operate with.

After the second ISF check, require the parents to pay in cash, by money order, or cashier check. Include a significant fee for all returned ISF checks, for example, $15 to $20.

NOTE: *Since most Christian schools operate on a tight budget, it takes all families paying their tuition on time for the educational plan to continue as scheduled.*

Automatic Payment. Some schools use an automatic tuition collection system; parents authorize the school to deduct from their savings or checking account the monthly tuition owed (See CSRK 5.2). The parent's bank makes an electronic transfer to the school's account on a specified day each month.

The advantage for the school is in knowing the day following the bank draft how much money transfers into the school's account, as well as which parent accounts do not have enough funds. The bank assesses a $15 ISF charge to each parent whose account had insufficient funds. The school in turn charges its own ISF fee. These ISF fees are strong encouragements for parents to have enough funds in their account at the time the automatic draft takes place.

Call parents with ISF notices immediately, asking them to bring in cash, traveler's check, money order, or cashier's check to apply toward the ISF draft. Require this payment within two days so their children can remain in school. This will help motivate parents to be on time with their tuition payments. A temporary suspension or withdrawal policy based on past-due tuition will increase the faithfulness of parents paying their tuition on time, if it is consistently enforced.

Educational Loan. Another technique for collecting tuition involves arranging with a local lending institution for parents to get an educational loan. Parents secure a loan from the lending institution as the school being the co-signer on the bank note. The lending institution transfers the loan dollars into the school's account.

The main advantage is that the school has its operating funds up front at the beginning of the school term. Furthermore, the lending institution pays the school interest on unused monies. Parents in turn deal directly with the bank on a nine- to twelve-month payment plan rather than with the school

The main disadvantage is the school assumes the parents indebtedness should they withdraw from school. Also, the bank charges parents interest on the loan. This encourages parents to increase their indebtedness, a challenge for those schools sponsored by a church that encourages members to be debt free.

Collection Agencies. Over the past few years there has been a strong, steady increase in the use of collection agencies for collecting tuition. The thought behind the use of an outside agency is that most Christian schools are poor bill collectors. Rather than pressing a parent to pay tuition on time, the school extends mercy. Although mercy is a positive trait, mercy will not pay the bills. Invariably, schools continue to allow accounts to go delinquent to a point where it jeopardizes the financial welfare of the school. In some cases, when the school decides to withdraw children because of past-due tuition, the school risks the loss of a past-due account amounting to hundreds, even thousands of dollars.

If you decide to use a collection agency, view the collection agency as an extension of your school. As such, draw up specific guidelines identifying what type of performance you expect, as well as the nature and tone of the collection activities. All it would take is one disgruntled parent with a poor attitude over how an agency tries to collect past-due tuition to have a negative influence on other families enrolling in your school. It is essential for a school to be familiar with an agency's record and methods of collection. Check out several references.

Credit Cards. The wide availability of credit cards provides a very attractive option for collecting tuition. The disadvantage to the school is the percentage charged by the credit card agency for participation. The school also must buy, rent, or lease card machines, maintain valid lists and fill out detailed records before it can receive payment. Furthermore, it encourages indebtedness and results in parents paying high interest rates on the unpaid charge account balances.

Fees

Schools assess several different fees, such as enrollment, books, athletics, music lessons, science labs and other fees.

Enrollment. Most schools charge an enrollment fee that is usually non-refundable and covers the cost of promotional packets, enrollment forms, entrance testing, supplies, etc. This fee should be high enough so parents will give careful thought to enrollment. The fee may range between $50 to $150 per child.

Books. There are two major decisions involving textbooks: rental vs. purchase and paperback vs. hardcover. Under a purchase plan, the school purchases books from vendors. Parents then purchase the books either at wholesale or retail prices. The books are theirs to keep. Books may be sold back to the school at the end of the school term, or sold to other parents during a book exchange day. If you choose a purchase plan, sell the books at retail prices, then use the money earned from the sale of books to purchase instructional aids.

The major advantage of a purchase plan is it places the responsibility for the condition of the books on the individual student. The major problem is the difficulty in estimating how many new books to order for the new year. If you underestimate your need for new books, you may start school without enough books for all students. On the other hand, over-estimation may result in having to return books, so as not to inflate your inventory. Some book vendors charge a restocking fee as high as 10 percent for returned books.

The rental plan places the responsibility for the care of books on both the student and the school. There are two advantages of this rental plan. First, the school collects all the books at the end of the year. This lets the school know exactly how many new books to purchase for the new school year. Second, the school can reduce the cost to the parent by prorating the costs over a two- to three-year period. Set an average rental fee for each school division, such as kindergarten, grades 1-3, grades 4-6, grades 7-8 and grades 9-12. This keeps the number of different fees to a minimum and eases accounting procedures.

The decision to purchase paperback or hardcover books should follow the decision to have students rent or purchase their textbooks. Hardcover books are best when you use a rental system. This extends the replacement time, thereby reducing the per student rental cost.

Consider the following policies:

1   Use paperback books when parents are required to purchase books.

2   Rate workbooks at full-cost for that year and have students keep them at the end of the school year.

3   Prorate paperback books over a three-year period.

4   Prorate hardback books over five years. Replace hardback books as new editions become available.

5   Require teachers to keep inventory logs that include the name of the student, assignment date, number of the book and its condition. All books other than workbooks are collected at the end of the school year and the count noted in the inventory log.

6   Assess a repair fee for damaged books.

7   Require students who lose books to pay the remaining portion of a replacement cost.

8   Have students cover all books they plan to return. Consider purchasing standardized school covers with your school logo and other information (calendar, code of conduct, policies, etc.) imprinted on the cover. Some schools use this idea as a special fund-raiser.

9   Whenever possible, purchase hardcover books, especially when you use a rental system.

10   Schools that are part of a church with a bookstore may get better prices from publishers by ordering their books through the church book store rather than the school. Sell books at a reduced price or use the additional income to purchase other resource materials.

11   Consider including other fees with the cost of textbooks. For example, a fee of $140 per student in grades 7-12 provides all books, lab fees, a student ID card, a copy of the school yearbook and accident insurance. This initial fee might appear high at first, but parents appreciate paying for everything at once rather than paying a variety of fees.

12   As a special incentive for early re-enrollment during a one-time re-enrollment period, consider waving a percentage of this fee, for example, 25 percent.

Athletic. Many Christian schools require payment of athletic fees to help offset athletic programs. For example, all students participating in a sport pay a $15 fee per sport at the elementary level, not to exceed a total of $30. At the junior and senior high school levels, this fee is $25 per sport with a maximum for any one student of $50. To help offset the cost for families with more than one child in athletics, have a maximum of $100 for a single family. In addition, some schools charge a student activity fee ($5-$10), or a family activity fee ($20-$30).

Other Fees. Many Christian schools require students to pay for special programs, such as private music lessons, science labs, home economics labs, etc. The rationale for this plan is clear: since not all students participate in all school-sponsored programs, only those students who use the services should pay. Usually, high school students are the ones who end up paying additional fees.

Another fee may be driver's education. This is due to the additional cost of insurance, fuel, and maintenance of the driver's education vehicle. This fee should be competitive to similar fees charged by public schools in the surrounding community.

Sales

Lunch tickets, bus tickets, athletic tickets, yearbook and newspaper advertisements are examples of general sale items. Lunch ticket sales should offset the cost of your food services program as bus tickets should provide the major revenue for your transportation expenses. Yearbook and newspaper sales, as well as revenue from the sale of advertisements, should offset publication expenses.

Consider purchasing supplies wholesale and repackaging them for resale during school registration. This affords a real savings for parents and insures that students have the recommended supplies. Other sale items could include Bibles and dictionaries [CSRK 6.8].

Fund-raising

Most Christian schools will use special fund-raisers to generate a portion of the income essential to carry on its programs. There are several elements for effective fund-raising projects:

1   Develop a plan with realistic goals.
2   Select the fund-raising project(s) that will help achieve your goal. Do not consider raffles and lotteries as a fund-raiser regardless of the cause.
3   Identify who is to be involved. Consider using professional fund-raising help and keep teacher involvement to a minimum so fund-raising activities do not interfere with instructional activities.

4   Organize your materials. Forms are essential to keep accurate and efficient records.

5   Communicate the need to staff, students and parents. Call attention to the cause, give goals, and motivate toward action.

6   Launch the project and set up a timetable of events.

7   Run the project for a two-week maximum period.

8   Close and evaluate the program.

In ministries where groups from the church and those from the school are doing fund-raising, it is a good idea to assign one person the task of reviewing and approving all fund-raising requests [CSRK 6.9]. Place all approved activities on a master calendar to avoid overlap.

Encourage groups to take fund-raising activities to different clientele rather than "hitting up" the same group every time. Also, for those families who do not participate in fund-raising events, consider assessing these families the full cost of tuition.

> **NOTE**: *Limit fund-raising to no more than 20 percent of the operating budget. Limit the number to no more than four major school-wide events per year. Going beyond these recommendations will eventually result in fund-raising overload.*

Other Sources of Income

Some Christian schools have been successful in securing funds and equipment through the following sources:

1   **Donations.** Seek donations of money and gifts of equipment from individuals or organizations [CSRK 6.10].

2   **Grants and bequests from foundations.** The school applies for funding by submitting a grant proposal or request to a foundation.

3   **Investments.** These include investment programs for cash holdings stemming from tuition paid by semester or year, earning interest on money not immediately needed.

4   **Clubs and organizations.** For example, booster clubs and parent-teacher organizations.

5   **Living gifts of life insurance, real estate, personal property, stocks and bonds.** (For a complete discussion of these gifts, see *Financing Christian Schools.*)

6   **Founders Club.** This is for individuals, organizations, corporations, or foundations that donate $500 to $1,000 to start the new school. For example, the 5:15:5 Club, where there are five hundred people pledging $15 per month for five years.

7   **Letter Campaigns.** Use this technique for a specific need.

8   **Sales for equipment programs.** Some schools can fund their bas-

ketball clock and high school wood basketball floors by entering into an agreement with vendors, such as Pepsi, to sell their products at all sporting events.

9 **Adopt-a-Student.** Implement this program to give individuals and churches an opportunity to adopt a student by helping with the Christian school costs.

10 **Memorials.** These include living memorials, or gifts given in memory of another person. Memorial gifts are tax-deductible for the giver.

11 **Matching Gifts.** Many companies will match gifts given by an employee to an educational institution. Have parents check with their employers to see if a gift-matching program is available.

12 **Sustaining Membership.** Contact special groups such as newly married couples with a new child and ask them to become a sustaining member of the school. Ask for a commitment to pray for the school, devote time and talents and plant financial seeds into the school ministry.

13 **Faith Promise Dinners.** This fund-raiser yields immediate cash flow, many small donors, and gives a pool of human resources for future volunteer projects.

14 **Radio Day.** Each year, Victory Christian School participates in selling radio spots to vendors in the community to sponsor a day of programming by the students on one of the local radio stations. The students make up ads and serve as disc jockeys for the entire program.

15 **Alumni.** Don't overlook the valuable resources that are in the hands of school alumni.

16 **Capital Drive.** This activity is more successful for raising large sums of money. Contact Christian schools or churches who have had successful capital-drive campaigns and secure the assistance of professionals who specialize in capital programs.

17 **Educational Endowment.** Establish an educational endowment fund whereby the money given to the fund earns interest that can be designated for several school-related projects or to help pay operational costs [CSRK 6.11].

Federal and State Funding

Although there is state and federal money available to private schools, be cautious of programs that might compromise the philosophy of your school, open your records to government audits, or require employment of certain groups of individuals, such as homosexuals, recovering drug users, etc. If your school accepts federal or state money, do not use these funds for basic programs. Thus, if you should decide to no longer accept federal or state funds, your basic program will not be affected.

Computer Alternative

Projecting the amount of income to expect each year requires careful tracking of enrollment figures, number of children attending per family, amount charged for textbooks and other fees, staff discounts, fund-raising income, etc. Performing this task constitutes a substantial commitment of time, three to four pads of paper, and a dozen pencils with good erasers.

Schools can recapture hundreds of hours of calculating time, enhance accuracy and increase forecasting effectiveness by placing income projections on a computer using spreadsheet software, such as *LOTUS 123*. Once all the variables influencing income are identified, they can be added to a financial spreadsheet and used to answer questions. For example, "What will my income be if we raise tuition by 5 percent, experience a 2 percent increase in enrollment, a significant change in the number of children coming from families with two or more children and a 10 percent increase in the discount given to children of school staff?"

What once took hours to figure now takes less than one minute. Mike McCutchin, Chief Finance Officer at Victory Christian Center, Tulsa, Oklahoma has created several comprehensive templates for *LOTUS 123* users. These templates allow opportunity to answer any number of "what if" questions. These templates are available on computer disk from DEL Publications.

Institute an Accounting System

There are three recommended approaches to Christian school accounting. These are cash basis, full accrual and fund accounting.

Cash Basis Accounting

The major components of this system include a checkbook, cash disbursement book, cash receipt book, employee compensation records, general journal, general ledger, written chart of accounts and trial balance. Revenues are recorded when they are received and expenditures are recorded only when cash disbursements are made. (For those who are unfamiliar with bookkeeping systems, consider *Bookkeeping for Nonprofit* or *Chumas Certified Accounting Manual*.)

This is a good system for small schools with a limited number of transactions, and it requires little special training or procedures. The major disadvantage is that it reflects only cash-on-hand and bills-as-paid. There is no record of money due or money owed.

Full Accrual Accounting

This system contains the same ingredients as a cash system with the addition of an accounts payable and accounts receivable register. Under this system transactions are recorded as they occur rather than when the cash itself is exchanged. This system of accounting requires a skilled bookkeeper or accountant who can produce reports showing budgeted and actual revenues and expenditures to date, encumbrances for each expense category, and unencumbered balances for expenditure accounts.

Fund Accounting

This system establishes a carefully developed chart of accounts and integrates components of cash and accrual systems of accounting. Fund accounting is especially helpful for it allows churches sponsoring schools to set up one set of books and one checking account, yet maintain a separate accounting of restricted and unrestricted income and expenditures for both church and school.

Chart of Accounts. A simple approach is to set up a common chart of accounts that allows you to spend dollars in direct support of program priorities and to evaluate the changes in program emphasis for different cost centers. This involves establishing detailed account groups and line items. The five major account groups are revenues (income), deductions from revenues, personnel expenditures, operating expenditures and capital expenditures.

Cost Centers. A key task in fund accounting is dividing the church and school into cost centers. For example:

1000 Administration
2000 Elementary School
3000 Junior High School
4000 Senior High School
4100 Athletics
4200 Student Services
5000 Food Services
6000 Library Services
7000 Transportation Services
8000 Facilities

Each cost center manager (often called departmental manager) is responsible for his particular portion of the school spending plan. In essence, it is a team approach to budget preparation. The center manager produces a list of program goals and objectives. Once the center manager identifies objectives and goals, he builds a spending plan using budget preparation forms. This involves estimating the cost to achieve each objective or goal and the amount of income generated by the cost center. For example, the athletic director plans expenses for the basketball program, then calculates the amount of income from gate receipts, business sponsors, tournament fees, sport participation fees, etc.

The advantage of a cost center approach and chart of accounts is that it allows financial accountability of the entire ministry, both church and school. You also can gather clear and complete information for ministry divisions (pastoral care, youth department, children's department, women's ministry, men's ministry, Sunday school, day school, etc.). The same information can be provided for centers within each division (for example, in the day school—administration, elementary school, senior high school, etc.), as well as ministry-wide summary information for each account group or line item. For example, salaries and wages, advertising, postage and freight, etc.

Some schools, especially those with an enrollment of more than 200 students may further divide each center into programs. Music, math, science, physical education and social studies are a few examples. This process provides the opportunity to "see that dollars are spent in direct support of program priorities and the change in program emphasis for different grade levels."[12] Since operating a high school costs more than operating an elementary school, this approach will further define these cost differences and provide information essential in establishing differential tuition scales for each level.

A complete fund accounting budget packet is available from DEL Publications. The packet contains sample budget packets, chart of accounts, account definitions, budget instructions, samples of revenue budget comparison reports, overview reports, and program planning forms.

Computer Systems

There are nearly a hundred church management systems on the market, ranging in prices from a few hundred dollars to a few thousand dollars. However, only a few incorporate a Christian school and church as an integrated package. *Automated Church Systems*, *Hunter Systems* and *Shelby Systems* are the three leading programs.

Schools interested in fund accounting might consider software designed for this purpose, such as *PC Fund Accounting*. As the business or school office receives requisitions (coded to show the budget classification as identified in the chart of accounts), they are checked against the budget information "on file" in the computer. Among other items, the computer shows whether an appropriation exists for such an expenditure, whether the expenditure has been approved, and whether the account fund balance will cover the expenditure.

Regardless of the system you choose, "You must keep all machine-readable records along with a complete description of the computerized portion of your accounting system. This documentation must be sufficiently detailed to show the applications performed, the procedures used in each application, and the controls employed to ensure accurate, reliable processing. These records must be kept for as long as they may be material in the administration of any Internal Revenue law."[13]

> **NOTE:** *"A computerized accounting system is only as good as the individual making the entries. Persons who do not have specialized knowledge of intricacies of the requirements of nonprofit corporations could make costly mistakes that would not be detected until an audit, inquiry, or investigation."*[14]

Identify a Budget Calendar

A well-organized budget calendar is important to the successful development and implementation of a budget. The calendar specifies the time schedule to follow in the collection of data for development of the budget. The following budget calendar will help new schools in proceeding through the budget development systematically: (The calendar assumes a January 1 decision to open a new school in September of the same year.)

Date	Budget Activity
Jan. 10	Develop chart of accounts
Feb. 1	Estimate enrollment
Feb. 10	Start revenue estimations
Mar. 1	Hold first budget discussion with pastor
Mar. 20	Confirm the school's educational plan
Apr. 1	Complete revenue projections
Apr. 10	Estimate start-up costs
Apr. 25	Establish salary schedules
Apr. 30	Compile non-salary compensation schedules
May 1	Submit preliminary budget to board
May 15	Revise preliminary budget
May 20	Conduct final work sessions on budget
June 1	Review and adopt proposed budget

June 10	Finalize accounting procedures
June 20	Formally adopt budget
July 20	Monitor enrollment
Sep. 10	Adjust budget based on final enrollment
Sep. 20	Adopt revised budget
Oct. 1	Review accounting system
Oct. 10	Review personnel records and staffing
Nov. 10	Review educational program and adjust
Dec. 15	Distribute budget preparation packets

The calendar presented assumes that the fiscal year of the school begins on July 1. The list is for illustrative purposes and should be modified for individual schools. Jordan cautions,

> "The budget calendar does not provide the panacea for all the problems and controversy of the school's financial affairs, but it does provide a structure through which staff members can make a positive contribution so decisions may be made in a more systematic fashion and may be based on carefully gathered information."[15]

Establish a System for Managing the Budget

The main purpose in establishing a system for managing the school's budget is to provide the necessary information to make good financial decisions and to provide information about the school's operation. Two of the major management tasks include setting up accounting journals and evaluating the budget.

Set up Accounting Journals

Contact a certified accountant or bookkeeper to help set up the necessary journals (See Figure 6.6):

Figure 6.6 Accounting Journals

• Receipts	• Disbursement
• Accounts receivable	• Payroll
• Accounts payable	• General journal

There are two primary journal approaches: single and double entry. Using a double-entry bookkeeping approach provides the necessary checks to assure accuracy of each transaction. The amount of debits must equal the total credits for the records to balance.

Bookkeeping and Service Bureaus

Small schools that use a simple cash basis bookkeeping system can assign the task of managing cash receipts, cash disbursements and keeping the checkbook to the school secretary. The school administrator can summarize the cash records and prepare the financial reports. As the number of transactions increases, consideration should be given to employing a part-time bookkeeper.

Another option is using an outside service bureau to keep all bookkeeping records. This may be less costly than hiring a part-time bookkeeper. The cost will vary depending on the range of services and volume of transactions.

In-house Accounting Services

Schools sponsored by churches with in-house accounting services should assimilate the school's fiscal processing into the churches bookkeeping system. Often, all churches have to do is expand their present chart of accounts to better reflect school expenses.

Evaluate Your Budget

"So how is the school doing?" To provide a meaningful answer, several actions must be taken.

Income and Expense Segments. First, divide budget income and expenses into monthly segments. Showing income and expenses for each month allows detailed comparisons of actual income and expenses across months. Furthermore, projecting actual income and expenses on a month-by-month basis rather than dividing the total annual budget equally over a school year provides a greater degree of confidence in the accuracy of the budget.

Estimates of Income and Expenses. Second, the budget must contain an accurate estimate of income and expenses. As Gross points out, "If expenses have been underestimated by 15 percent and income has been overestimated by 10 percent, there will be a deficit of 25 percent, and unless the organization has substantial cash reserves it could be in serious difficulty."[16]

For new schools with no history of income, expenses and no cash reserves, the accuracy of these estimates and classification of expenses becomes extremely critical. Established schools can estimate monthly income and expenses according to the previous year's actual income and expenses, then adjust those months where the school expects differences. For example, adding a new high school class in the second semester.

Financial Reporting. A third action is financial reporting. The reports must be useful; that is, they provide the necessary information to make sound decisions and to answer the question "How is the school doing?" Some of these reports include: statement of revenues and expenditures, balance sheet and statement of changes in fund balances.

The type and extent of reporting depends on the size of your school, intricacy of your budget format and technological assistance available to your school. Prepare these reports according to accepted accounting principles and within a time frame that is no later than ten days after the end of the accounting period and sooner if the school's cash balance is low.

Statement of Revenues and Expenditures. This statement helps the school determine how much was budgeted, how much was spent, and how much is left to spend. This report can be adjusted to various formats depending upon the information desired. For example, as a minimum, include income and expenses for the current month and year-to-date as well as the amount of deviation (variance) and a narrative summary of the reasons for these variances. Figures can be summarized by cost center, account and function. A sample of these and other financial reports are part of the Christian School Budget Packet available from Del Publications.

Balance Sheet. A balance sheet is prepared from the General Ledger. Income and expense accounts and opening inventories are recorded. Fixed assets are identified as well as liabilities and fund balances.

Be Alert to Financial Difficulty

Managing the budget is important to assure the school's financial success. Closely monitoring the budget will alert school officials to financial difficulty if it should occur. The sooner a school identifies financial challenges, the greater will be the chance of intervention. In addition to using monthly financial reports in helping to identify financial challenges, administrators, pastors and boards need to be familiar with several key indicators of financial difficulty. Consider the following indicators of financial difficulty. If a statement is true of your school, place a check mark in the box.[17]

☐ Have budgeted expenditures exceeded budgeted revenues for two consecutive years?

☐ Has the pupil/teacher ratio dropped to less than 20:1?

☐ Has the school been delinquent in paying salaries or invoices on time?

☐ Has enrollment been declining?

☐ Has the school's revenue increase been less than the increase in inflation?

☐ Has there been an increase in the number of accumulated sick leave days per employee?

☐ Has there been a disproportionate increase in fixed expenditures as percentage of total expenditures?

☐ Have fund-raising activities accounted for more than 20 percent of the expected revenues?

☐ Have administrative costs increased beyond 11 percent of the total expenditures?

☐ Has there been a steady increase in repair and maintenance costs?

☐ Is the percent of uncollectible tuition greater than 5 percent?

☐ Has the school engaged in short-term borrowing?

☐ Has there been excessive transfers of funds from one budget group to another?

Be Prepared to Adjust Your Budget

When it becomes apparent that expenses are greater than revenues, the administrator and board must act and change the spending plan or increase the school's revenues. Elve recommends that schools gather all pertinent facts, weigh them from all possible angles, and then decide what can and what cannot be changed to reduce the costs of education.

Before deciding to reduce or drop a program, prepare an impact statement [CSRK 6.12]. Include in this statement the following expectations:[18]

- The number of students affected.
- The number of staff affected.
- Facility implications.
- The results of reducing vs. discontinuing the program or service.
- Possible impact on other programs or services.
- Implications regarding accreditation requirements.
- The amount of dollars to be saved.

There is a balance in cost cutting and cost saving. As Elve warns,

"Often in life quality and costs are tied tightly together and therefore to cut costs can mean cutting the quality of the education your child is receiving."[19]

Consider a Financial Council

As there is a need for wise counsel and assistance during the formative stages of the school, there is also a need for advice in the fiscal affairs of the school. A financial advisory council is one way of meeting this need. Some responsibilities include:

- Reviewing cash management practices.
- Monitoring the school budget—income and expenses.
- Reviewing financial reports, balance sheets, fund-raising events, capital campaigns.
- Reviewing and recommending financial policies and procedures.
- Reviewing utilization of current assets.
- Examining the use of school land.
- Assessing insurance programs and financial audits.
- Exploring staff benefits.
- Helping to establish the financial success of the school.

Practice Sound Accountability Measures

Sound financial procedures and accounting practices are essential in the administration of all funds. A good administrator accounts for all receipts and expenditures regardless of whether it is a $1,000 tuition check, or ten cents received for a school pencil.

Develop a Cash Flow Statement

The cash flow statement helps you determine how much money the school can expect to receive. Reporting may be weekly, bimonthly, monthly, or as needed. Balance this information with the monthly spending plan.

Careful monitoring cash flow and expenditures will assure that financial resources will be available at the time the school anticipates expenses. Constructing a monthly cash flow report will ease spending decisions should your cash flow be underprojected. Providing a quarterly cash flow statement should provide sufficient time to adjust to avoid a cash shortfall.

Formulate a Good Payroll System

It is not unusual for about 75 to 80 percent of the school financial resources going to meet payroll.[20] Therefore, you must set up a sound payroll system as an integral part of the total school accounting system.

The following guidelines are provided:

1   Institute policies governing issuing of contracts for salaried staff and time sheets for hourly employees [CSRK 6. 13]. When possible, convert to an automatic time clock or time-care system.

2   Develop standardized forms for requesting leave and reporting absences from work [CSRK 6. 14; 6. 15].

3   Purchase preprinted payroll checks with sufficient space on the tab to print deductions and year-to-date information.

4   Determine how often staff will be paid. Consider using 24 to 26 pay periods. The costs for preparation are higher, but this schedule is more convenient for the employee and contributes to employee morale.

5   Reconcile your payroll each pay period. It is best to get the first payroll correct so it can act as a control measure for future comparisons.

6   Maintain a good set of payroll records. Include the following: employees earnings and deductions—federal, state, social security, insurance, and employee absences and vacation days earned and used.

7   Set up a report tickler system to assure that required state and federal reports are filed on a monthly, quarterly and annual basis.

8   As soon as possible, computerize your payroll system.

Some schools use a bank or service bureau to process the entire payroll, prepare payroll tax reports, maintain payroll records and issue W-2 forms.

Maximize Financial Resources

Since financial resources are always scarce, hard decisions must be made in distributing monies that are available.[21] Strive to be good stewards of the financial resources that are placed at your disposal. The following list of suggestions will assist in maximizing financial resources:

1   Shop around for the best price.

2   Institute energy conservation programs.

3   Defer capital spending until you establish replacement reserves.

4   Place spending priorities on essential programs.

5   Maintain maximum class sizes. This may require using combined classes.

6   Reduce insurance costs through safety awareness programs.

7   Evaluate in-house compared to outside services; e. g, custodial, printing, etc.

8   Train staff to waste less, for example, paper supplies, towels, etc.

9   Use least expensive means, for example, ditto vs. copier.

10   Use more efficient procedures or equipment, for example, fewer buses.

11   Utilize volunteers, especially for non-instructional tasks.

12   Consider cooperative services with other Christian schools, for example, data processing, pooling use of maintenance specialists, volume purchasing, etc.

13   Use copy counters to control the number of copies. When copy counters are not possible, use a manual recording sheet [CSRK 6.16].

14   Centralize inventory control.

15   Establish standardized supply lists to take advantage of bulk purchasing.

16   Schedule salaried and nonsalaried payrolls so they do not meet in the bank at the same time.

17   Use students and staff to clean buildings.

18   Require administrators and counselors to serve as substitutes two days per year.

19   Use U.S. Postal Service library rate, not book rate, for book shipments.

20   Replace long distance field trips with shorter ones.

21   Employ temporary help for peak work loads rather than regular clerical help.

22   Reduce the temperature in the classroom by two degrees in the winter and increase by two degrees in the warmer months.

23   Reduce or eliminate unnecessary lighting.

24   Conduct an energy audit.

25   Compare differences between purchase orders and invoices. Actual costs may vary dramatically from quoted prices because of price changes, mailing/shipping charges, quantity discounts, etc.[22]

26   Train staff to complete all information on all financial documents. For example, purchase orders, petty cash requests, check requisitions, etc.

27   Try new materials using a field-testing option. Publishing companies wanting to field test a new product will usually provide a free class of materials for each grade level for whom the materials are appropriate.[23]

Pitfalls to Avoid

1. Settling for second best. Don't fall into the trap of agreeing that "as long as you can train your children in a Christ-like environment, it really doesn't matter if you have second-hand equipment and secular school throw-outs." God wants your school to have the best. Why shouldn't He? He gave the best that He had—Jesus. God always gives the best.

Several years ago Victory Christian School fell into this trap in the selection of chalkboards. Because of the shortness of time in preparing the school to open at a new location, low quality, quick-ship, wood-framed, painted masonite chalkboards were purchased. At the end of the first year of operation, the chalkboards had seen their better day. Half of the boards had to be replaced at the end of the first year of operation—the school had settled for a less than quality product in order to save a few dollars.

Many times, schools go without because they fail to ask. Matthew 7:11 (NASB) states, "**...how much more shall your Father who is in heaven give what is good to those who ask Him!**" We encourage you to have your "expecters" out, looking for the blessings to come to your school. Deuteronomy 8:17,18 says that God gives you power to get wealth in order to establish His covenant with you:

> **"And thou say in thine heart, My power and the might of mine hand hath gotten me this wealth.**
>
> **"But thou shalt remember the Lord thy God: for it is he that giveth thee power to get wealth, that he may establish his covenant which he sware unto thy fathers, as it is this day."**

2. Failing to start a replacement and upgrade program for all equipment. Furniture and equipment do wear out! Have as a goal replacing all used and outdated equipment and furniture over a three- to five-year period. Once your school has been operating for a year or so, consider using a percentage replacement amount for the value of the equipment owned by the school.

> **NOTE**: *Add a 2 percent per year replacement percentage. The 2 percent figure is based on the dollar value of the equipment.*

3. Not knowing how much of the operating cost the sponsoring church or churches will underwrite. Expecting a new school to pay for itself the very first year is a very tall order. Churches that sponsor schools usually underwrite much of the initial start-up costs. Some churches continue supporting the day school by paying for many of the school's indirect costs, such as utilities, maintenance, etc.

It is a good idea for the church to know exactly what these costs will be for any given school year. Once known, the church can decide to underwrite whatever cost it deems necessary. The church should then prepare a written agreement between the church and school about the amount to be underwritten.

Knowing how much to expect from the church allows the school administrator to prepare the budget accordingly. It also allows the church to distribute financial resources to the day school on a regular basis, as it does any other department within the ministry.

This procedure is much better than an open-ended oral agreement making the church responsible for whatever deficits are created by the school. Under this arrangement, neither the school nor the church knows what is expected. This lack of expectation may lead to difficult times should the church cash flow be less than expected and the church be forced to cut its support to the school.

> **NOTE**: *The goal for a church-sponsored school is for the school to bear all of the direct costs and a fair (reasonable) share of the indirect costs. This amount may change as the school improves its financial base.*

4. Improperly using work-study programs. We caution schools who have work-study programs where parents exchange work, such as secretarial or custodial, for tuition. In the sight of IRS, this in interpreted as tax-free income and should be subject to income tax. If the IRS audits a parent's taxes, the school increases its risk of being audited.

To help parents avoid the unreported income challenge, consider the following:

- Establish a certain number of work-study jobs.
- Write a job description for each position.
- Hire the parent and pay them by check.
- Have the parent sign the check back over to the school. Apply this amount to their child's tuition or use a payroll deduction.
- Include the work-study program as part of the scholarship application process.

The only challenge to this plan is that the school must consider the parent an employee and is therefore responsible for withholding taxes and paying social security and worker's compensation.

5. Failing to institute effective tuition collection procedures for past-due tuition. Regardless of the plan your school chooses to collect tuition, the following recommendations will improve your collection rate:

Parents Ability to Pay. Evaluate the parents' ability to pay the tuition before accepting the student's enrollment. As part of your application process, ask the parent to identify the family income range before taxes. The higher the income level, the greater the chances of the family to pay tuition. Check to see the type of job each parent has. Check to see if they have an outstanding balance at any other Christian school. If there are questions about the parents' ability to pay, conduct a credit check.

Written Agreement. Require parents to commit in writing (a covenant between them and the school) to pay tuition on time. The logical result of failure to meet their tuition debt is to withdraw their children from school. Schools do an injustice to parents when they allow delinquent accounts to continue to accumulate to a point where what was once a few hundred dollars becomes thousands: the small molehill becomes a mountain. Furthermore, it is not right for some parents to go through extreme sacrifice and self-denial to keep their accounts current, while others fall further and further behind, yet keep their children in school.

Follow up. Provide for immediate follow up on all accounts. First, mail account statements. Second, accounts that become delinquent should receive a letter followed by a personal phone call, then a request to withdraw [CSRK 6.17].

Confirmation Letter. Confirm phone conversations and arrangements to pay past-due tuition with a confirmation letter. Put the letter in the mail as soon as possible, preferably by the following day [CSRK 6.18].

Income Projections. Adjust your income projections to consider accounts that are past due. Regardless of how hard you try, there will always be those parents who fall behind in tuition and withdraw their children before you can collect past-due tuition. Once withdrawal takes place, the chances of collecting tuition diminish. In the first year, project a 90 percent collection rate, then work toward a goal of 100 percent.

Penalties. Set up a policy of withholding report cards and sending out official transcripts for students whose accounts are past due. Include this as part of your payment agreement. Tell parents in advance that records will be withheld [CSRK 6.19].

Cleared Accounts. Require parents with outstanding accounts from the previous year to have their account cleared to re-enroll for the new school term (See CSRK 5.2).

Family Budget. For those families who show a history of payment challenges, require them to develop and submit a family budget. Set up an appointment to review their budget and provide financial counseling where needed. Consider adding a class on financial management to your Sunday school program or hold a class on Saturday mornings in the school. Require all parents with outstanding accounts to attend. (See Larry Burkett's *Christian Financial Concepts Series*.)

Teaching. Train your parents to believe God for supernatural provision. the Word of God says,

> "**Give, and it shall be given unto you; good measure, pressed down, and shaken together, and running over, shall men give into your bosom...**" (Luke 6:38).

Encourage parents to give of their time, talent and finances in meeting the needs of others, then to believe God for the meeting of their own needs.

6. Failing to properly educate finance advisory council members of their role in the fiscal affairs of the school. Individuals who invest their time in serving on advisory councils or committees often find themselves going beyond the boundaries of the position. Others are offended when the school fails to implement their recommendations, or when they are given no "say-so" or opportunity for worthwhile input. In these cases, quality people will not serve very long without becoming frustrated and resigning.

Wager offers this advice, "Committee members should be briefed (probably by the superintendent) on the school's general lines of delegated authority and accountability. In particular, committee members should be aware of any responsibilities that the board and school finance officer cannot legally delegate. Committee members also should know what school resources will and will not be available to them—staff time, typing, copying, printing, staff records, student records, and so forth."[24]

In selecting council members, apply some of the same standards that apply to school boards, such as a strong Christian testimony, agreement with vision of the school, members of the sponsoring church. In addition, appoint members who have expertise in business and finance. The superintendent or Chief Finance Officer should chair the council and provide leadership.

7. Failing to report unrelated business income. Generating income to pay for the many programs of the Christian school leads to creative income producing activities, some of which might be suspect as unrelated business income. If an activity is determined to be unrelated to the school's exempt purpose, the school will need to file a Form 990-T and pay appropriate taxes, excluding the first $1,000 of non-exempt income.

To be considered as an unrelated trade or business, the following conditions must be met:

- The activity must be a trade or business that produces income from the sale of goods or performance of services.

- The activity must occur on a regular basis.
- The activity must not be substantially related to the school's exempt purpose.

A trade or business would be exempt if substantially all the work is performed by volunteers, the activity is conducted for the primary benefit of the church or school for the convenience of its members, students or employees, and selling merchandise where most of it has been received as a gift or contribution.

8. Some schools get into trouble because they do not establish sound accounting measures. The following guidelines for avoiding pitfalls are in checkbox format. Place a check in the box of all that apply to your school.

☐ Issue receipts when funds are received. Maintain a record of the receipt [CSRK 6.20].

☐ Utilize a ticket system in all activities where admission is charged. Use a ticket tally form for all ticket sales [CSRK 6.21].

☐ Pay all bills by check, except if under $15; then use a petty cash voucher [CSRK 6.22].

☐ Verify all petty cash expenditures with receipts. Avoid keeping large sums of money in petty cash (over $300), and ensure that it is closely managed in accordance with established petty cash procedures.

☐ Keep supporting documents for each disbursement.

☐ Utilize a two-signature check system. This is to insure that no one person can disburse funds, and then cover up an improper disbursement in the records.[25] Use a check requisition [CSRK 6.23].

☐ Make deposits in the bank daily. Do not allow deposits to accumulate. Use proper deposit slips. This will provide a record of all receipts and disbursements.

☐ Excess cash should be kept in a separate interest-bearing account, and require two signatures to withdraw the money.

☐ Use two individuals to count cash and sign the deposit slip. This is especially critical where receipts are not issued.

☐ Make purchases using an authorized purchase order. Standard purchase order forms are available from office suppliers. When possible, develop your own form in multiple copies. One is sent to the vendor, one is retained by the purchasing center, one is used for receiving and a fourth copy is sent to the accounting office. The accounting office matches the invoice with the receiving copy before paying the vendor.

☐ Use competitive bidding on major purchases, for example, furniture, vehicles, insurance, etc.

☐ Establish a fixed asset inventory system to include the cost, age, location and condition of the asset. Consider using a tag system to identify equipment and furnishings. Include in the inventory any school-owned textbooks. The inventory is important in providing fire insurance records. Computerize these assets.

☐ Start a quality inventory control system for supplies and textbooks. The inventory system can be a simple card system containing the item's description, location, and number on hand. When items are used, an entry is made on the card. The card reflects the status of the item. When the supply reaches a low point, reorders are issued. Complete an inventory of all textbooks and supplies before the end of the school term to allow for sufficient restocking time. Consider computerizing your inventory.

☐ Establish a policy so no school employee will receive any compensation or reward of any kind from a vendor for any sale of supplies, materials, or services.

☐ Require pre-approval of any travel, transportation or subsistence. Reimbursement for expenses is received by submitting an expense voucher [CSRK 6.24; 6.25].

☐ School equipment should not be loaned to staff. If it is, staff should sign for the equipment to assure the lender's responsibility for, and return of, all equipment [CSRK 6.26].

☐ School employees who are responsible for funds should be bonded, with the amount of the bond determined by the estimate of the amount of money the school will handle.

☐ Issue prenumbered receipts for all income at the time it is first received. Deposits should indicate the receipt numbers, be issued in duplicate, noted in the receipt book and a comparison made between the total receipted and the amount deposited in the bank. Account for all receipt numbers [CSRK 6.27].

☐ Use only a few designated personnel to collect money. This includes the sale of tickets and collection of student fees, among others. Those authorized to collect funds should have clearly written instructions on how to handle and process the funds; and if much money is involved, the individual is bonded.[26]

☐ Pay all invoices on time (request payment terms on all purchases, then keep these terms).

☐ Student activity funds should be kept in a separate restricted account with all expenditures being approved by the activity sponsor and principal. Require all clubs, class activities and other groups to maintain individual receipts and expense journals. Review these on a monthly basis [CSRK 6.28].

☐ Before initiating any new program, estimate the cost of human and financial resources. For example, the decision to add another secretary not only includes the cost of wages, but also the cost for a desk, typewriter, filing cabinets, phone and phone line, etc. Estimate not only the initial one-time start-up cost, but the ongoing cost as well [CSRK 6.29].

☐ Avoid having cash in obvious places and never leave cash unsecured where it offers the opportunity for theft.

☐ When adding new programs, anticipate all "hidden" costs anticipated, such as staff, supplies, training, equipment, etc.

☐ Are only those new programs added that are able to be sustained over time?

☐ Tuition write-offs should be approved by someone other than the person receiving and posting tuition payments.

☐ Use a person other than the person writing the checks to reconcile bank statements. This prevents the person from covering up fraudulent practices.

☐ Place excess tuition funds in interest-bearing treasury bills or certificates of deposit.

☐ The budget provides for a contingency cushion (begin with a goal of 5 percent).

☐ Reduce losses of inventories by using lockable cabinets or closets and restricting access.

☐ Arrange for internal and external audits of all accounts. An audit is not an attack on the integrity of the school. Its main purpose is to provide good suggestions for improving accounting procedures, and protecting all of those who have been responsible for handling school funds. The audit should be by a certified accountant or auditing firm that is independent of the school or ministry. The school determines the scope and nature of the audit. Fees are generally based on a predetermined basis, flat fee, or maximum fee.

During an audit, auditors will need access to all school financial records and documents. An internal audit should be conducted on a yearly basis and an external independent audit at least once every two years (a comprehensive financial audit). An alternative to an audit is to request a CPA to review financial statements. Although it is less expensive than an audit, it does not provide the same level of credibility.

The audit should include:

- Board minutes that pertain to financial decisions and transactions.
- Official budgets.
- All journals, ledgers, registers and financial summary reports.
- Justification records for all school expenditures.
- Bank deposit records, investments in certificates of deposits, etc.
- School insurance policies.
- Verification of school inventories.
- Proof of prices, quantities and receipts of purchased goods and services.
- All student activity accounts.

Father, show me the programs and services this school is to offer. Instruct me in developing an income and spending plan to meet the goals and vision of the school. I accept Your supernatural financial provision. Let the rewards of obedience be poured out upon this school and its students, parents and staff.

A well-planned financial program based on the uncompromised Word of God, sound financial principles and procedures is critical for the growth and development of every Christian school.

Christian School Resource Kit

6.1   Written Bid System

6.2   Supply Requisition Form

6.3   Purchase Order

6.4   School Equipment Inventory

6.5   School Instructional Materials Inventory

Endnotes

1   Philip Elve. *Financing Christian Schools*. Grand Rapids, MI: Christian Schools International, 1984. p. 5.

2   International Christian Accrediting Association. *Elementary and Secondary Christian Schools: ICAA Official Visitors/Site Chairman's Manual*. Tulsa, OK: Oral Roberts University Educational Fellowship, 1987, p. 28.

3   Forbis K. Jordan, Mary P. McKeown, Richard G. Salmon, and Dean L. Webb. *School Business Administration*. Beverly Hills, CA: Sage Publications, Inc., 1985, p. 151.

4   Malvern J. Gross Jr., William Warshauer, Jr., and Richard F. Larkin. *Financial and Accounting Guide for Not-For-Profit Organizations*, 4th Edition. New York, NY: John Wiley & Sons, Inc. 1994, p. 383.

5   *Tulsa World*, Tulsa, OK: March, 26, 1989.

6   Edward F. DeRoche. *An Administrator's Guide for Evaluating Programs and Personnel*, 2nd Edition. Boston, MA: 1987, p. 294.

7   Forbis K. Jordan, *op. cit.* p. 132.

8   Richard D. Gatti and Daniel J. Gatti. *New Encyclopedic Dictionary of School Law*. New York, NY: Parker Publishing Company, 1983.

9   Ralph D. Mawdsley and Steven P. Permuth. *Legal Problems of Religious and Private Schools*. National Organization on Legal Problems of Education, 1983.

10   Philip Kotler and Karen F.A. Fox. *Strategic Marketing for Educational Institutions*. Englewood, NJ: Prentice-Hall Inc., 1985, p. 243.

11   Adapted from James Deuink. *The Ministry of the Christian School Guidance Counselor*. Greenville, SC: Bob Jones University Press, 1985.

12   Ivan D. Wager and Sam M. Sniderman. *Budgeting School Dollars: A Guide to Spending and Saving*. National School Boards Association. 1055 Thomas Jefferson St., N.W., Washington, DC 20007, 1984. p. 15.

13   Michael Chitwood. *Church, Management and Tax Conference Manual*. Clergy, Tax and Law, Inc., Suite 500, Osborne Office Center, Chattanooga, TN 37411, 1993, p. 84.

14   *Ibid.,* p. 84

15   Forbis K. Jordan, *op. cit.*, p. 170.

16   Malvern J. Gross Jr., *op. cit.*, p. 386.

17   Adapted from Ivan D. Wager, *op. cit.*, p. 236.

18   *Ibid.* p. 18.

19   Philip Elve. *op. cit.*, p. 181.

20   Forbis K. Jordan. *op. cit.*, p. 37.

21   Larry W. Hughes and Gerald C. Ubben. *The Elementary Principal's Handbook: A Guide to Effective Action.* 2nd Edition. Boston, MA: Allyn and Bacon, Inc., 1984, p. 309.

22   Adapted from Robert D. Ramsey. *Secondary Principal's Survival Guide.* Englewood Cliffs, NJ: Prentice-Hall, 1992, p. 207.

23   Adapted from Marcia Kalb Knoll. *Elementary Principal's Survival Guide: Practical Techniques and Materials for Day-to-Day School Administration and Supervision.* Englewood Cliffs, NJ: Prentice-Hall, Inc., 1984, p. 176.

24   Ivan D. Wager, *op. cit.*, p. 236

25   Malvern J. Gross, *op. cit.*, p. 441.

26 Clayne R. Jensen. *Administrative Management of Physical Education and Athletic Programs.* 2nd Edition. Philadelphia, PA: Lea and Febiger, 1988, p. 150.

References

American Fundware, Inc. *PC Fund Accounting.* P.O. Box 773028, Steamboat Springs, CO 80477; (800) 227-7575.

Automated Church Systems. Computer Dimensions, Inc. P.O. Box 3990, Florence, SC 29502; (800) 669-2509.

Burkett, Larry. *Christian Financial Concepts Series.* Chicago, IL: Moody Press, 1982.

Chitwood, Michael. *Chumas Certified Accounting Manual.* Chitwood and Chitwood, Chattanooga, TN 37411, 1993; (800) 225-5849.

Horngren, Charles T. *Cost Accounting: A Managerial Emphasis.* Englewood Cliff, NJ: Prentice-Hall, 1977.

Hunter Systems. 100 Century Park South, Suite 206, Birmingham, AL 35226; (800) 326-0527.

McCutchin, Michael. *Christian School Budget Packet.* Tulsa, OK: DEL Publications, (In Preparation).

Public Management Institute. *Bookkeeping for Non-profits.* PMI, 333 Hayes Street, San Francisco, CA 94102, 1979.

Shelby Systems, Inc., 65 Germantown Court, Suite 303, Cordova, TN 38018; (800) 877-0222.

STEP 7

SELECT TEACHERS

One of the most important steps in starting a Christian school is selecting teaching staff. No other element in the educational process has a greater affect upon the pupil than the Christian teacher. Luke 6:40 says, **"A pupil...after he has been fully trained, will be like his teacher"** (NASB).

Identify the Type of Teacher You Want

The primary goal in teacher selection is to hire the type of teacher needed to carry out the vision of your school. Look for teachers who are equipped for service—spiritually, academically, professionally and personally.

Spiritual Qualifications

Several important spiritual ingredients must be present in each teacher candidate. Consider the following as a minimum.

Born Again

Being spiritually born-again is a prime requisite. H.W. Byrne stresses the importance of the born-again experience:

> "The kind of heart a person has determines the kind of world view he exercises. If the heart is not Christian, it is certain that the world view will be unchristian. Of necessity, therefore, the only place that a Christian philosophy can start is with a Christian consciousness. Such a consciousness must come through the distinctive Christian experience called regeneration. Regeneration comes through the revelation of God in Christ, and the transformation which comes thereby when received."[1]

Only through the conversion experience is the teacher's mind open to receive the revelation knowledge of God, and only then is he qualified to reveal God to others. Unless a teacher allows Jesus Christ to be Lord of his life, it will be difficult for him to motivate students toward Christ-likeness.

Called of God

The teacher should also be able to give testimony that he has a sense of God's will, that teaching is God's calling, and that teaching at your school is God's direction. Roy W. Lowrie, Jr. makes this comment,

"An unsettled teacher does not make the strong contribution to the life of the school that is essential to its progress, for he is always thinking or wishing he were somewhere else."[2]

There will be times during the year when teachers will need to possess a deep conviction of God's leading to your school. From this conviction will be born a confidence in God's provision that will sustain them as they face difficult times. Paul provides this word,

"Who hath saved us, and called us with an holy calling, not according to our works, but according to his own purpose and grace, which was given us in Christ Jesus before the world began" (2 Timothy 1:9).

Since God truly calls teachers to serve in your school ministry, there can be the added confidence that God also equips them to do the task. When circumstances come against the teacher that would lead him to question God's calling and leading, the teacher needs to hold fast to his confession of faith and expect the circumstances to line up with God's calling and direction.

The call of God motivates teachers towards excellence. Teachers who are called of God will be doing what God wants them to do, and they will do it well.

Filled With the Holy Spirit

The teacher is a channel through whom the power of God flows. It is the active work of the Holy Spirit in the life of the teacher that becomes a transforming force in the very life of the school. When the Holy Spirit in the teacher is given full release, He will:

- Guide them into all truth (John 16:13).
- Tell them the thoughts of God (Col. 2:3, 1 Cor. 2:10).
- Quicken their understanding (1 Cor. 2:9-15).
- Facilitate teaching and make learning happen (1 John 2:20, 27).
- Transfer the wisdom of God (1 Cor. 1:30).
- Give authority over all power of the enemy (Luke 10:19).
- Teach them all things (John 14:26).
- Act as an intercessor in their behalf (Rom. 8:26).
- Provide access to God the Father (Eph. 2:18).
- Warn of coming deception (1 Tim. 4:1).
- Forbid or restrain actions (Acts 16:6,7).
- Give power (Acts 1:8).

- Deliver them from demonic spirits (Matt. 12:28).
- Produce fruit in their life (Gal. 5:22,23).

God wants His power to flow out of the teacher to students. When a teacher touches his students with the power of God, students who are being held captive educationally, emotionally, socially, psychologically and spiritually, will be set free.

The active presence of the Holy Spirit in the life of a teacher causes creativity to flow so lesson planning becomes an easy task. The teacher who allows the Holy Spirit to work in his life can expect to walk in the ability of God, "**...Not by might, nor by power, but by my spirit, saith the Lord of hosts**" (Zechariah 4:6). Jesus says,

> "**Verily, verily, I say unto you, He that believeth on me, the works that I do shall he do also; and greater works than these shall he do also; because I go unto my Father**" (John 14:12).

The indwelling presence of the Holy Spirit enhances classroom management by convicting tendencies to let things go, do less than expected, go the minimum mile, or not to care about the conduct of students. The Holy Spirit will not allow a teacher to accept sloppiness or laziness. When the Holy Spirit is released in the life of teacher, the teacher will be infused with a deep sense of responsibility; and they will be better able to bring academic, spiritual and behavioral stability in the classroom.

Believes and Acts on the Word of God

Teachers need to have a full understanding of the uncompromised Word of God and be able to use it with great authority, putting it to use against situations and circumstances. The Word of God is the power of God (Romans 1:16). The power of God has been entrusted to the teachers in your school; therefore, they need to be diligent with this power.

Kenneth Copeland likens being trusted with the power of God as a father who takes his son out to shoot a shotgun. When he shoots the gun for the first time and is not prepared, the recoil will take him back a couple of times because of the force and power of it. After about two or three times, he is able to handle the power of the gun. Only after his son had used the gun and was able to handle the power, was he able to take the gun out and shoot it by himself.

Unless teachers are trustworthy with the power of God, they will be held back. God has given teachers power and authority, and they need to be able to use it effectively.

Jesus said that His words were spirit and life (John 6:63). It stands to reason that in order for the teacher to live in the blessings and victory that God has given, he must know how to effectively use God's Word to bring into his own life those things that He has promised.

John Osteen, pastor of Lakewood International Outreach Center, in Houston, Texas, said,

> "We are not to occasionally speak God's Word and use it only in isolated situations that occur in our lives. God wants you (teachers) to become saturated in the Word, so that you will have an abundance of His Word in your heart and in your mouth."[3]

Matthew 12:34 says, "**...out of the abundance of the heart the mouth speaketh.**" God is looking for teachers whose hearts are full of His Word and who are willing to speak His Word. As they speak His Word, God will perform it. Jeremiah 1:12 says, "**...For I will hasten my word to perform it.**"

Since Jesus is seated at the right hand of the Father and is the High Priest of their profession (Hebrews 3:1), teachers can speak God's Word over situations and circumstances, and Jesus takes these words to the Father. The Father acts upon His Word by placing all His spiritual authority into operation to create those things that the teacher believes and declares. For example, when facing a difficult circumstance, the teacher declares God's promise found in Romans 8:28—All things are working together for good in my life. Everything is fitting into God's perfect plan for my life. I am called according to God's purpose.

An Active Prayer Life

Look for teachers who have an active prayer life, those who will be intercessors, ones who understand the importance of Mark 11:24 "**...What things soever ye desire, when ye pray, believe that ye receive them, and ye shall have them.**"

Look for teachers who know how to pray the Word of God. Praying the Word of God brings the will of God into existence. In 1 John 5:14,15, we read,

> "**And this is the confidence** (success) **that we have in him, that, if we** (teachers) **ask any thing according to his will, he heareth us: and if we know that he hear us, whatsoever we ask, we know that we have the petitions that we desired of him.**"

Seek out those teachers who are willing and are able to take authority over spirits, mechanical failures and circumstances. This commitment to prayer will save a lot of wasted time discussing challenges that should be overcome in prayer. Through prayer, teachers will come to their classrooms prepared for success.

Involvement in Christian Service

Employ teachers who have a record of participation in a local church body in the area of attendance, tithing, prayer and service. Their involvement and level of participation in a church before college, during and after college, are good indexes of commitment. Your church can use the leadership of these teachers. You should be able to count on them being ready to serve.

Bill Kelly offers this advice for interviewing teachers:

"Always look for signs that the applicant has already demonstrated a burden to serve and motivate others. It is important to note that the emphasis is upon past proof, not present desire... If your teacher applicant has been waiting for a job in your school before demonstrating their willingness to work with kids, don't be disappointed if they never get involved."[4]

Should teachers be required to attend your church? We have worked in both situations and have come to acknowledge the importance of the teaching staff being active members of the sponsoring church. This helps to:

- Strengthen unity among ministry staff.

- Provide opportunity for teachers to hear what the Spirit of God is saying to the church, so that the same message can to be communicated in the classrooms.

- Provide a focal point for agreement, allowing all to speak the same words.

- Increase the willingness of church members to provide prayer and financial support. When members see teachers committed to the local church, they are more willing to provide prayer and financial support.

- Inspire commitment. When people see that church is important to the teachers, church will become important to students and parents. A teacher must realize that people watch his life before they listen to his words. Faithful attendance in the sponsoring church allows students and parents to view the teacher's life and the example he portrays.

Academic and Professional Preparation

It is important to carefully evaluate teacher credentials in several key areas. These include degrees and licenses, subject preparation, experience and classroom management.

Degrees and Licenses

The importance of degrees and licenses is voiced by Harris: "Undoubtedly the most important influence on the quality of an instructional program is the collective competency of the professional staff."[5] However, the very fact that a teacher has a college degree and a teaching license does not guarantee that he will be a "good" teacher. The key is to find teachers who know their subject and can teach it well; a person cannot teach what he does not know (2 Tim. 2:2). This idea does not diminish the importance of having degreed staff.

Deuink and Herbster conclude,

"Christian schools claiming to offer an education that is academically comparable to that offered by other private and public schools cannot depart from traditionally accepted standards of professional competence and preparation and expect to maintain the respect of the community."[6]

Byrne recommends looking for a teacher whose "academic preparation...is characterized by good balance between general and professional education. A college degree should be considered minimum and the master's degree imperative at the upper levels of Christian education."[7]

Although Bible school training is important, it is not essential. However, having six to twelve credits in Bible is highly recommended. Furthermore, training in a Christian liberal arts college or university compared to a secular institution should yield an educational philosophy that is more compatible with the Christian philosophy of education.

Teachers who do not hold a degree should be required to enroll in a degree program as part of their professional development plan. Most accrediting agencies have this as a requirement.

Subject Preparation

Give special attention to the course training required for the various levels of the school. Consider adopting those guidelines established by your own State Department of Education. For example, most states require teachers to have 12 to 18 semester hours in a specific subject area in order to teach.

It is important to look for teachers who are qualified to teach in more than one content area. The more subjects a teacher can teach, the greater value that teacher will be. This is especially true in smaller schools where one teacher may be required to teach two or three subjects. Also, seek teachers who are able to help with extracurricular activities; namely, coaching, drama, publications, ministry trips and worship.

Experience

Experience is an important ingredient. More experienced teachers will have fewer behavioral challenges in the classroom, display more confidence, be more productive, better organized, more familiar with the curriculum and teaching methods, know what works and what does not; however, don't overlook the first-year teacher. As Kelly comments,

> "There's something exciting about the spark and vitality that the new teachers bring to a staff. There's no substitute for the raw enthusiasm of youth...The inexperienced teacher will make his mistakes, but the energy of his efforts tends to be infectious. So the challenge to the Christian school administrator is to properly orchestrate a balance between the zeal of youth and the wisdom of experience."[8]

Increase the success of first-year teachers (as well as new teachers) by assigning a veteran teacher to them who will assist them during their entry year. Also, providing a reduced teaching load for first-year teachers will lessen first-year burnout.

Classroom Management

The teacher must be able to establish a classroom environment that is smooth-functioning and well-ordered where everyone is at the right place, at the right time, doing the right thing in the right way. The teacher you hire must have a passion for improvement and be earnest about the business of training (disciplining) young people.

One of the greatest frustrations facing teachers who move from secular education into Christian education is a false assumption that there will be few discipline challenges. Since each student is at a different level of spiritual maturity, they will be at different levels of self-discipline. Regardless of the level, students need to be held accountable for their behavior.

Many of the same classroom management principles that worked in the secular school work in the Christian school. The added advantage is the teacher is able to utilize the power of God to see behavior changed.

A teacher who establishes himself in the classroom as the authority holds students accountable for school work, good behavior and living consistent Christ-like lives, will gain the respect of students. This teacher will become an effective minister, so, when the teacher speaks, the students will listen and heed the teacher's words. When students hear and obey their teacher, they are more likely to hear and obey the Spirit of God.

God calls the teacher to have dominion in the classroom and not for the classroom to have dominion over him. Behavior challenges are not to have him bound with indecision as to what to do. God expects the teacher to deal with and handle every situation.

Getting an idea of how a teacher applicant would respond to behavior challenges comes by asking the applicant to respond to simulated behavior situations. For example: "What would you do if after telling a boy to stop tapping his pencil on his desk, the boy continues to tap his pencil?" After the teacher gives his response, ask "But what would you do if he continues to tap his pencil?" After the teacher responds a second time, answer "Yes, but what if he continues to tap his pencil?" This type of questioning will uncover the depth of behavior management skills.

The presence of the Holy Spirit in the classroom is an important aspect in establishing a positive classroom climate. A classroom that is filled with the presence of the Holy Spirit will see teachers and students become sensitive to the convicting power of the Holy Spirit. This will happen to such a degree that the slightest deviation that grieves the Holy Spirit will be evidenced by teachers and students. Obedience to the Holy Spirit results in classroom harmony.

What teachers often see as misconduct is little more that the outward manifestation of an inward conflict that has a spiritual basis, such as rebellion directed toward teachers. You need teachers who can deal with the behavior (symptom) as well as take authority over the spirit (Eph. 6:12). When teachers learn to manage the spirit of the student rather than the behavior, the behavior will change to match the spirit.

Sometimes it becomes necessary to employ teachers who have had little classroom experience or have had no course work in classroom behavior management. It then becomes necessary to provide a workshop in classroom management as part of your teacher-orientation program. When there is evidence of a major weakness in this area, consider requiring course work before employment. If no courses are available, require independent reading. Consider the following books:

- *Classroom Discipline and Control* by Fred B. Chernow and Carol Chernow
- *The Strong-Willed Child* by James Dobson
- *School Discipline Desk Book* by Eugene R. Howard

- *The Effective Teacher* by Arthur Nazigian
- *Spirit-Directed Discipline* by Dennis Demuth and Carol Demuth.

A Zeal for Life

Hire teachers who have an inner excitement about life in general. Teachers who display a zeal and excitement that is grounded in the Scriptures will influence students. When teachers display aliveness and are bright and optimistic, their teaching will be interesting, student response will be stimulating, communication will flow and lives will be influenced.

Ask yourself this question, "When this teacher that I'm thinking about hiring stands before his class, will the students detect a vibrant spirit that radiates the joy of Christ?" If the answer is "Yes," then hire the teacher. Remember, the student will become like his teacher.

An Acceptable Lifestyle

Look for teachers who are willing to commit to a twenty-four hour lifestyle based on Romans 12:1,2,

"**Therefore, I urge you, brothers (teachers) in view of God's mercy, to offer your bodies as living sacrifices, holy and pleasing to God—this is your spiritual act of worship.**

"**Do not conform any longer to the pattern of this world, but be transformed by the renewing of your mind. Then you will be able to test and approve what God's will is—his good, pleasing and perfect will**" (NIV).

Schindler and Pyle state,

"It's how the teacher responds to his own life situations that will be transmitted to the students. It's how the teacher handles his problems, his heartaches, his sins, his mistakes, and those people that despitefully use him—that is what is learned by the students."[9]

Gene Garrick, pastor of the Tabernacle Church in Norfolk, Virginia comments,

"The influence on students is not just in the classroom but in the total life of the teacher—attitudes, habits, character, associations, interests, priorities, motivations, reactions and relationships."[10]

Paul says that teachers will be an open book read by all men whether at church or elsewhere (2 Cor. 3:2-5). Students need to see the teacher as a consistent example, whether the teacher feels like it or not. It takes a quality decision to be an example in character and attitude: an example that leads the teacher to say, "Follow me as I follow Christ." This means they must do all the right things 24 hours a day.

Select the Right Number of Teachers

The number of teachers you require is directly related to the projected enrollment. Follow these steps:

1   Identify the student to teacher ratio.

2   Divide the number of students enrolled at each grade level by the student to teacher ratio. This will show how many classes or sections you will need.

3   Allocate instructional and support staff to each class. Use the Staff Allocation Chart found in Figure 7.1 to record the number of teachers you need.

Figure 7.1 Staff Allocation Chart

Grade	Ratio	Enrollment	Teachers
K4 & K5	__/1	_____	_____
Grade 1	__/1	_____	_____
Grade 2	__/1	_____	_____
Grade 3	__/1	_____	_____
Grade 4	__/1	_____	_____
Grade 5	__/1	_____	_____
Grade 6	__/1	_____	_____
TOTAL		_____	_____
Special Teachers			
Art		_____	_____
Music		_____	_____
Physical Education		_____	_____
Resource		_____	_____
TOTAL Special Teachers		_____	_____
GRAND TOTAL		_____	_____

At the elementary level, the number of special teachers will vary according to the number of grades and the number of class periods per week. At the secondary level, the diversity of course offerings, state guidelines for teacher loads, and class size restrictions influence the number of teachers needed.

Locate the Teachers You Need

After identifying the kind of teachers you want and how many you need, your task shifts to finding and persuading talented and well-prepared individuals. The key is diligence. Begin searching for staff as soon as the school is announced. Consider appointing a search team to find prospective candidates who meet all the qualifications. Here are some strategies to investigate.

Look From Within

Current staff and members of the supporting church are excellent sources for teachers. There may be some teachers in your church who are supportive of your vision of a Christian day school and have been waiting in the wings for an opportunity to teach in a Christian school.

Once the school is announced, walk-in applicants from the community will be plentiful. Generally, unsolicited candidates are attracted to the school because of its close affiliation to the sponsoring church or churches, especially because of their reputation or visibility. Be careful to discern whether or not walk-in applicants have a Christian philosophy of education. If you want to employ an applicant who has no knowledge of a Christian philosophy of education, place in their hands reading material such as Paul Kienel's book, *The Philosophy of Christian School Education*, or H.W. Byrne's book, *A Christian Approach to Education*. After reading the material, interview them concerning understanding and agreement with the philosophy.

NOTE: *Make no offers for employment when disagreement is evident.*

Contact Christian Liberal Arts College

Christian colleges offer a value source for teachers. Consider the following services.

College Placement Services. Most colleges have active placement services. When sending a notice, be specific about the grade level and subject fields. In addition, make a personal call to the department chairman and ask for the names and addresses of the top teacher candidates. Furthermore, many professors are good sources of information for quality candidates. Write a personal invitation to each of them enclosing information about your school and ask for names and phone numbers of their top students [CSRK 7.1]. Where possible, attend college placement days on campus, arranging interviews ahead of time.

Harris encourages smaller schools to engage in "early contracting."[11] College students who are close to graduation and have received an excellent practicum evaluation can be issued a contract contingent upon graduation and certification. Some colleges will permit the teacher to take their practicum at your school, even if it is located 1,000 miles away.

College Alumni Associations. As Nadler points out, "Major alumni associations sometimes offer a placement service for their members. The quality and extent of this service vary considerably depending on the association and the college's budget. Frequently, when recent college graduates are considering job changes, they return to their alma mater for help in making a move."[12]

College Placement Fairs. College placement fairs are good sources for recruiting students. Be prepared with a good display, samples of yearbooks, textbooks and plenty of pictures. Although there may not be much time to speak with individual students, the most critical task is to keep good records of all students who visit the booth so follow-up contacts can be made. Plan for some extra time following the fair to interview the most promising recruits.

Try Other Teacher Recruiting Strategies

Every recruiting avenue should be investigated. In addition to those strategies already mentioned, consider the following:

Contact Other Christian Schools

Many established Christian schools have more applicants than they have openings, especially when the school is larger (those with an enrollment of 200 or more students). Contact the school administration for names of applicants, their telephone number and area of teaching preparation.

Contact Christian Placement Organizations

Many of the major Christian school associations, such as the Oral Roberts University Educational Fellowship, Association of Christian School International and Intercristo, have active placement programs. In addition, they frequently publish membership directories which provide an excellent source for recruiting teachers. Some associations publish a placement newsletter.

Advertise in Local Newspapers

Advertising in a local newspaper will generate a number of inquiries. Place in your ad specific requirements to narrow your target audience.

Also, consider advertising in an evangelical newsletter or magazine.

Open House

New schools will find an open house to be a positive way to expose the school staffing needs to the public, especially when a number of different positions are available. Conducting an open house has the advantage of including tours of the facilities, displays of instructional materials, and special presentations on the vision of the school. Keep records of the number and quality of candidates from each source so that future teacher recruiting can be enhanced.

Prayer

The Bible says, "**...yet ye have not, because ye ask not**" (James 4:2). Jesus said "**And all things** (including teachers), **whatsoever ye shall ask in prayer, believing, ye shall receive**"(Matt. 21:22).

Jesus instructs in the book of John,

"**...Verily, verily, I say unto you, Whatsoever ye shall ask the Father in my name, he will give it you. Hitherto have ye asked nothing in my name: ask, and ye shall receive, that your joy may be full.**" (John 16:23,24).

Attract Quality Teachers

Attracting quality teachers means compensating them for their training and experience, providing extra pay for extra work, being willing to establish a good benefits package and providing excellent working conditions. With strength in these areas, recruiting teachers will be an easy task.

Compensate for Training and Experience

Providing a staff member with a just compensation is one of the greatest challenges facing Christian schools. However, making a strong commitment in this area is a key to recruiting and maintaining quality teachers and administrators. Although there is no set formula to calculate salaries, there are several variables to consider.

Adhere to Scriptural Principles

There are several scriptural principles to follow. For example:

- A worker is worthy of his hire (Luke 10:7).
- Do not take advantage of a hired man (Deut. 24:14,15).
- Provide your staff with what is right and fair (Col. 4:1).
- Give the appropriate wage for work assigned (Jer. 22:13-17).

- Use an accurate wage scale (Ezek. 45:10).
- Help remove financial pressure (Mal. 3:5).

Consider Established Salaries

Conduct a survey of teacher salaries in the surrounding communities. Christian school teachers should be making no less than their public school counterparts. We realize that this may be a controversial statement, but why pay a Christian school teacher, who in most cases works harder, gives more of his personal time, has a greater sense of commitment and loyalty, and generally has more students, more parent contact and is imparting eternal values, any less than a public school teacher who has little or no eternal affect upon students?

Most schools point to finances as the reason for low salaries. There is nothing more draining on Christian school teachers than having to keep a second job to make ends meet. Dare to believe God for the finances to pay an adequate salary. Set as your first-year goal to be within 75 percent of the starting salary for public school teachers from districts of equivalent size; then, be committed to a plan that would continue to close this gap.

In addition to salaries within the community, consider the salary structure directly associated with the sponsoring church. Avoid salary inequities by evaluating all ministry positions on a comprehensive scale. An additional step is to prorate teacher and administrative salaries over a twelve-month period which is usually paid in a nine- to ten-month period. This helps relate school salaries to other ministry salaries paid over twelve months.

Award Prior Experiences and College Credit

Schools will attract teachers with more experience when additional compensation is given for prior experience and college credit, especially when this experience has been in a Christian school. Many schools set a limit on the number of years of experience they will compensate, generally up to six years.

As shown in Figure 7.2, the base salary is multiplied by the corresponding multiplier. For example, given a base salary of $15,000 with three years of experience, multiply $15,000 X 1.15 to obtain a salary of $17,250. Advancement to class B through E requires completion of corresponding number of graduate credit hours.

Once placed on the schedule, each year the teacher moves to the next step. After reaching step 6, an incremental increase is provided. This increase takes into account the change in the cost of living index, as well

Figure 7.2 Teacher Compensation Scale

Yr Exp.	A Bachelor's	B Master's	C + 30	D + 60	E Doc.
0	1.00	1.05	1.10	1.15	1.20
1	1.05	1.10	1.15	1.20	1.25
2	1.10	1.15	1.20	1.25	1.3
3	1.15	1.20	1.25	1.30	1.35
4	1.20	1.25	1.30	1.35	1.40
5	1.25	1.30	1.35	1.40	1.45
6+ $200 - $500 Increments.					

as the pool of monies generated by a reasonable tuition increase or an increase in student enrollment.

Some schools incorporate a special compensation plan as part of a "master teacher" program, often called "career ladders." For example, teachers progress to subsequent higher levels of designation, starting as an "apprentice teacher," moving to "professional teacher," "senior teacher," and finally "master teacher."[13] Reaching each level of attainment requires meeting different standards, such as years of service, certification, demonstration of skills and knowledge of content areas, etc. [CSRK 7.2]. With each level of attainment comes an incentive pay supplement.

Provide Pay for Extra Duty

As a school grows and expands its programs and student activities, there will be a need to assign staff to cover these areas, all requiring special work and responsibilities beyond the normal school day and hours (See Figure 7.3).

Staff who are assigned extra duties should receive compensation for the extra time. Compensation may take several forms, such as reducing the standard teaching load either in the form of number of courses taught, number of preparations, or number of students. Another method is to provide a stipend for extra services. This may be a flat amount consistent with those amounts offered within the Christian and public school communities.

Compensation must be equitable. Differences in pay are only permitted when based on a system of seniority, merit pay, measures of

Figure 7.3 Extra Duty

• Department Head	• Athletic Coaches
• Spelling Bee Sponsor	• Class Sponsors
• Curriculum Coordinator	• Pep Band Sponsor
• Fund-Raising Coordinator	• Chapel Coordinator
• Yearbook Sponsor	• Music Director
• Christian Service Sponsor	• Special Events Sponsor
• Newspaper Sponsor	• Cheerleader Sponsor
	• Government Sponsor

quality and quantity of productivity rather than gender (See Equal Pay Act of 1963). Challenges usually arise when coaches of boys sports receive a higher level of compensation than coaches of girls sports.

Jensen suggests a very simple method for establishing a just compensation across activities and gender. His system uses a compensation index built upon the following factors: [14]

- The number of extra hours per day (E).
- The number of months of involvement (I).
- The number of hours in the school day (H).
- The length of the school year (Y).

The formula **E/H x I/Y** provides a multiplier index that is applied to the base salary. For example, a basketball coaching job requires 2 extra hours per day either in practice or in games (E = 2); the standard work day is 8 hours (H = 8). The basketball season lasts 4 months (I = 4), and the school year lasts 9 months (Y = 9).

Apply the formula 2/8 x 4/9 = multiplier = .111. Given a teacher's base salary of $17,500, the extra compensation would amount to $1,943 (that is, $17,500 x .111 = $1,943).

Plan Staff Benefits

Fringe benefits for educators are like other wage-earning groups. Consideration for a fringe benefit program comes only after the teachers have an adequate living wage. However, certain benefits are considered basic, such as medical and hospitalization insurance. Regardless of the benefits provided, they need to be equally available to all employees. Figure 7.4 shows a list of benefits afforded educators.

Under IRS Section 125, schools can establish a cafeteria plan for all employees whereby participants may choose among several benefits (See

Figure 7.4 Staff Benefits

Time Off with Pay	Social Security
Holidays	Tax-Sheltered Annuity
Military Training	
Professional Absences	**Incentives and Improvements**
Personal Absences	
Vacations	Department Head
	Expense Allowances
Protection	Journals and professional
Health and Accident	Books
Insurance	Professional Affiliations
Hospital and Medical	Professional Improvement
Insurance	Credit
Liability Insurance	Scholarships
Life Insurance	Training Programs
Dental Insurance	Tuition Payments
Pensions	Tuition Refunds
Retirement	Unit Leadership
Severance Allowance	

IRS–PLR9034078). The percentage of benefit contribution of the school and that of the teacher will vary depending on the revenues available. An added blessing of fringe benefits is "they can be provided without the increased income taxes that would accompany the increase in salary if employees paid for the benefits themselves"[15]

NOTE: *Generally, benefits should comprise 10 to 15 percent of staff costs.*

Provide Excellent Working Conditions

Kelly lists "failing to maintain proper working environment" as the second highest contributor to staff turnover.[16] Bright, colorful classrooms, furnishings in good repair, clean floors and carpeting, proper heating and cooling systems, uncluttered offices and inviting classrooms influence employee decisions. Likewise, the availability of audio-visual resources, and an atmosphere where love and appreciation can be sensed, all enhance the appeal to commit to a contract.

Choose the Right Teachers

The major task in the selection process is getting as much information as possible on the prospective teacher. This information along with the confirmation of the Holy Spirit, form the basis for a selection decision.

Once that decision is made, only time will tell whether the decision was good. Brubaker comments,

> "Although it may be difficult to choose among several well-qualified persons, one will always be glad he searched diligently...The temporary anxiety of the decision-making process will yield to the long-term satisfaction and joy of seeing an effective and cooperative member serving in the school at God's call."[17]

Develop a Selection Process

The selection process includes several stages. The first is to develop an application and tracking system.

Employment Application

The initial step is to design an application form that will collect information in the following areas: personal, academic, educational, teaching experience, spiritual, teaching certification, previous employment, health, and Christian school philosophy. A sample application is available as part of the Christian School Resource Kit [CSRK 7.3].

Include in the application a request for written references, transcripts and college placement records. Have them sent directly to the school. All transcripts should be original copies [CSRK 7.4].

Once an application is received, place the application in a file folder. On the tab affix a label to identify the area for which the candidate is seeking employment. Consider using a color dot coding system for identifying folders by categories, such as elementary teachers, secondary teachers, administration, and so forth. Next, design a 3 x 5 card that can be filed in an A to Z file. This will provide a ready access system to locate teacher candidates. Include as a minimum, name, address, phone number, area of certification, and where they are in the application process such as application received, transcripts requested/received, references contacted, and letters sent from the office. In addition to these tasks, record on this card where the candidate is in the application process [CSRK 7.5].

There are several computer programs on the market; for example, *Hire*, designed to keep track of all the people who apply for specific jobs. The program allows you to merge files for writing letters to applicants, record whether or not they submit supporting documents and monitor the status of each applicant. Later in the school year, if it is necessary to find a replacement, the program automatically screens all applicants according to criteria you establish.

Appraise the Application Information

Check to see that the application is complete. Look for any discrepancies. As Hughes suggests,

"One technique used to uncover discrepancies is to search for missing information. Common problem areas are efforts to conceal unfavorable past activities by excluding dates and not listing appropriate reference sources. Look particularly at references from previous employers to make sure each employment situation is represented. Read between the lines on health records. Look for gaps in employment or school records."[18]

Contact References

Use telephone inquiries to follow up on letters of recommendation. If the prospect looks good and the letters of recommendation are positive, make telephone contacts with the references. This is important, for as Harris point out, "The openness of records in recent years, together with the fear of litigation that might result from negative statements in letters of recommendation, has undoubtedly contributed to the problems associated with the use of such devices..."[19] It is also evident that most people will make more complete and frank statements orally than they will in writing.

Conduct an Interview

We have come to value the personal interview as more important in the selection process than a teacher's credentials and college records. The interview allows you to:

- Clarify any discrepancies on the application;
- Gather more in-depth information on such areas as commitment to teaching, knowledge of subject matter, knowledge of current teaching techniques;
- Involve more that one person;
- Experience the teacher's personality first-hand;
- View the person's manner of dress, speech, diction, reaction under stress, enthusiasm, flexibility and cooperation;
- Review the job description with the applicant [CSRK 7.6];
- Assess physical and mental vitality;

- Discover the teacher's willingness to accept out-of-class responsibility;
- Confirm the teacher's calling and identify future professional plans;
- Identify personal preferences and convictions;
- Investigate classroom management techniques.

It is important to prepare for the interview so the information received is not biased, and that it is relevant to effective performance on the job.[20] Your opening remarks should center around informal conversation to get acquainted and to establish rapport. Ask about their background and interests.

Asking the right questions is critical to the interview process. Consider the following questions:

1   Why did you choose teaching in a Christian school? *Listen for:* Pleasure in working with students.

2   Why do you think we should hire you? *Listen for:* Desire to fulfill God's call; benefits of their gifts, talents, ability, hard work, etc.

3   Tell me about your philosophy of Christian education? *Listen for:* Theistic world view, God and Bible centered; requirement of God to parents to teach and train their children.

4   What are some of your best ways of managing behavior in the classroom? *Listen for:* Variety of techniques.

5   Why are you leaving your present position? *Listen for:* God's calling, absence of strife.

6   What are the two things you wish to avoid in this position? *Listen for:* Anything that you would require them to do that they would rather avoid.

7   What would your last principal tell me about your two greatest strengths, two greatest weaknesses? *Listen for:* Any positive traits, skills, etc. that would fit in with the vision and the needs of the school.

8   What are some important goals in your life for the next three years, spiritually, financially, professionally? *Listen for:* Long-range planning, goal completion, stay in teaching.

9   How do you want your students to view you? *Listen for:* Caring, firm but loving, understanding, a good disciplinarian.

10 Would you describe a teacher who ministers to the needs of students? *Listen for:* Listening, praying, caring, being in agreement for God to work miracles, going the extra mile, listening to the Spirit of God on how to minister to students.

11 What is God saying to you? *Listen for:* Teacher's desire to line up

with the will of God, spiritual growth.

12 Tell me about the methods and techniques that work best for you in teaching. *Listen for:* A variety of approaches, methods, and techniques.

13 Describe a well-organized teacher. *Listen for:* Routines for teacher and students; systems for assigning students to groups, collecting homework, follow up on assignments, partitioning of grade book.

14 How do you make learning fun in your classroom? *Listen for:* Variety, creativity, doing rather than telling.

15 What kind of lifestyle is important in a Christian school? *Listen for:* Example setting, fruit of the Spirit, holiness, determination to please God.

16 How would you deal with bad reports, negative comments and behavior of other staff? *Listen for:* Matthew 18:15-17 principles.

17 How can you bring the Word of God to bear upon the situations and circumstances you face in and out of the classroom? *Listen for:* Authority of the Word of God, faith in positive outcomes, overcoming attitude; things that are temporal are subject to change; uncompromising of the Word of God.

18 How does God guide you in your classroom? *Listen for:* Sensitivity to Holy Spirit and prompting of the Holy Spirit, the peace of God; receiving directions through Word of God and from those who are appointed as authorities in the school.

19 In what two areas do you feel you will need the most assistance? *Listen for:* Willingness to admit needs exist, and openness and willingness to receive assistance.

20 How are you involved in service in your church? *Listen for:* Active involvement, support of the pastor.

The Christian School Resource Kit contains an interview recording sheet that allows you to rate the responses to each of the questions [CSRK 7.7]. This questioning period should be no less than 30 to 40 minutes. Finally, share with the teacher applicant the school's pay scale and fringe benefits. Provide opportunity for questions. Explain the procedure from this point on. Request any information or credentials not included in the application. Conclude the interview with prayer. Request that the teacher candidate pray first, and then you conclude in prayer.

Other Considerations

Consider going beyond the traditional interview. Request work samples, videotapes of teaching, auditions and writing samples.[21] Invite the teacher to be a guest teacher.

Involve Others

Consider involving other teachers or administrative staff in the interviewing process. Proverbs 11:14 says that "**...in the multitude of counsellors there is safety.**" This is especially helpful where the candidate will be functioning in teaching teams or reporting to a department head. Provide an opportunity for each person involved in the interview to complete an interview form [CSRK 7.8].

Make the Decision

Sometimes you will feel prompted to offer a candidate a teaching position on the spot. However, wait for at least two to five days. This allows time for the Holy Spirit to confirm His choice by quickening your spirit, so that you have confidence that you know that you know that this in the right choice. Waiting also allows the peace of God to swell up inside of your spirit—"**And let the peace of God rule in your hearts...**" (Colossians 3:15).

Brubaker encourages, "Trust...God to provide a staff that is of the highest quality spiritually and professionally."[22] In many schools, the board reserves the final authority to hire teachers based on the administrator's recommendation.

> **NOTE**: *Even if you are a few weeks away from opening school, do not compromise the confirming work of the Spirit of God, or you may end up settling for a teacher that is not the best choice.*

Communicate Your Decision to the Candidate

Once a decision is made, communicate it to the applicant. Since an applicant may be applying to several schools, it is important that you inform them as soon as possible of your decision, especially if it is your intention not to offer them employment. In some cases, it may be necessary to require a follow-up interview. At this time, the applicant should know whether more applicants are to be considered before the final decision and the timetable for the final decision.

After deciding, provide the applicant with a letter of intent to employ. You may wish to include in the letter the areas of assignment, orientation schedule, and dates that a contract will be issued along with any other important information [CSRK 7.9].

Get Teachers Started

There are a number of steps to take once a decision is made to employ. Consider the following:

Plan a New Teacher Visitation

Once a teacher agrees to teach, invite them to re-visit the school. If they have not taken a tour of the facilities, do it at this time. If room assignments have been made, show them their room and then welcome them back to begin their room preparation.

Provide teachers with a copy of the staff handbook, teacher editions of textbooks, curriculum guides, record book and lesson plan book and staff list. Hughes shares, "Providing advance information is one of the most productive ways of helping a new teacher to get off to a good start."[23]

Design a Teacher-Orientation Program

"How much time do you need?" When asked this question, we usually respond, "As much time as is necessary." The standard is two to four days. However, some schools, especially new schools, spend one to two weeks. The purpose in teacher orientation is to open communication, establish the vision, generate team spirit, and discern what the Spirit of God desires to be accomplished in the life of the school.

During the second year of operation, it is advantageous to divide your orientation into two segments, those items to be shared with the entire group, and those items specific to new teachers. Returning teachers should be assigned to each new teacher to help clarify any questions, show where resource materials are located and help prepare their rooms.

Your orientation program should include the following:

- Introduction of staff. Welcome staff and tell a little about each one. (Provide a teacher directory complete with pictures of each staff person.)
- Share the vision of the school and its relationship to the church goals and objectives.
- Cover the school's philosophy of education.
- Present an overview of the organizational structure.
- Present policies and procedures that the teacher will be held accountable for following.
- Cover the availability of resources.
- Distribute teacher desk materials, textbooks, lesson plan books, workbooks, gradebooks, curriculum guides, etc.
- Review school calendar.
- Present financial information, such as, W-4 forms, pay periods, staff contracts, application for benefits, credit union, etc.
- Review ancillary services; for example, food services, health

services, transportation, etc.

- Assign classrooms and keys.
- Present final teaching assignments.
- Tour the building.
- Provide mini workshops on specific critical topics, such as, Classroom Management, Speaking the Word over Students, Teachers as Ministers, etc.
- Cover the schedule for the first week.
- Provide time for teachers to prepare their rooms.
- Allow plenty of time for questions and answers.
- Establish a strong spiritual foundation of prayer.

We have noticed that regardless of how well you plan your teacher orientation, it is unlikely that your teachers will retain all the information they need to know to be successful. Therefore, consider carrying the orientation into the first month of school where specific time is set aside for this purpose.

NOTE: *Plan the orientation schedule so it can easily flow into an in-service training program that continues throughout the school year.*

Assign Staff

One of the greatest responsibilities in starting a Christian school, improving instruction, or maintaining existing programs is organizing and assigning staff. This task involves identifying the best match between available staff and instructional needs.

It is not always possible to make explicit assignments or reassignments until just before the start of the school year, mainly because of retaining factors. For example: number of students enrolled, availability of facilities, course offerings, limits on class size, limits imposed as a result of unavailable qualified staff and the allocation of financial resources. Assigning staff involves three aspects: determining staffing patterns, assigning teachers to units or departments and determining teacher instructional loads.

Determine Your Staffing Pattern

Most first-year schools select a traditional staffing design of a simple unit, commonly known as a self-contained classroom, where one teacher is assigned to a single group of students housed in a single classroom and teaches all subjects. The group of students may be a single grade level, or a combination of grade levels.

Self-Contained Classrooms

Reasons for choosing self-contained classrooms are as follows:

- Staff hiring is simplified since you will need one teacher for each classroom.
- Most churches adding a Christian day school already have buildings designed for self-contained classes.
- Most teachers have experience and training in the self-contained classroom concept.
- Teachers can concentrate on getting to know a small group of students very well. This enhances the teachers ability to "pastor" and to minister to the spiritual needs of the students.
- Teacher consistency in dealing with a single group of students improves discipline.
- Scheduling and supervision of staff and students are simplified.
- Instructional flexibility is advanced, since the teacher can shorten and lengthen an instructional time segment depending upon the needs of the students on any given day.

Specialized Classrooms

Depending upon your financial resources, you may modify the self-contained classroom unit by introducing specialized assignments, such as art, music, or physical education. Not only will your curriculum be enhanced, but you will have specialized programs to include in your promotional campaign.

A good technique to use in deciding whether or not one should add specialized teachers is to answer this question, "Would adding a special music (or any other special teacher or program) result in additional students enrolling in the school?" When promoted in a positive fashion, adding a specialized teacher may draw a sufficient number of new students to cover the increased cost. This is especially true in those communities where public schools have eliminated or reduced specialized programs.

Specialized teachers may be scheduled to the regular classroom a few times a week or the students can go to a specialized room for several periods each week. This gives the self-contained classroom teacher additional preparation time.

Figure 7.5 shows an example of a special teacher schedule. Using this schedule, each class receives three days per week of health fitness, one day of swimming (consider transporting your students to a neighborhood pool, YMCA), two days of choral music and one day of art. The total staff size is increased by the number of specialists needed. If it is

Figure 7.5 Special Teacher Schedule

Activity	Day	Time	Location
1st Grade			
Health Fitness	MWF	10:00-10:30	Girl's Gym
Choral Music	T&TH	1:45-2:15	217
Art	F	8:15-9:15	125
3rd Grade			
Health Fitness	T&TH&F	8:45-9:15	Boy's Gym
Choral Music	M&W	2:15-2:45	217
Art	T	9:15-10:15	125
4th Grade			
Health Fitness	T&TH&F	8:45-9:15	Boy's Gym
Choral Music	T&TH	2:15-2:45	217
Art	W	9:15-10:15	125
5th Grade			
Health Fitness	T&TH&F	8:45-9:15	Girl's Gym
Choral Music	T&TH	12:45-1:15	217
Art	M	9:45-10:45	125
6th Grade			
Health Fitness	T&TH&F	8:45-9:15	Girl's Gym
Choral Music	M&W	12:45-1:15	217
Art	M	1:15-2:15	125

not possible to employ full-time specialists, consider a cooperative arrangement with other schools in your community.

Instructional Teams

While most Christian day schools utilize self-contained classrooms, some organize their staff into teams where certain teachers are assigned subject specialization. In this approach, one teacher handles a specific content area, such as language arts and social studies, while a second teaches only math and science. Teachers can move between classrooms, or students move from classroom to classroom. This staffing pattern works best when the instructional needs of a large portion of the students require individualized attention.

Don't overlook the use of paid and volunteer aides to team with professional staff for instructional as well as clerical support. Make sure that volunteers and paid aides are properly selected and trained. They should meet the same qualifications as teachers except in the area of academic preparation, be involved in an orientation program, and be placed according to their individual talents and abilities.

NOTE: *When assigning staff, the important issue is to discern God's staffing plan for meeting the instructional needs of the specific population of students.*

Assign Teachers to Units or Departments

Regardless of whether you are organized with self-contained classrooms or teams, assigning teachers to units or departments will help in the successful administration of the school. Appoint experienced teachers to lead each unit or department. Their responsibilities might include the following tasks:

1   Work with the principal and other unit leaders/department heads to identify and coordinate goals, objectives and practices.

2   Meet with unit/department members to coordinate objectives and practices within the unit/department.

3   Serve as the line of communication between the principal and the classroom teacher in terms of new development, announcements, curriculum, textbooks, etc.

4   Assist unit/department teachers in the handling of day-to-day problems of instruction and act as resource persons for department teachers on curriculum questions.

5   Assist the principal with budgeting, ordering and receiving of supplies and equipment for the unit.

6   Take charge of the unit's or department's books and equipment inventories.

7   Assist the principal in evaluating teacher performance and make recommendations to the principal regarding unit/department personnel.

8   Provide orientation and in-service training programs.

9   Assist in identifying and using community resources.

10   Implement an ongoing program of curriculum evaluation.

11   Provide the principal with course outlines for all unit/department offerings.

12   Assist the principal in interpreting grading policies, promotional policies, and the school's instructional program to parents.

13   Devise experimental programs designed to improve the curriculum and instructional techniques.

14   Be responsible for cataloging supplementary and audio-visual materials and making them available for the unit.

15   Work three days before new teachers arrive and three days after school is out.

16   Write a yearly report on the achievements, outstanding accomplishments and problem areas of instruction within the unit.

17   Keep informed on educational innovations and trends as they relate to unit/department concerns.

Determine Teacher Instructional Loads

Assigning teachers to elementary classrooms is simply a matter of matching teachers with the most appropriate grades. At the junior and senior high school level, this task is a little more involved. The following suggestions are provided to assist you in making these assignments.

1   A teacher trained at the secondary level with a major in science and a minor in math can probably teach four or five courses in those fields. However, assigning him to teach in four different subjects, such as science, math, Bible, and history, is sure to reduce the overall effectiveness of the teacher.

2   Hire teachers to fill instructional vacancies according to their specialization.

3   Notify teachers as soon as possible of their tentative assignments with the possibility of last-minute adjustments.

4   Consider the instructional desires of the teacher as they interface with the overall staffing needs.

5   Where possible, assign teachers to areas they have previously taught, unless they are the best candidate to fill another need.

6   The teaching load of new teachers should be lighter than that of more experienced teachers.

7   Assign new teachers earlier than experienced teachers. Avoid giving new teachers "what is left over."

8   The typical secondary teacher should not carry a class load that exceeds 180 students per day.

9   The most expert teachers should be assigned to honors classes and remedial classes.

10   The teaching load should be spread evenly among the teachers. Take into consideration extra assignments.

11   Each teacher should have at least one free period daily for planning and conferencing.

NOTE: *Make each assignment following prayerful consideration. Strong schools are built on strong teachers.*

Evaluate Staff

Staff look forward to evaluations as eagerly as they look forward to going to the dentist. Find an administrator who looks forward to conducting teacher evaluations, and you've found someone who's about to retire. Very few educators look forward to being evaluated or conducting evaluations.

Establish a Philosophy of Assessment

Christian schools must employ staff that are willing and competent to contribute to the goals of the school. The major purpose of evaluation is to assess staff effectiveness in contributing to these goals. Achieving the goals of the school leads to fulfilling the vision of the school. The challenge for many administrators is establishing an effective evaluation program that will help staff fulfill this calling.

Many times the terms *evaluation* and *assessment* are used interchangeably. We view assessment as the sum total of all activities (for example, teacher observations) and measures (e.g., checklists, self reports, etc.) used to obtain information on a particular staff. Evaluation goes beyond observation activities and measurement; it is more than analyzing information. Evaluation involves the application of value judgment to the information. For example: satisfactory, unsatisfactory, needs improvement, superior, etc. It is placing this value judgment on performance that causes staff apprehension.

Assessment Strategies

Although special efforts go into recruiting and selecting staff, it is difficult to determine with complete precision the effectiveness of those employed. As Lovell and Wiles point out,

> "Sometimes an individual is employed without the necessary motivation and or competence. Often organizations and position requirements change so that individuals must adapt or organizations must find new employees. In many cases individuals change and lose their effectiveness. These are some factors that make it essential for organizations to provide an effective and efficient system for the continuous evaluation of the performance of organizational members. Such a system should provide

an effective system of support for individual improvement and a basis for personnel decisions."[24]

In his book *Appraising Teacher Performance,* James Lewis concludes,

> "Researchers seem to arrive at the same findings that regardless of the techniques or methods employed, e.g., rating scale self-analysis, classroom visitation, etc., few if any 'facts' seem to have been reached concerning teacher and administrative effectiveness. Furthermore, no generally agreed upon method of measuring the competence of educators has been accepted and no method of promoting growth, improvement and development have been generally adopted."[25]

Although Lewis was speaking of secular education, we feel the same conclusion is apparent in the Christian school setting. Most Christian staff assessment systems center around a critical review of a staff person's performance. These systems have the advantage of being quick and easy to administer; the disadvantages are threefold: they generally constitute a treat to self-esteem; tend to alienate the evaluee from the evaluator, especially when performance is unacceptable; and provide little direction in motivating professional growth.

Scriptural Principles

Four key biblical principles are important to Christian school staff evaluation. These are the principles of fruit-bearing, growth, works, gifts and talents. They form the foundation for an assessment philosophy and provide direction for instituting a comprehensive staff appraisal system.

The Principle of Fruit-Bearing. Most Christian school administrators will agree that the primary determinate for employment is the "unquestionable" call of God. Experience, training, personal characteristics, and philosophy are important, but unless a staff person has a definite call to Christian education in general and to your school in particular, they will most likely not be employed—unless a school is just looking for a "warm body" (a common hiring pitfall).

The Christian school teacher, having accepted God's call, faces a challenging expectation—fruit-bearing. Every staff person is chosen and called to your school to bear fruit. Thus, your assessment instruments should indicate whether or not fruit-bearing is taking place. What is the fruit expected of each staff? For the teacher, fruit is the change in the lives of his students—academically, behaviorally, spiritually, socially, and physically. Fruit is the end result of time spent in the classroom. It is the total curriculum brought to manifestation in the life of the students.

The scriptures identify three degrees in fruit-bearing: "fruit," "more fruit,"and "much fruit" (See John 15:2,5,8). There is also the expectation that the fruit would remain.

NOTE: *It can be said that the real success of a Christian school is not how its students perform while they are in school, but what they do with their lives after leaving the school.*

Since the goal of each staff person is to bear "much fruit," the administrator assumes the role of fruit husbandman and inspector rather than judge. His task is to assist in adding "more fruit" to their account (Phil. 4:17). Just as a husbandman is responsible for seeing to a bountiful harvest, the administrator is responsible for the success of his staff—providing them with the necessary materials, resources, supplies, facilities, training, supervision and instructional leadership, to increase their effectiveness in producing "much fruit."

The Principle of Growth. Growth is a biblical principle important to the evaluation process. Colossians 1:10 speaks of this principle, "**That ye (staff) might walk worthy of the Lord unto all pleasing, being fruitful in every good work, and increasing in the knowledge of God.**" Again in Ephesians 4:15, we read, "**But speaking the truth in love, may grow up into him in all things, which is the head, even Christ**" (4:15). "All things" includes professional skills and competencies.

Regardless of the level of experience and amount of training, staff are expected to show signs of continual growth. Growth means progress and development. Paul says, "**...press toward the mark for the prize of the high calling of God in Christ Jesus**" (Phil. 3:14). This verse indicates clear direction toward pre-determined goals. It is the administrator who is responsible for formulating professional goals along with performance indicators.

Assessing growth requires a minimum of two measuring periods. Historically, staff receive only one performance measure during a typical school term. Unfortunately, the administrator has no way of knowing what the performance was like before and after the measure: there is no sign whether the performance being measured or seen is variable or constant.

The first assessment should be taken by mid-November and a second assessment the first part of March. For those staff who continue to experience performance difficulties, conduct a third assessment no later than the first week of May. Consider waving the second assessment for those experienced teachers who have been with the school for three or more years and have shown continual growth and development. For these teachers, use the previous year's assessment to determine growth.

The Principle of Works. Scripture indicates that God believes in good works, not as a condition for entering heaven (Eph. 2:9), but as the basis for eternal reward (Matt. 25:21), based on performance here on earth. God expects Christian educators to be effective workers, **"Work hard and cheerfully at all you do, just as though you were working for the Lord and not merely for your masters"** (Col. 3:23, TLB). **"But let everyman prove his own work, and then shall he have rejoicing in himself alone, and not in another"** (Gal. 6:4). In fact, Paul said, **"For we are his workmanship, created in Christ Jesus unto good works, which God hath before ordained that we should walk in them"** (Eph.2:10).

Employ and retain Christian school staff who are committed to "good works." These good works are the result of a high level of quality in performance. "Good works" for a Christian school teacher include such items as: daily lesson plans designed to achieve identified objectives, accurately written records of student progress, and grading patterns that are fairly administered and based on identified criteria.

When assessing staff, ask yourself the question, "What behaviors could I observe to lead me to conclude that this is good work?" For example, the following observable behaviors are evident of good lessons plans: Lesson plans

- describe techniques and methods to be used to teach the lesson;
- state expected minimum mastery of lesson objectives;
- show how the lesson objectives are consistent with the school's objectives and mission—learner outcomes;
- contain a clear logical, sequential format, not just page numbers;
- provide a variety of evaluation activities; and
- describe lesson activities in clear terms. [26]

Principle of Gifts and Talents. There are a variety of spiritual gifts in the Body of Christ (See 1 Cor. 12; Eph. 4; Rom. 12). Included among these gifts are administration and teaching. When these gifts are put to service, they become a ministry, the purpose of which is equipping God's people (students, parents and staff) for the work in His service. Teaching or administration as a ministry are different from teaching or administration as a vocation. For instance, teaching as a vocation requires skills in such areas as instructional methods and techniques, organizing the teaching-learning process, etc.

Teaching as a ministry refers to a divinely given skill to teach others the things of God. A teacher may be able to plan and deliver a smooth, creative lesson, yet, if not anointed, no spiritual truth will be imparted that results in changed lives. A Spirit-gifted teacher, regardless of progress in the vocational aspects of teaching, can be greatly used of God.

It is the responsibility of each staff member not to neglect the gift that is in them (1 Tim. 4:14). It is the administrator's responsibility to agree with teachers for the gift of teaching (John 16:24) and to ensure that all gifts are exercised—**"And since we have gifts that differ according to the grace given to us, let each exercise them accordingly"** (Rom. 12:6, NASB). Since stepping out in faith in exercising a gift may include making mistakes, administrators need to be supportive rather than critical when mistakes are evident, helping the person correct the mistakes and to move on.

Since God has called your staff as Christian educators, they need to exercise their gifts with all boldness and faith, having confidence that God has equipped them for the task. It is the administrator's responsibility to provide opportunities for staff to exercise their gifts. For example: appointing teachers with administrative gifts to serve as unit leaders.

Design an Appraisal System

Each of these principles needs to be incorporated into a staff appraisal system. This system should include assessment prerequisites, a sequence of implementation and a plan for improvement (growth).

Assessment Prerequisites

Each Christian school should develop its own set of suitable assessment procedures. There are three prerequisites to consider.

1 **Policies and Procedures.** Clearly written and communicated policies and easy-to-follow procedures set the stage for staff accountability. When staff know and understand the kinds of fruit they are expected to produce, quantity and quality of good works, requirements for growth and utilization of gifts and talents, they are less likely to make mistakes, experience fewer instances of frustration, and are more supportive of new policies, procedures, or programs that they must follow.

2 **Performance Standards.** Carefully defined performance criteria are essential to any evaluation program. Stating these standards as behavioral indicators helps those doing the evaluating to determine whether the standard has or has not been met. Stating performance standards in measurable terminology allows staff to know exactly what is expected of them. Figure 7.6 presents prayer as an example of a performance standard.

Figure 7.6   Spiritual Performance Indicator - Prayer

Area: Prayer

Performance Indicator: The teacher incorporates prayer as an essential ingredient in Christian Education.

Behaviors (Works):

1. Maintains a consistent personal quiet time.
2. Begins and ends the class with prayer.
3. Encourages students to pray for one another's needs.
4. Exhibits a sensitivity to the spiritual needs of students.
5. Applies the Word of God in prayer.
6. Is punctual to staff devotions.

---

3   **Availability of Resources**. Achieving acceptable levels of performance depends on the availability of a number of different resources, such as finances, time, materials and supplies, training and equipment. For example, requiring teachers to develop education plans for each student is very time demanding. Since time is an essential factor in achieving objectives, it must be made available. Without additional time, it will be difficult to hold staff accountable for achieving this goal.

Assessment Sequence

Implementing a successful staff appraisal program involves several basic steps. Consider the following:

1   **Criteria Identification**. Hold a conference with each staff before the assessment to determine the criteria to be included in assessing his performance (works, fruit, growth and utilization of gifts and talents) along with specific performance indicators. Assist the staff person in pinpointing challenge areas that need to be included in the observation. For example, student time on task [CSRK 7.10].

2   **Select Assessment Measures**. Part of the pre-observation conference includes agreement on the assessment measures, such as classroom observation, peer-reporting, student-surveys, parent questionnaires, etc. Include a self-assessment. Paul instructs us to "...examine yourselves...prove your own selves..." (2 Cor. 13:5). The Christian School Resource Kit contains a sample of a performance

assessment instrument [CSRK 7.11]. The kit also contains an example of a spiritual self-assessment [CSRK 7.12].

3   **Identify Records and Products.** Determine which records and products will be required, such as individual student test scores, lessons plans, grade book, disciplinary records, homework samples, etc., and who will be responsible for producing them.

4   **Select Time and Place.** Arrange for agreed upon dates, times and places where the data will be collected. In planning classroom observations, include more than one observation and no less than fifteen minutes for observing each activity. Obtaining more than one sample of performance over a period of time will increase the reliability of the findings.

5   **Schedule a Review Conference.** Once all assessment data are complete, schedule a review conference. Avoid the traditional format of starting out with a few positive strokes, complimenting the person before lowering the boom. (The only place a boom should be lowered is on a construction site.) The purpose of the conference is to present and explain essential information about the performance indicators, "discussing and pooling ideas and arriving at recommendations for solving problems, setting objectives, developing action plans, and improving performance."[27]

Using a performance approach based on the principles of fruit-bearing, good works, growth and gifts, removes much of the anxiety associated with staff assessment and evaluation. Usually, teachers will welcome the administrator's ideas for improving (becoming all that God intends in order to better fulfill His calling).

NOTE: *When correction is needed, the administrator should approach it in a spirit of restoration, not harping on faults, but restoring the person to the standard, and helping to clearly identify specific areas of improvement and the process to bring it about. Expect repentance and forgiveness to flow.*

Develop a Plan for Improvement

Include every area needing improvement in an individual staff development action plan. The plan should contain a statement of the problem, measurable objectives and specific actions to be taken with time lines. The Christian School Resource Kit provides a sample of part of an action plan of a school guidance counselor, classroom teacher and elementary school principal [CSRK 7.13]. This plan then becomes a tool for conducting a follow-up appraisal.

Administrators can facilitate change in staff by adhering to several key approaches:

1   Believe that the improvement plan is ordered by God. "**The steps of**

a good man are ordered by the Lord: and he delighteth in his way" (Ps. 37:23). "A man's mind plans his way, but the Lord directs his steps and makes them sure" (Prov. 16:9, AMP).

2   Recognize any amount of progress resulting in improved performance. Jesus said of Peter, "...Thou art...thou shalt be..." (John 1:42). Jesus pointed to Peter's possibilities.

3   Encourage the leading of the Holy Spirit in the life of the staff person. "But the Comforter, which is the Holy Ghost, whom the Father will send in my name, he shall teach you all things, and bring all things to your remembrance, whatsoever I have said unto you" (John 14:26).

4   Remove all constraining factors hindering improvement. For example: lack of supplies, inadequate training, etc. (Eph. 3:20).

5   Keep all commitments. For example, promising to provide teachers with release time (Matt. 12:36,37).

Arrange for Staff Development

Staff development is a valuable ingredient of any successful educational institution. The ultimate result of a staff development program is improvement of the entire school. Staff development begins the moment a decision is made to establish a Christian school, continues until school begins and is maintained as long as the school is organized.

Prior to the School's Opening

Staff development begins long before a new school opens. Activities include: visiting established Christian schools; collecting and reading Christian school administrative books, manuals and other resource materials; attending local, state, regional and national Christian school conferences, new school workshops and Christian summer school institutes (for example, Oral Roberts University) and accreditation conferences (for instance, International Christian Accrediting Association). Include in these activities church and school board members, the school administrator, teachers, pastor and other key church and potential school leaders.

Another important "prior to opening" activity is planning and conducting a thorough staff orientation. The quality of this activity prepares staff for continual growth throughout the school year.

After School Begins

Consider formulating a staff development team. Most educators agree that involving teachers in planning, implementing and evaluating development activities results in a more effective development program. Under the leadership of the administrator, a staff development team conducts a needs assessment, formulates written objectives, arranges planned activities to accomplish these objectives, and implements a plan for evaluating these activities. Consider two distinct plans—a school-wide staff development plan and an individual development plan for each administrator, faculty member and support staff.

School-Wide Development Plan

The focus of a school-wide development plan is on activities and topics designed to help the school better achieve school goals and fulfill its purpose and vision. Consider the following process:

1   Use small discussion groups for brainstorming a list of ideas. Ask each group to narrow their list to the top ten ideas. One school came up with the following topics:

- Implementing a Philosophy of Education in the Classroom
- Developing Strong Moral Character
- Establishing Self-Discipline in Students
- Effective Classroom Management
- Creative Teaching Strategies for History
- Training in the Fruit of the Spirit
- Conducting Effective Parent Conferences
- Avoiding Educational Malpractice
- Applying Scriptural Principles in the Classroom
- Ministering Reconciliation
- Meeting the Needs of Students from Single Parent Families
- Extending the Curriculum to the Home

2   Collect the top ten ideas from each group. Consolidate these lists to a single document and give the entire staff an opportunity to rank order each development item as to its importance.

3   Tabulate the ranking and produce a final list of the top ten priorities; ask staff for written recommendations of individuals (staff and outside speakers) who can conduct the development activity.

4   Divide the staff into two groups. For each development topic, ask each group to produce a written plan using a standardized planning form [CSRK 7.14]. The plan should include the following points:

- The title of the activity.
- A brief description of the activity.
- Proposed personnel to receive training (elementary, secondary, office, etc.).
- Amount of release time required.

- Specific objectives.
- Dates, time and place of activity and length of training.
- Staff person responsible to coordinate the activity.
- Individuals who will do the training.
- Special resources used in the training (films, video, etc.).
- Outcomes to include in the evaluation [CSRK 7.15].
- Estimated costs and source of funds.

5   Collect all planning sheets. The staff development team reviews each planning sheet and places the activities on the master school schedule[CSRK 7.16]. Schedule development activities periodically throughout the year. Setting aside three to five school days over the course of a school term for staff development is an acceptable expectation in most states. Generally, days used for staff development count as part of the required numbers of total school days.

NOTE: *The time spent in staff development translates to improved classroom instruction and growth in the quality of the school. Consider 10 to 15 days per year, including orientation.*

Individual Staff Development Plan

One of the primary objectives of a staff development program is upgrading the skills of staff. In addition to school-wide development activities, each staff person should have an annual development plan. Most accrediting agencies require some form of individualized staff development plan. For example, as part of the accreditation process, the International Christian Accrediting Association (ICAA) requires an individual plan that includes the following areas: Spiritual, Physical and Professional. A sample of an actual individual development plan is included in the Christian School Resource Kit [CSRK 7.17].

Spiritual Development Plan. This plan includes activities for the individual staff member in the area of spiritual growth (for example, Bible studies, daily Bible reading and devotions, Christian tapes, courses, seminars, independent reading and study, and in-service instruction and special events).

Physical Development Plan. Activities include the area of personal fitness development, nutrition, and exercise appropriate to the staff member. Staff members are encouraged to participate in individual programs and community opportunities.

Professional Development Plan. This part of the staff's plan includes activities appropriate to the staff member's employment and may include participation in degree programs or refresher courses, subscription to professional journals, certification and/or licensing, listening to Christian educational tapes, vocational training (job-related), independent reading and study and in-service opportunities.

Some schools use a point method for keeping track of staff participation in development activities. Staff earn points as follows:

- One point for each clock hour in an approved development activity.
- Fifteen points for each college course.
- Maximum of eight points for travel (for example, a history teacher traveling to a state historical site).
- Two points for each clock hour when presenting a workshop.

An appropriate goal is for each staff person to earn at least fifteen staff development points per year and 75 points during a five-year cycle. The school administrator maintains a record of each person's points, proof of activities completed, copies of transcripts, travel brochures, etc. He should notify each person at the end of the year about the number of points earned [CSRK 7.18; 7.19].

Consider providing a financial incentive for exceeding the yearly goal. For example: award $25 to staff accumulating 20 to 49 total points and $50 for those who earn 50 or more points. An incentive system increases staff motivation and provides a means whereby schools that do not have educational assistance benefits, can provide a financial incentive for completing staff development opportunities. Schools unable to provide financial incentives might consider placing the name of the top point earner on a five-year plaque (one plaque for each school division, for example, elementary, secondary, support staff) [CSRK 7.20].

Pitfalls to Avoid

1. Providing written contracts before enrollment is finalized. Once you inform a teacher in writing of your decision to employ them, obtain written acceptance of the applicant's "intent to be employed." It is extremely important to pay special attention to oral agreements (they are often viewed as a form of contract). This may be the case when a teacher is influenced to leave his previous teaching position, or not apply for other positions, because of oral promises of employment and benefits.

Since new schools do not have a solid enrollment base to generate the needed tuition income to pay salaries, offer contracts only after you have an adequate enrollment so the income generated will pay teacher salaries. In place of a contract, provide a letter of intent to hire, then hire teachers based on a specified teacher student ratio [See CSRK 7.9]. If is set at 1 to 25, offer one contract for every twenty-five students

?lve points out,

> "Class size economics can be lost if contracts are given to more teachers than are actually needed. In times when there are teachers in need of positions, it may be well to under-contract for the projected school year."[28]

A private religious school is under no obligation to provide written teacher contracts. When issuing contracts, add a clause that provides for a means of dismissal should enrollment projections fall short. Check your state's position on employment "at will," that is, the employee acknowledges and agrees that his employment and compensation can be terminated, with or without cause, and with or without notice, at any time, at the option of either employer or employee.

2. Overselling the school. Be realistic about the school's strengths and weaknesses. This keeps the applicant (as well as the students and parents) from acquiring any false, preconceived "halo" impressions that later may be proven to be false.

> **NOTE:** *Don't promise anything that you are not committed to deliver.*

3. Attempting to cover all policies during teacher orientation. Although many of the policies will be reviewed during the teacher orientation time, it is not possible to cover all areas, and even if they were covered, teachers would not be able to retain the information. Therefore, all school policies and procedures should be written down and placed in the hands of the teachers.

Consider distributing policy handbooks the first day, then ask staff to review it for discussion the next day. Do not assume that everyone understands each policy. Spend a block of time each day until all policies are reviewed. Require teachers to sign a statement that they have read and understand all policies.

4. Failing to employ substitute teachers who will "teach school" rather than just "keep school." There will be times when classroom teachers are absent for one reason or another. This is especially true of secondary teachers whose school-related duties take them out of the classroom.

During a teacher's absence, very few parents want to pay tuition to have substitute teachers who merely keep the students under control until the regular teacher returns. They want a substitute teacher who will continue with the educational, behavioral and spiritual growth of their children.

It takes a very special person to be able to step into an unfamiliar classroom, exercise control and at the same time complete the lesson plan for the day. Consider the following strategies:

- Require substitute teachers to meet the same requirements for employment as regular teachers.

- Pay substitutes to attend the teacher orientation held at the start of the school term.

- Schedule substitutes to observe at least a day in those classes they intend to serve as a substitute.

- Invite full-time substitutes to attend faculty meetings.

- Establish a reporting system from the time of notification to the close of the school day.

- Require all classroom teachers to prepare and to continually update a substitute folder containing special instructions for substitutes, classroom procedures, seating charts, location of teacher keys, supplies and staff list.

- Ensure that all daily lesson plans are completed by classroom teachers at least one week in advance and that daily changes are made on their desk copy.

- Prepare a substitute teacher guidebook. Include topics, such as qualifications, getting off to a good start, how to respond to students, how to end the day or class period, daily schedule, classroom routines, reimbursement procedures.

- Set the wage of substitute teachers at a competitive level for the community.

- Give substitute teachers an opportunity to evaluate their participation and the school's preparedness [CSRK 7.21].

- Provide recognition and appreciation to substitutes by checking in with them at the end of the day. (For more information on substitute teachers, see *Substitute Teacher: Standing in the Gap.*)

5. Not having job descriptions for staff. One of the first tasks in selecting school staff is writing a job description for each position. When staff know what is expected of them, they are more likely to be supportive of the school's line of authority, have a greater sense of accountability for functions and responsibilities assigned, and be more receptive of performance assessments.

The essence of accountability demands performance standards.

Including these standards as part of a job description provides a foundation for meaningful supervision and effective management. Consider the following suggestions:

- Create a single job description for all classroom teachers.
- Include a well-defined set of tasks with acceptable performance standards.
- Make compliance to policies a part of each description.
- Provide an opportunity for applicants to review the job description before a formal interview.
- Design the job description around the position rather than an individual, then look for a person to fill the position.
- Review a job description periodically for changes.
- Make certain job descriptions have a final statement such as "and any other related duties as assigned" so that the excuse "that isn't my job," has no grounds.

Although this chapter has as its main focus selecting teaching staff, of near equal importance is hiring staff for all other assignments within the school regardless of the position.

NOTE: *Even those positions that may seem insignificant, such as custodians, cooks, or teacher's aides, can add a major contribution to the success of your school.*

6. Not following the established teacher compensation scale. Publishing a teacher compensation scale that is based on an increase in compensation for years of experience (for example, moving from one step to the next) leads to the assumption that each year there will be an automatic increase in pay. In other words, there is the belief that an automatic raise in pay happens based on completion of a successful academic year.

As long as there is sufficient revenue to provide raises, there are few challenges. However, in most Christian schools, it is not possible to provide automatic pay increases. Furthermore, schools operating under a ministry-wide compensation schedule may be restricted to awarding raises only as raises are awarded to the entire ministry.

If schools hire new teachers with the same number of years of experience as teachers already employed and place the new teachers at a higher level on the pay scale, this action will cause discontent among the present staff, who are already locked into a ministry-wide pay scale. Over time, this action will cause a large disparity in compensation within the teaching staff, especially when the teacher compensation scale represents a 10 percent increase from one step to another and the ministry-wide pay increase is only 5 percent, or when there are no raises.

One solution is to use a "flexible" compensation scale that is based on the present year's salary structure and then adjusted as raises are provided. New teachers are hired based on the present salary scale; they are placed on the scale at the same level as currently employed staff. Adjustments are made to the compensation scale based on raises provided across the ministry or after final adjustments are made in the school's income and spending plan, once enrollment stabilizes (approximately the end of September).

7. Failing to Release Staff. Employees will be the first ones to spot people who need to be let go. When the school takes no action, the administration is tolerating incompetency. Respect is lost for administration when incompetence is allowed to continue. In many cases, this results in others letting up on their own productivity. As a result, new standards of performance are indirectly established.

On the other hand, wrongful discharge results in lowering morale. When discharge is done in the right way, morale goes up. Contained in the Christian School Resource Kit is a termination checklist along with several special prepared letters used during the dismissal process [CSRK 7.22].

8. Not dealing with a challenge situation when it arises. Rather than facing problems, some tend to ignore them, hoping they will go away. Lovell and Wiles admonish, "If a vital problem is ignored by official leadership, feelings begin to build, and the acids of anger and fear begin to erode the objectivity of the participants."[29] Be committed to resolving problems quickly.

> "Father, we call forth those teachers You have ordained to be at this school—those teachers and staff who have been preparing for such a school as this. Any thought or circumstance that would prevent them from answering Your divine calling, let it be stopped. We release staff to fulfill their calling. In the name of Jesus, we call them in! Amen."

> **The goal is to achieve a total staff that works in harmony in carrying out the vision of the school.**

Christian School Resource Kit

7.1   College Teacher Placement Request
7.2   Master Teacher Levels

Endnotes

1   H. W. Byrne. *A Christian Approach to Education.* Milford, MI: Mott Media, 1977, p. 42.

2   Roy W. Lowrie, Jr. *To Those Who Teach in Christian Schools.* Whittier, CA: Association of Christian Schools International, 1978, p. 5.

3   John Osteen. Lakewood International Outreach Center, 7400 East Houston Road, Houston, TX, 1991.

4   Bill Kelly. *A Guide for Principals and Board Members on Christian School Growth.* Whittier, CA: Western Association of Christian Schools, 1976, p. 88.

5   Ben M. Harris, Kenneth E. McIntyre, Vance C. Littleton, Jr., Daniel F. Long. *Personal Administration in Education.* Newton, MA: Allyn and Bacon, Inc., 1985, p. 103.

6   James W. Deuink and Carl D. Herbster. *Effective Christian School Management.* 1st Edition. Greenville, SC: Bob Jones University Press, 1982, p. 87.

7   Byrne, *op. cit.*, p. 128.

8   Kelly, *op. cit.*, p. 90.

9   Claude E. Schindler, Jr. and Pacheco Plye. *Educating for Eternity*. Whittier, CA: Association of Christian Schools International, 1979, p. 30.

10 Gene Garrick. Foreword to *To Those Who Teach in Christian Schools*, by Roy W. Lowrie, Jr., Whittier, CA: Association of Christian Schools International, 1978, p. iii.

11 Harris, et. al., *op. cit.*, p. 96.

12 Leonard Nadler. *Recruiting, Training, and Recruiting New Employees*. San Francisco, CA: Jossey-Bass, Inc., Publishers, 1987, p. 91.

13 Ronald W. Rebore. *Personnel Administration in Education: A Management Approach*. 2nd Edition. Englewood Cliff, NJ: Prentice-Hall Inc., 1987, p. 240.

14 Adapted from Clayne R. Jensen. *Administrative Management of Physical Education and Athletic Programs*. Philadelphia, PA. Lea and Febiger, 1988, p. 260.

15 K. Forbis Jordon, Mary P. McKeown, Richard G. Salmon, and Dean L. Webb. *School Business Administration*. Beverly Hills, CA: SAGE Publications, Inc., 1985, p. 95.

16 Kelly, *op. cit.*, p. 83.

17 J. Lester Brubaker. *Personnel Administration in the Christian School*. Winona Lake, IN: BMH, 1980, p. 42.

18 Larry W. Hughes and Gerald Ubben. *The Elementary Principal's Handbook*. Newton, MA: Allyn and Bacon, Inc., 1984, p. 220.

19 Harris, *op. cit.*, p. 109.

20 *Ibid.* p. 110.

21 Robert D. Ramsey. *Secondary School Survival Guide*. Englewood Cliffs, NJ: Prentice-Hall Inc., 1992, p. 65.

22 Brubaker, *op. cit.*, p.47.

23 Hughes and Ubben, *op. cit.*, p. 256.

24 John T. Lovell and Kimball Wiles. *Supervision for Better Schools*. 5th Edition. Englewood Cliffs, NJ: Prentice-Hall, Inc. 1983, p. 10.

25 James Lewis, Jr. *Appraising Teacher Performance*. West Nyack, NY: Parker Publishing Company, Inc. 1973, p. 11.

26 Adapted from *Oklahoma Minimum Criteria for Effective Teaching and Administrative Performance*. Oklahoma City, OK: State Department of Education, 1989.

27 Lewis, *op. cit.*, p. 156.

28 Philip Elve. *Financing Christian Schools*. Grand Rapids, MI: Christian Schools International, 1984, p. 177.

29 Lovell and Wiles, *op. cit.*, p. 87.

References

Association of Christian Schools International. P.O. Box 4097, Whittier, CA 90607-4097; (213) 694-4791.

Chernow, Fred B. and Chernow, Carol. *Classroom Discipline and Control.* West Nyack, NY: Parker Publishing Co., Inc., 1981.

Demuth, Dennis M. and Demuth, Carol M. *Spirit-Directed Discipline.* Tulsa, OK: DEL Publications, In Preparation.

Demuth, Dennis M. and Demuth, Carol M. *Substitute Teacher: Standing in the Gap.* Tulsa, OK: DEL Publications, In Preparation

Dobson, James. *The Strong-Willed Child.* Wheaton, IL: Tyndale House Publishers, Inc., 1978.

Howard, Eugene R. *School Discipline Desk Book.* West Nyack, NY: Parker Publishing Co., Inc., 1978.

Intercristo. Career Specialists, P.O. Box 33487, Seattle, WA 98133; (800) 426-1343.

International Christian Accrediting Association (ICAA). 7777 South Lewis, Tulsa, OK 74171; (918) 495-7054.

Kienel, Paul A. ed. *The Philosophy of Christian School Education.* 2nd Edition. Whittier, CA: Association of Christian Schools International, 1978.

Nazigian, Arthur. *The Effective Teacher.* Whittier, CA: Association of Christian School International, 1983.

Oral Roberts University Educational Fellowship. 7777 South Lewis Avenue, Tulsa, OK, 74171; (918) 495-7054.

Computer Software

HIRE. Louie Crew as listed in *PC-SIG Encyclopedia of Shareware.* 4th Edition. Sunnyvale, CA: PC-SIG, Inc. 1991.

STEP 8

PLAN THE CURRICULUM

What will you teach in your Christian school? Answering this question forms the basis for planning the curriculum. In its broadest meaning, the curriculum is life inclusive; it includes all activities and experiences encountered by the students. Its purpose is the fulfillment of 2 Timothy 3:17, **"That the man of God may be perfect, thoroughly furnished unto all good works."** In its narrowest sense, a curriculum is the area of subject or content matter that will be studied.

Planning for the curriculum involves the following tasks:

- Develop educational goals.
- Adopt an educational approach.
- Select content matter and subjects.
- Select curriculum guides.
- Select textbooks.
- Establish school parameters.
- Institute a high school credit system.
- Develop grading and reporting systems.
- Schedule teachers and classes.

Develop Educational Goals

H. W. Byrne addresses the importance of educational goals in the following comments,

"Generally speaking, aims and goals provide direction for the whole educational process. More specifically, there are values for the teacher and pupil. Aims and goals give the teacher the inspiration of a worthwhile endeavor. He is constantly motivated by a sense of destiny and purposefulness. Furthermore, aims and goals serve as guidelines in the selection of materials and methods by which the pupil is moved toward the objectives set up...They provide the means whereby integration and correlation of the Christian curriculum is made possible...aims and goals become practical guides in providing unity and integration for a God-centered and bibliocentric philosophy of education and curriculum construction."[1]

There are four primary areas of goal formation. These are spiritual, academic/mental, physical/behavioral and social/cultural. Developing school-wide and individual goal statements and methods of assessing each are important tasks in curriculum development.

Spiritual Goals

Proverbs 22:6 provides direction for spiritual goals, **"Train up a child in the way he should go: and when he is old, he will not depart from it."** The curriculum area that establishes the uniqueness of the Christian school is its spiritual program.

Two primary school-wide goals are:

- 100 percent of the students will be born again (John 3:3).

- 100 percent of the students will be water baptized (Mark 16:15,16).

In addition to these school-wide goals, consider the following goal statements:

1   To be spiritually mature (1 Cor. 14:20).

2   To be able to view the whole of life from God's perspective (Eph. 2:10; 5:16; 2 Peter 1:3).

3   To be effective in the area in which God has called him to serve (2 Peter 1:3; Heb. 10:24,25).

4   To be conformed to the image (likeness) of Jesus, to think like Him and to act like Him (Matt. 5:48; John 15:4).

5   To understand the basic doctrines of the Bible (Titus 2:1).

6   To be a bold witness for Jesus Christ (Romans 10:15-18).

7   To be submissive to those in authority from God's perspective (Romans 13:1-7; Heb. 13:17; Eph. 6:1-3).

Achieving these goals will necessitate "programs of daily Bible instruction for each grade level appropriate to the students' current spiritual development and needs and school-wide programs, such as chapel, for the spiritual training and edification."[2] Although there are several fine Bible curriculums available, begin by selecting the Bible curriculum that best addresses the meeting of goals. Most Bible curriculum publishers will provide free samples of their curriculum.

Academic/Mental Goals

Secondary to spiritual goals are academic/mental goals. Examples of school-wide goals are,

- 100 percent of the students will score at the 85 percent level as measured by the yearly standardized achievement test.

- 90 percent of the graduating seniors will score no less than 21 on the ACT test.

Other goal statements could encompass the following:

1   To have an informed mind (Rom. 15:14), quickened judgment (1 Cor. 2:15) and exactness of thought (Col.4:6) .

2   To voice the Christian point of view in the social sciences—Economics, History, Geography, Sociology, Psychology, Political Science, Law, Anthropology (Prov. 14:34; Rom. 13).

3   To recognize God's revelation of truth through the natural sciences— Chemistry, Physics, Mathematics, Anatomy, Botany, Geology, Physiology, Zoology (Gen. 1:1; Ps. 19).

4   To embrace God's place in the humanities—Art and Music, Literature (Deut. 31:19; 2 Tim. 3; 1 Cor. 2).

5   To effectively communicate in every facet of Christian living and service—writing, reading, speaking and thinking (Ex. 17:14; Prov. 29:11; James 3).

6   To use good study skills and habits (2 Tim. 2:3-7).

7   To know how to research and to reason logically from a biblical perspective (Heb. 5:14; Rom. 12:2).

Physical/Behavioral Goals

Physical development is an important aspect of the Christian school curriculum. Examples of appropriate school-wide goal statements include the following:

- 100 percent of the students will score at the 75 percent level as measured by the President's Physical Fitness Test.

- 100 percent of the students will be able to pass the school's field test. Students in grades K5 to 3rd will be able to jog 3/4th of a mile without stopping. Students in grades four to twelve will be able to jog 1.5 miles without stopping.

Further physical goals may include the following:

1   To maintain a lifestyle of physical fitness (3 John 2; 1 Thess. 5:23; Ps. 92:12-14).

2   To take care of the body as the Temple of the Holy Spirit (1 Cor. 3:16; 1 Cor. 6:19,20).

3   To participate in quality leisure-time and sport activities (Gal. 5:7-9,16,24; Prov. 3:1,2).

Social/Cultural Goals

School-wide social/cultural goals are more difficult to formulate and assess. Some schools use rating scales and surveys to assess growth in this area. For example:

- 100 percent of the students will display Christlike attitudes and positive character traits as measured by the annual School Behavior and Attitude Survey.

Other goal statements for individual students might include the following:

1   To be a good citizen (Rom. 13:1-7).

2   To display good ethics (Rom. 13:9).

3   To respect rights and property of others (Rom. 14:13).

4   To foster a good attitude (1 John 2:15-17).

5   To become a positive example (1 Tim. 4:12).

6   To contribute positively to Christ-centered homes and families (Eph. 5:22,23; 2 Peter 3:18).

7   To foster wholesome, Christ-pleasing relationships (1 Thess. 4:1-7; 1 Tim. 4:12; Gen. 2:18-25; Eph. 5:22,33).

Explore Curriculum Strategies

Once you identify your goals, you can explore curriculum strategies that will lead to attaining these goals. Implementing these strategies results in accomplished goals. Rating scales, surveys, questionnaires and tests are examples of instruments that provide a qualitative measure of success in attaining goals. Careful and consistent monitoring help determine whether or not a school is moving toward its goals. Often, a curriculum that looks good in a curriculum catalog fails to produce the desired results. When this happens, adjust the present strategies or identify new curriculum strategies until you reach the goal.

Develop Course/Subject Goals and Objectives

Having established the school's educational goals, the next task is to ensure that course goals and learner objectives are available for each academic course and subject. This task usually follows the purchasing of textbooks, teacher editions and curriculum guides. Contained within these resources is the necessary information needed to formulate course goals and learner objectives. In developing these goals and objectives, use a standardized recording format that includes the following components [CSRK 8.1]:

- Course Description
- General Course Objectives
- Spiritual Significance
- Course Content
- Methodology
- Evaluation
- Enrichment Resources
- Approved Textbooks

Developing goals and objectives for each course and subject provide the foundation from which teachers can prepare quarterly objectives, develop instructional units and construct daily lesson plans. The Christian School Resource Kit contains a sample course/subject document containing these components [CSRK 8.1].

Adopt an Educational Approach

Selecting the right curriculum begins by identifying an educational approach. There are two basic approaches: independent and teacher-directed.

Independent Approach

The first approach is independent study. In this approach, each student moves through a content area as the curriculum directs. The teacher assigns students a series of ten to twelve booklets. Achieving success on the first book, students progress to the next until they have successfully mastered the subject content. The two major publishers of curriculum directed materials are Accelerated Christian Educators (ACE) and Alpha Omega Publications.

Some schools select this approach for reasons other than the individual pace; for example, schools that lack the financial base to pay for teachers. Some schools elect this approach when they have classrooms with a few students at several grade levels or ability levels. A teacher can administer a simple diagnostic test, the results of which tell the teacher exactly where to start the student in a particular subject. This approach has also found usefulness by schools where there is a limitation in the square footage needed for a large traditional classroom.

NOTE: *Independent study schools are able to increase their success by employing experienced teachers who can direct the education process, ensure that sufficient interaction among the students takes place and provide for development of listening and note-taking skills, a major criticism of the individual approach.*

Teacher-Directed Approach

The second approach is the traditional teacher-directed approach. It is by far the most popular. In this situation, the teacher is the one who plans the content and decides what to teach within the prescribed curricula. The setting is a traditional classroom with the teacher presenting the daily lessons. The expectation is for students to progress through the curriculum as a group, going from one grade level to the next.

A Beka Books and Bob Jones University Press are two major publishers of teacher-directed curricula. These publishers produce materials specifically for Christian schools; the materials have as a foundation the integration of a Christian philosophy of education.

Principles Approach

Still another approach that has found acceptance over the past few years is the principle approach. It is better thought of as a methodology rather than an approach; it centers on researching, reasoning, explaining, recording and relating principles found in the Word of God to practical aspects of life.

It takes several weeks of training, much prayer and study to begin to renew the mind to this approach. Some subjects, such as History, are easier to apply the principle approach because of the amount of materials available.[3] The strength of this methodology is its reliance on the Bible as the underlying and final authority in all subjects.

Another strong point is the type of thought-provoking questions that require students to apply, analyze, synthesize and evaluate information in addition to simply recalling facts. The main challenge with this methodology is finding teachers who have a high level of mastery of their subject(s) and have quality time for class preparation. Since very few published materials are available, teachers and students are very much on their own. For more information about the principle approach, write Foundation for American Christian Education, American Christian History Institute and Heritage Institute Ministries.

The Best Approach

When asked which approach works best, we respond, "Any one will work if you work it." There are many examples of successful schools using each approach. There are also examples of schools who use a combination of approaches. Some teacher-directed schools use independent study materials with students who are self-motivated, who have schedule challenges, or need extra units of credit for graduation. Likewise, some independent schools offer teacher-directed courses.

Schools that have been in existence for several years soon find out that a single curriculum does not guarantee success. Schools have had to adapt and adjust approaches to meet the needs of a particular population of students. Victory Christian School in Tulsa, Oklahoma, provides a good example of this, where the A Beka Phonics and Reading approach has been changed to include Sing, Spell, Read & Write. Abundant Life Christian School in Madison, Wisconsin, supplements the A Beka Language Program with materials from Merrill Publishers. It is not unusual to find an ACE school modifying its curriculum with teacher-directed materials, or a teacher-directed school including aspects of the principle approach, such as Bethany Christian Academy in Baker, Louisiana.

Select Content Matter and Subjects

The task of selecting a curriculum is very easy. Given the number of good Christian curricula available today, there is no need to reinvent the wheel. Someone once said, "Selecting a curriculum is like finding a good horse and riding it as long as you can."

Investigate Local and State Curricula

Before selecting the curriculum, we suggest obtaining curriculum publications from your local and state education departments. Although you may disagree about the specific content taught, carefully consider the scope and sequence. Schools can avoid confusion when students transfer from secular schools to Christian schools by adhering to the approved scope and sequence. It also eases scheduling at the high school level.

Many forces have an influence on curriculum decisions, not the least of which are legally mandated requirements stating the subject areas to teach. A careful review of your state's private school curriculum requirements is a good place to start. For example, in first through sixth grades, the State of New York requires the teaching of the following subjects—Arithmetic, English, Language, Reading, Writing, Music, Geography, Health Education, Physical Education, Science, United States History and Visual Arts.

Begin With the Basics

Schools can categorize the basic content for study into four levels: early elementary, upper elementary, junior high and high school. The strategy at each level is to build a solid foundation in the basics, such as Bible, Reading, Writing, Arithmetic, Science and Social Studies. The Green Bay Packers based their domination of football in the 60's on the explicit execution of a few basic plays. So it is with your school. Concentrate on the basics, then add electives as the school grows. Consider the curricula content outlined in Figure 8.1.

Enhance the Curriculum

Following the implementation of the basic curricula, consider several curriculum enhancements. For example: mini courses, outdoor education, enrichment programs and independent study programs.

Mini Courses

These courses of study are usually of one to six weeks duration and

Figure 8.1 Curricula Content

Early Elementary K-3

Bible

Writing

Reading (Phonics)

Arithmetic (Numbers)

Social Studies

Science

Fine Art (Music and Art)

Physical Education

   and Health

Upper Elementary 4-6

Bible

Penmanship

Language Arts (Reading,

   Spelling, Grammar,

   Poetry)

Arithmetic

History/Geography

Science

Fine Arts (Music and Art)

Physical Education

   and Health

Junior High 7-8

Bible

Language Arts (Literature,

Grammar, Vocabulary,

   Spelling and Writing)

Mathematics

Social Studies (History,

Geography and Civics)

Science

Fine Arts (Music and Art)

Physical Education

   and Health

Senior High 9-12

Bible 4 years

English 4 years

Math 3-4 years

Social Studies 2-3 years

Foreign Language 2-3 years

Sciences 3-4 years

Electives

Computer Literacy

Home Economics

Family Living

Vocational Education

Music, Art, Drama

Speech, Debate

can be formed quickly according to student interest. Eugene R. Howard offers the following suggestion,

"Mini courses can be jointly planned by students and staff; they can be book- and paper-centered or activity-centered; they can encourage student creativity and increase the level of responsibility that pupils take for their own learning. Such courses can offer alternative ways for pupils to gain credits, both in required and elective courses. As mini course offerings are expanded, the opportunity for more pupils to become involved in learning activities of interest to them increases."[4]

Outdoor Education

Consider expanding the curriculum to include outdoor education experiences. Each year, Abundant Life Christian School of Madison, Wisconsin, takes its eighth graders on a week-long wilderness adventure to the Apostle Islands on Lake Superior. Students and staff live in cottages and assume all of the daily life tasks, such as getting water from the well, preparing meals and doing dishes.

Teachers take advantage of the informality of the outdoor setting to minister to students individually and to challenge them in their personal walk with God. Throughout the day teachers integrate the work previously presented in the classroom into nature-challenging experiences, requiring students to draw from scientific, mathematical and communication skills. Students practice skills in map and compass reading, wilderness ethics, backpacking, equipment maintenance and first aid.

Enrichment Programs

Adding enrichment activities to the basic curriculum provides opportunity for parent involvement and furnishes leadership opportunities for students. Although enrichment activities can take place throughout the school term, presenting them sometime between January to March helps add variety to one of the longest non-vacation stretches in the traditional school year.

Some schools will set aside a one- to two-hour, weekly enrichment block of time for three to four successive weeks, usually held on Friday. Use pupils, parents, staff, grandparents or friends of the school community who have special skills, or competencies to present activities, such as stamp collecting, model airplane building, pet grooming and gourmet cooking. Obtain this information from a simple survey (See Figure 8.2).

Give a second survey to each student to determine how much interest each activity generates (Figure 8.3). After compiling the final enrichment list, students select three activities in order of preference. Groups are kept as small as possible to encourage close interaction and 100 percent participation.

Independent Study Programs

Most think of independent study only as an option at the college

Enrichment Program Survey 1

We invite you to be part of this year's Enrichment Program. You may have some special interest or competency that you would be willing to share with the student body. We would like to offer a wide variety of activities. Over the years, students, staff, parents, grandparents, and friends have enriched the lives of our students with topics such as fly fishing, go-cart building, horsemanship, pet grooming, model airplane building, jewelry making, archeology, movie making, and many more. With your help, this year's Enrichment Program can really make a difference in our school. You do not have to be an expert to participate.

Name:
_____
Circle One: Student   Parent   Staff Other-Explain
_____
Address:
_____
City/Zip:
_____
Home Phone:
_____
Best time to call:
_____
Work Phone:
_____
Best time to call:
_____
Have you every presented an enrichment activity in the past?
_____
_____

If so, what was the competency?
_____
_____
_____

What competency or interest are you willing to present this year?
_____
_____

What special supplies will you need?
_____
_____

What special assistance will you need?
_____
_____

Figure 8.2 Enrichment Program Survey 1

Enrichment Program Survey 2

This year's Enrichment Program will be from 1:30 to 3:00 p.m. Friday, February 2, 9 and 16. From the list of activities, please select five that would be of interest you. Place a number 1 next to your first choice, a number 2 next to your second choice. Do the same for your third, fourth and fifth choices. We will make every effort to schedule you into one of these five choices.

Activity	Selection
Babysitting training	_____
Motocross	_____
Waterskiing	_____
Using a modem	_____
Oil painting	_____
Small engine repair	_____
Single living	_____
Pet grooming	_____
Tennis tips	_____
Landscaping	_____
Puppeteering	_____
Politics	_____
Air traffic Controlling	_____
Basic Electronics	_____
Computer Troubleshooting	_____
First Aid	_____
Archery	_____
Missions Preparation	_____
Teaching Pet Fish Tricks	_____
Organic Gardening	_____
Stamp Collection	_____

Name: _____

Grade: _____

Homeroom Teacher: _____

Figure 8.3 Enrichment Program Survey 2

level. However, independent study programs are helpful for senior high school students. At the high school level, independent study programs provide several advantages, such as overcoming scheduling conflict or studying a subject not offered as a traditional course. Other advantages include making up work in a course previously failed without having to sit through the entire course content, and preparing a student for college where the student is more responsible for their own learning.

Eugene Howard offers several suggestions for establishing independent study programs. They are as follows:

1. Make it clear in the program's guidelines that pupils are expected to develop, with the assistance of their teachers, a clearly stated plan of work.

2. The plan should specify: the purpose of the study; a description of what the pupil expects to learn; a list of anticipated learning activities; a description of how the effectiveness of the study is to be evaluated; and an estimated completion date.

3. Keep a record of a pupil's independent study activities as part of his cumulative record.

4. List these activities on the pupil's high school transcript so college admissions officers can see evidence of the pupil's capability of learning independently.[5]

Plan Field Trips

Every Christian school needs to plan for field trips. However, planning a field trip for the sole purpose of having "something to do" is not justifiable, mainly because of additional costs and the amount of school time missed. Therefore, all field trips should be supportive of the school's educational goals and fulfill specific learner objectives.

If the students are to gain full benefit from a field trip, they should participate in the planning, especially for upper elementary students and above: as much value may be derived from planning activities as from the actual trip. Consider the following:

- Stimulate class interest through class discussion, photographs, bulletin boards and testimonials from students who went on similar trips.
- Clarify with the students the purpose of the trip. Use these objectives later in evaluating the trip.
- Develop background information on the trip by consulting reference materials well in advance.
- Identify the points to observe.

Evaluating a field trip is another important component. Were the objectives met? How were attitudes of students and hosts affected? Was Christlike behavior exemplified? What new activities did the field trip stimulate? What evidence is there that the field trip further developed a spirit of inquiry and curiosity? Establish a central file for field trip ideas, containing brochures, names of contact people, expectations, planning tips, evaluation information, etc.

Careful planning of field trips will maximize their effectiveness and reduce potential liability risks. A school cannot exculpate its legal liability by using standard field trip forms. However, it can reduce its legal risk by the following actions:

1   Provide parents with a written description of the trip, objective of the trip, departure time, arrival time and what to do for late return.

2   Develop an emergency plan so parents know what to do in case of a bus accident and how they will be contacted, and what will be done with an unruly child. Communicate behavioral expectations in writing before the trip.

3   Ensure sufficient supervision of students. Base this rational on the nature of the trip and maturity level of the students. The higher the potential for injury, or the lower the maturity level, the greater will be the need for supervision.

4   Maintain an accurate attendance accounting throughout the trip to ensure that no one remains behind.

Obtain Curriculum Materials

Most curriculum publishers are willing to provide samples of their curriculum. Many publishers have regional representatives who will make a personal visit to your school and answer any questions you might ask. Contained in the Christian School Resource Kit is a current list of the most prominent publishers of Christian school curriculum materials [CSRK 8.2].

Consider the Teacher

If you select a teacher-directed approach, the real key to its success is going to rest with the teacher. You can place a superior curriculum in the hands of a less than adequately trained teacher, and your results will be less than optimal. Any curriculum, when placed in the hands of a skillful teacher, will end up being the very best. What are we saying?

NOTE: *Teacher selection is critical to the success of your curriculum: it is the teacher who makes the curriculum come alive.*

Select Curriculum Guides

Curriculum guides serve as blueprints. A good guide includes the following aspects: identifies specific measurable objectives, skills to be taught and activities to be used; cites instructional resources; specifies time parameters; and lists pupil learning outcomes.[6] Curriculum guides provide for accountability, planning, continuity and integration. In addition, they should help the teacher address student questions, such as: "Why do I have to learn this stuff?" and "How will I ever use this?"

Accountability

A published curriculum provides for scope and sequence of a subject by grade. Everyone knows what is being taught and the specific skills to master. When a child completes a grade, one knows the skills that have been mastered, and there is the assurance that the child is prepared for the next level of mastery

Planning

Placing a planned curriculum in the hands of a teacher reduces the amount of preparation time essential to successful teaching. This is especially true of first-year teachers. The published curriculum provides teachers with proven instructional methods, presents a suggested classroom schedule, identifies goals and other teacher information. Published curriculums and accompanying guides are very valuable, especially in smaller schools where a single teacher makes three or four different subject preparations.

Continuity

A published curriculum and curriculum guide provide continuity over time. When teachers are the source of the curriculum rather than a published curriculum, as teachers change so may the curriculum. At times, the curriculum may disappear. For example, one school administrator over five years had to use five different teachers to teach journalism. Since there was no established curriculum, each year the new teacher had to develop the course content from scratch. Unfortunately, when each teacher left the school, they took with them what they had created. Further complicating matters was no published Christian journalism textbook.

Finally, the administrator decided to adopt the State Department of Education's Journalism Curriculum Guide and to use a textbook published by a secular publishing company. He gave the next new teacher an additional preparation period to integrate biblical truth to topics in the curriculum and to develop a curriculum guide that would be kept by the school.

Integration

One of the main criticisms of using secular materials is the total lack of the Word of God in the subject content. The task of producing an integrated lesson plan is very time consuming and difficult, even when reference materials abound, such as the four volume series *Bible Truths for School Subjects.*

Ruth C. Haycock, author of this series says,

> "Implementing the Bible into the school curriculum goes deeper than the use of scientific facts to illustrate spiritual truth, though such use is clearly scriptural. It goes deeper too than merely quoting Bible verses which refer to scientific subjects; it involves finding the scientific facts and principles which are taught in the Bible and incorporating them into the teaching where they are relevant to the subject at hand, thus consolidating truth gained from Bible study and from observation by men... In order for this kind of integration to take place, teachers must be engaged in solid Bible study which makes them increasingly familiar with what the Bible says. In addition, every teacher must make a serious effort to learn what is taught in the Scriptures that relates to topics in his own curriculum."[7]

Requiring a teacher to be solely responsible for integrating biblical principles in daily subject content is like asking a mechanic to change a tire on a moving vehicle. If teachers are to be responsible for adequately integrating biblical truth in their subject, provide sufficient time for this task, not just during the school term, but weeks before the start of classes. Providing for integration of a biblical viewpoint in every subject, whether this is accomplished through a published curriculum from a Christian publisher, or left up to the teacher, allows the student to view the Bible as God's divine revelation to them and the absolute truth which assume a position of primacy in all of life.[8]

Cautions

Along with the positive points of using published curriculum guides, there are some cautions. First, teachers and administrators need to see the curriculum guide as a guide and allow the teacher flexibility to adjust the lesson according to the needs of the students and sensitivity of the Holy Spirit.

Lee C. Reno comments,

> "The guide is something like the rules of a ball game. It must

be there in order for the coaches and players to have a firm base for what they are doing. In basketball, for instance, the purpose of the game is to make more baskets than the opposing team. If every player understands the rules of the game, he will be better able to know the importance of the position, even if he is not the one who always scores the points. Similarly, when a teacher knows what is expected and what must be covered in a course, the basics are established. Within the basic framework, the teacher will use professional skill and sensitivity to the Holy Spirit and will reach the departmental goal. Each class and teacher is unique. It is important that the goal be reached, but the exact process will vary according to the make-up of class and teacher."[9]

Second, success in the classroom is dependent on more than just covering the curriculum. Success is always a result of a positive interaction among the student, the teacher and the curriculum. Guard against the "curriculum" becoming an instructional bondage to the students and teacher. Provide the teacher with the freedom to have her daily lesson ordered by the Holy Spirit and to take the time to meet the personal needs of her students. One teacher put it this way, "Stay on track while staying free to discuss ideas or questions that come up within the boundaries of that track."

NOTE: *Do not allow the curriculum guide to stifle spontaneous teaching. Yet, do not allow spontaneity to become an excuse for not following the curriculum guide.*

Select Textbooks

Textbooks are expensive. Making a quality purchase decision the first time will eliminate future problems, since what you select, you will most likely keep for several years.

Christian vs. Secular Textbooks

The situation is not as critical as it was ten to fifteen years ago when there was a shortage of quality Christian textbooks in many subjects beyond the junior high school grades. Today, you can find textbooks on most high school subjects written from a Christian perspective.

When selecting textbooks from a Christian publisher, there is the assurance that the books are true to the Word of God with biblical principles incorporated throughout the content. The activities and approaches are consistent with the Word of God.

Purchasing an entire K-12 curriculum from a single Christian publisher ensures a proper integration across subjects and a balanced scope and sequence throughout the grades. Fragmentation and overlap happen when schools select different publishers for different grades or different subjects. Base your textbook selection on their ability to help students achieve learning objectives and the school's educational goals rather than on the experiences of one or two teachers or comprehensiveness of the textbook.[10]

Textbooks that are not published by a Christian publishing company run the risk of exposing students to a host of ungodly influences, such as new age concepts, one world order, humanism, situational ethics, satanism, witchcraft, occult, acceptance of alternative lifestyles, attacks on traditional values, authority and morality, to name a few. Very few Christian schools selecting secular textbooks take the time to do an exhaustive review of their contents. Fortunately, there is a group of concerned Christians who have taken the time to research textbooks published by major secular publishers. Copies of these reviews can be obtained from Educational Research Analysts, The Mel Gablers, P.O. Box 7518, Longview, TX 75601.

Leaving God out of textbooks sends the message to the student that the Bible does not have any relevancy to this subject. Therefore, God must not be important. A. A. Baker, vice-president of Pensacola Christian College and A Beka Book Publications says,

> "It would be well to note that Christian textbooks also provide an excellent advertising tool in selling parents on the benefits of your Christian school program. I can see no reason whatsoever to justify the use of secular, public school textbooks in the Christian school unless there is no other alternative. If parents are paying for a Christian education, they should not expect their children to have to use the same godless humanistic textbooks that are used in the public school system."[11]

> **NOTE:** *Textbooks, although important, are only part of the curriculum. The curriculum also includes the teacher's knowledge, didactic tools, supplemental resources and materials, field trips, and much more. The whole curriculum is much broader than any of its parts. Thus, when making textbook selections, be sensitive to how well the text fits into the total curriculum.*

Textbook Tracking

Once you select your textbooks, create a three-by-five-inch card file containing all essential textbook information, such as author, publisher, edition, cost, condition of book, location, copyright date, number of new books, number of used books, etc. This system will save you hours of research when it comes time to reorder books [CSRK 8.3].

Consider using a computer to facilitate this task. Use a database program for this purpose, or purchase a software program specifically created for tracking textbooks. For example, *Textbook Inventory*. This program tracks student names, ID numbers, the date the book was issued and the date the book was returned, in addition to all the variables mentioned earlier. The program provides a number of specialized reports including a printout of the entire inventory and a listing of books not returned.

Textbook Distribution

The simplest and easiest method for distributing books is to handle the books through a central distribution point. A second way is to distribute books through the homeroom. Regardless of the method of distribution, establish a strict accounting and inventory system [CSRK 8.4].

Some textbook publishers place a student identification stamp on the front, inside cover of the book. Numbering the books in sequential order on the edge is an easy method of accounting for them at the end of the school term. Conduct textbook inspections quarterly so students will retain the correct book number and have a sense of responsibility in caring for school property.

Purchase Curricula Resources and Materials

Curriculum resources are what teachers and students use in teaching and learning. Resources and materials are as necessary to teaching and learning as dishes and utensils are to eating—you can survive without them, but not without frustration.

Most curriculum guides provide a listing of essential resources and materials needed to carry out the curriculum. Make every effort to purchase these resources. These may include: special books and pamphlets, pictures, films, videos, records, tapes, transparencies and the necessary equipment for viewing and listening to these resources and materials. Don't fall into the trap of waiting until classroom teachers are hired or after school begins to order these resources. Review each curriculum guide when it arrives and order the required resources.

Good teachers probably never have enough instructional materials and equipment to satisfy their needs. [12] A school can maximize a limited number of resources by developing school-wide schedules around shared resources. An area in the school library or a place designated as an instructional materials center make wonderful places for gathering materials, managing resources and coordinating the use of equipment.

When no classrooms are available to house a resource center, consider using the end of a hallway, or even the hallway itself, the entrance to the school or church, or an unused church balcony. Some schools have found much success in creating an instructional materials task force to assist in obtaining essential resources as well as helping coordinate the use of these resources.

Establish School Parameters

School parameters include the school year, day and class periods. Determining these parameters are important tasks in organizing your school. The amount of latitude you enjoy depends on your individual state statutes regarding private schooling.

Length of School Year and School Calendar

Most state compulsory attendance laws require students to receive instruction for a specified number of days, somewhere around 180 days. For example, the Oklahoma State Statutes require all students, public and private, to attend school not less than 180 days. Schools can use five (5) days for attendance of professional meetings. In addition, parent-teacher conferences held during the school day count toward a school day and are part of the 175 days of classroom instruction.

Most Christian school accrediting agencies require Christian schools to adhere to the state mandated length of school year, even when not required by the state to do so. For example, Standard Four of the International Christian Accrediting Association (ICAA) states, "The school has developed an academic calendar to the needs of its programs and services. The length and amount of school days shall be no fewer than that required by the state in which the school is located, or a minimum of 180 days."[13] To fulfill this requirement, the school must submit a copy of its state regulations regarding attendance and the minimal number of instructional days required, including the required length of the school day. In addition, the school is required to submit a copy of its academic calendar.

A school can enhance the process of developing and maintaining a school-wide calendar through the utilization of computer software, such as *Calendar Creator Plus*. This program allows various departments of a school and church to produce their own individual calendar of events. Combining several calendars into a master calendar is as simple as one, two, three. The program allows organizing every activity in the school and church from single fixed events, such as vacations and holidays, to recurring events, such as teacher meetings. Print formats include daily, two-day, weekly, two-week schedules, monthly, six-month or annual calendars.

The beginning date for school is usually left up to individual school districts. Christian schools that draw students from several public school districts should consider using the starting and ending dates of the largest district. This will help avoid conflict in families with children in both private and public schools. Furthermore, community events pattern themselves after the largest school district.

Length of School Day

As with the length of the school year, the term of day is subject to state law. For example, Oklahoma law reads, "A school day for any group of pupils shall consist of not less than six (6) hours devoted to school activities, except that a school day for nursery, early childhood education, kindergarten, and first grade shall be as otherwise defined by law or as defined by the State Board of Education."[14]

Kindergarten children attend school two and one-half hours, while first graders attend for a minimum of five hours. Some junior and senior high schools, in an attempt to include all traditional subjects as well as Bible, provide for a lengthened school day; a seven-period day is not uncommon.

The daily starting and ending times are left up to individual school districts. These decisions should consider community traffic patterns and needs of those families being served. For instance, starting school ten minutes earlier or later may help parents avoid traffic congestion within the community. In addition, starting elementary school a few minutes ahead of the secondary school has its benefits; for example, offering an opportunity for more orderly and safer hallways.

Length of Class Period

Most state boards of education determine the length of the class period for grades seven through twelve. Although several states permit 45-minute periods, the standard is a 50- to 60-minute period with three to five minutes allowed for passing between periods. Some experimentation may need to be made regarding the optimum length of class periods.

After several years of using different class periods, Victory Christian School settled for a 50-minute period with four minutes between periods. Their periods are as follows:

- Period 1   8:04 – 8:54
- Period 2   8:58 – 9:48
- Period 3   9:52 – 10:42
- Period 4   10:46 – 11:36
- Lunch   11:36 – 12:18
- Period 5   12:18 – 1:08
- Period 6   1:12 – 2:02
- Period 7   2:06 – 2:56

Attendance Policy

Establishing a simple, yet effective attendance policy is critical to the success of every school. The U.S. Department of Education states, "Absences are a major problem at all levels of school. Students who miss a lesson lose an opportunity to learn. Too many missed opportunities can result in failure, dropping out of school or both."[15] The following activities will help improve attendance:

1 **Enhance the curriculum.** Students who are actively involved in learning experiences and believe they are worthwhile and meaningful are seldom truant. Improving the school climate and its programs results in increased attendance.

2 **Inform parents.** Research indicates parents want to hear promptly when their children have unexcused absences. Accomplish this manually using staff members to check attendance records and then phone the parents of absent students [CSRK 8.5]. Since many parents of absent students with attendance problems are not home during the day, consider calling in the evening. Some schools use an automatic absentee calling device that leaves a pre-recorded message with parents and will call back if nobody answers. For more information on automatic call systems, contact McGraw-Hill School Systems.

3 **Establish streamline reporting procedures.** Quick, accurate and consistent reporting of absences by teachers are essential. Create a tracking and reporting system that is free of inefficiencies or bottlenecks [CSRK 8.6; 8.7; 8.8]. Consider replacing the manual card and paper system with a computerized attendance system. Over the course of a school term, a computerized attendance module will recapture hundreds of hours spent on attendance taking and tracking. It is an excellent technique for keeping track of individual student attendance profiles so administrators are able to correct chronic attendance challenges at an early stage. Some computer systems automatically generate a letter to parents of a student who is absent from a particular class for a certain number of consecutive days [CSRK 8.9].

4 **Improve supervision of hallways, washrooms and school grounds.** Some students become expert transients; they are always somewhere between two classes. Improving supervision will reduce single period absences. Use student aides and parent monitors for this task [CSRK 8.10].

5 **Initiate a student counseling program.** Providing an opportunity for students to receive help in dealing with personal and learning challenges improves attendance. When a certified counselor is not available, make room in the daily schedule for teachers to visit with students on a one-to-one basis [CSRK 8.11].

6   **Do not use out-of-school suspension as punishment for truancy**. Suspending a student from classes for being truant only adds to missed opportunities to learn. It also increases the likelihood of failure.

7   **Do not lower a student's grade for excessive absences**. Instead, use incentives for being in class. Positive reinforcement is more affective in the long run. Byron Hansford offers this comment,

> "If grades are to reflect the individual's progress as measured against what he should be doing, the effect of several absences will automatically be shown without the arbitrary lowering of the grade. On the other hand, if grades are for the purposes of comparing the achievement of one individual with that of the rest of the class, lowering his grade arbitrarily because of absences would invalidate the comparison. If grades have any validity, and if evaluation for the purpose of grading is properly done, any absence from class should automatically show in the grade assigned."[16]

8   **Institute a special absent request process**. There are times when students have a legitimate reason for being absent. When these reasons are other than normal, such as illness, a death in the family, school-sponsored trips, etc. require students to complete a special absence request. Place on the request the student's name, reasons for absence, length of absence, classes to be missed and parent and principal signatures [CSRK 8.12].

Establish a Credit System

It is important for new schools to establish a system of credits that includes graduation requirements and grade classification. Schools differ in what they require. As a rule of thumb, students should meet all state graduation mandates. Also, requirements should parallel those of the public school, thus facilitating a smooth transfer of credits in and out of the school.

The school should provide students with a list of college prerequisites. In most schools, the number of credits for graduation range from 21 to 24. Figure 8.4 provides a list of graduation requirements for a typical school that offers a seven-period day. Out of a maximum of 28 credits, graduation requires 24 credits. Using this system, the minimum number of credits for grade classification is set at five credits for a sophomore, eleven for a junior and eighteen for a senior.

Course Plan Sheet

Students entering high school for the very first time, either as freshmen or as transfer students, should complete a course plan sheet

Figure 8.4 Graduation Requirements

Graduation Requirements	Credits
Bible (1 credit for every year in school)	4
English (4 credits including Senior English)	4
Social Studies (State History, U.S. History, World History, Government)	3
Math (3 years of math or 2 years math and 1 year foreign language)	3
Science (2 laboratory sciences)	2
Physical Education (1 credit)	1
Speech (1 credit, junior or senior year)	1
Electives	6
Total Credits Needed to Graduate	24
Varsity athletes may earn .25 credits per sport.	
College Prerequisites	
English	4
Foreign Language	2
Math	3
Science	3
Social Studies	2

[CSRK 8.13]. Try to see that every student has a four-year course program. Develop each plan carefully and accurately, keeping in mind the capabilities, interests, vocation or post-secondary education ambitions of the students; also, the plan should allow opportunity for change, depending upon the counsel of the student's parents and leading of the Holy Spirit. Part of the responsibility of the school is to assist the students in tuning in to the voice of the Spirit of God and the Word of God and tuning out confusing impulses from any other sources.

The Figure 8.5 displays a typical four-year program for a student entering school as a freshman. Some courses require prerequisites. For example, Math Analysis—must have Algebra I and II and Geometry; Spanish III—must have Spanish I and II; Algebra II—must have Algebra I and teacher recommendation; Calculus—must have Math Analysis and teacher recommendation; Driver's Education—must be fifteen and one-half years old by October 1st or February 1st for second semester.

Some schools publish a high school course description catalog. In some cases, local junior college, trade schools, colleges or universities may be willing to pay for the printing of this catalog. In exchange, the

Figure 8.5 Projected Four-Year Course Program

Freshman	**Junior**
English	English
Bible	Bible
Science - Physical Science	Science - Chemistry
Math - Algebra I	Math - Algebra II
History - State	History - World History
Physical Education	Elective _____
Elective _____	Elective _____
Sophomore	**Senior**
English	English
Bible	Bible
Science - Biology	Science
Math - Geometry	Math
History - U.S. History	Elective _____
Elective _____	Elective _____
Elective _____	Elective _____

Christian school gives the sponsoring institution opportunity to promote their institution in the catalog.

Develop Grading and Reporting Systems

Central to grading and reporting systems is the requirement for maintaining lesson plans and grade books. Careful attention to these documents increases the academic accountability of the teachers and ultimately the school.

Require Lesson Plans and Grade books

Teachers have been debating the pros and cons of lesson planning for years. Lorber and Pierce offer the following reasons in support of lesson planning: lesson plans are to teachers as a budget is to a finance officer. It is a tool that keeps teachers and the school on course to accomplishing its educational goals.[17]

1   Lesson plans specify the instructional objective of the lesson and thus help keep the main purpose of the lesson clearly in focus.

2   By containing all the important content, lesson plans assure that no crucial points will be accidentally omitted.

3   Lesson plans include teaching-learning activities that are determined

to be most likely to help students achieve the instructional objective(s), thus eliminating or at least decreasing the need for improvision.

4   Lesson plans provide a basis for determining how effective practical teaching-learning activities are in helping students achieve particular objectives and thus provide a basis for modifying instructional methods.

5   Lesson plans facilitate long-range planning by providing a record of what is taught during each lesson, thus assisting in maintaining continuity.

6   Lesson plans are essential if a substitute teacher is to do more than conduct a supervised study period in the teacher's absence.

7   Maintain a system for tracking the completion of lesson plans. The Christian School Resource Kit contains a Lesson Plan Tracking System [CSRK 8.14].

Institute a Grading System and Report Cards

Every school needs a grading system. Don Petry, internationally known educational consultant, says,

"Grades are evidence of a student's good works, just as achievement test scores are evidence of a school's good works."[18]

Grading System

The issuing of grades is extremely important. Not only do grades affect a student's progress through school, they influence college admissions decisions and predetermine the type of education and employment.

There are several grading systems available to Christian schools. Some systems, such as "grading on the curve" and "no-fail," are not supportive of a Christian philosophy. Grading on a curve means that a student's grade depends as much on what the other students in the class do as what he does. The same grade on a test may be an "A" in one class and a "C" in another class. Since the normal curve has been found to best represent chance, or random processes, those schools that grade on the curve must assume that students have been assigned to classes by a random process. Furthermore, it provides no way of adequately evaluating performance from one class to another or from one grade to another.

A "no fail" system teaches a child that regardless of what he does, he will not fail. Over time, this type of system teaches students that the world is a world without responsibility and ultimately implies that anything they do is acceptable.

Some schools use a "pass-fail" grading strategy at the high school level. The reasoning behind the "pass-fail" system is that it encourages students to take a course they would not normally take because they would be afraid of endangering their grade point average; and, second, it is supposed to eliminate the worry about what grade the student will receive. Unfortunately, such a system is very advantageous to students who usually receive an "A" and "B" grade, but devastating to students who usually receive "D's" or "F's". Furthermore, just because a student passes a subject does not automatically mean they will be self-motivated to take additional course work in the same subject. It would be more encouraging for students to receive a grade of "A" for passing and "I" for an incomplete if they fail. Then, give students an opportunity to clear the incomplete.

Most Christian schools prefer a grading system based on a standardized grading scale so that if all do well, all get good grades. The grade in a course should accurately reflect mastery of learning objectives and not just an average of several aspects of the grade, such as attendance, homework, quizzes and tests. It is better to award several grades per subject than to average several elements into a single letter grade.

NOTE: *When a teacher gives a letter grade of "B" representing a certain percentage, he also should be able to provide a list of those objectives or items within the subject content that represent the percent that was mastered and not mastered.*

Many Christian schools adopt a grading scale similar to that found in Figure 8.6. A failing mark in first through sixth grade is recorded as an "unsatisfactory" for the first nine weeks.

Grading at the kindergarten level needs to consider performance on daily worksheets. Figure 8.7 illustrates a special grading system for kindergartners. This grading scale allows teachers to assess performance on seven different tasks with a different range of points. For example, a score of 2 on a 6 item exercise has the same weight as a score of 8 to 9 on an 20 item exercise or a score of 40-49 on a 100 item assignment These scores represent an C+ on a D- to A+ traditional grading scale or a S- on an unsatisfactory to satisfactory grading system.

Some schools use a skills inventory at the kindergarten and lower elementary grades in addition to or in place of a traditional letter grade. The skills inventory changes with the curriculum requirements for each grading period. The Christian School Resource Kit presents an example of a kindergarten skills inventory [CSRK 8.15].

It is essential that all teachers use the same grading system and that the grading system employ similar weighing. For example, all math teachers will use weekly mastery tests to count for 25 percent of the final grade, unit tests count for 25 percent, and the nine-week's final counts

Figure 8.6 Traditional Grading Scale

		97 –100	A+
A	90s	93 – 96	A
		90 – 92	A-
		87 – 89	B+
B	80s	83 – 86	B
		80 – 82	B-
		77 – 79	C+
C	70s	73 – 76	C
		70 – 72	C-
		67 – 69	D+
D	60s	63 – 66	D
		60 – 62	D-
F	50s	Below 59	F

Figure 8.7 Kindergarten Grading System

		10	12			20	97-100	A+	O
	8	9	11	15	17-18	18-19	90-96	A	S+
6	7	8	10	13-14	15-16	16-17	80-89	A-	S+
5	6	7	9	11-12	13-14	14-15	70-79	B+	S
4	5	6	8	9-10	11-12	12-13	60-69	B	S
3	4	5	6-7	7-8	9-10	10-11	50-59	B-	S
2	3	4	5	5-6	7-8	8-9	40-49	C+	S-
1	2	3	4	3-4	5-6	6-7	30-39	C	S-
0	1	2	3	2	3-4	4-5	20-29	C-	S-
	0	1	2	1	1-2	2-3	10-19	D+	N
		0	1	0	0	1	5-9	D	N
			0	0	0	0	0-4	D-	N

for the remaining 50 percent of the grade. Likewise, a final Bible grade may consist of 25 percent for memory work, 25 percent for application, 25 percent for research and 25 percent for tests. Schools that use a common grading scale and a consistent strategy for weighing various components of a grade have a solid basis for student assessment and course evaluation. The Christian School Resource Kit contains a unique grading sheet for recording daily grades and averages. Grades are based on a maximum point system [CSRK 8.16].

For more information on grading topics, such as establishing a grade book, dealing with failing papers, grading homework, raising grades, calculating reading grades, grading incompletes, paper headings, grading written work, progress reports, grading exams, establishing testing schedules, see *Christian School Administration: Administrator and Teacher Guidelines.*

Report Cards

Hughes and Ubben declare, "Report cards are usually demanded by parents, feared by children, and considered inadequate by many educators."[19] The primary purpose of the report card is to report pupil progress to parents. Thus, design the card with this purpose in mind.

Report cards vary from a simple letter grade for individual subjects, to comprehensive and complex computer printouts of the student's progress. Other systems provide a written assessment of a child's mastery of specific learner outcomes. The type of indicator may be in the form of letter grades, number grades, percentage grades, or verbal indicators, such as "satisfactory," "outstanding," "superior" and "unsatisfactory" [CSRK 8.17].

The content of most report cards includes a measure of individual progress on a number of subjects, courses, topics or activities. For example: math, English, Christian service, citizenship, Christian character. The frequency of reporting should be no less than quarterly (end of each nine-week grading period). Some schools issue a progress report as a mid-quarter assessment [CSRK 8.18; 8.19]. Other schools produce a report card every three weeks. Report cards provide a vehicle for monitoring students' progress. Frequent and systematic monitoring of pupil progress makes it easier to identify strengths and weaknesses in learning and instruction and to make adjustments to ensure maximum success on the part of students, as well as teachers. Furthermore, providing parents with a written report of incomplete assignments helps them motivate their children to "good works" [CSRK 8.20].

NOTE: *Inconsistency in the use of the reporting system between one teacher and another causes parents to become confused and fail to understand this message from the school. As all teachers make a sincere effort to use the report card in a manner intended, it will make its maximum contribution to the growth of students and communication with the parent.*

Computerization of Grades and Report Cards

Now that personal computers are becoming very affordable, many teachers and schools have taken advantage of grading and report card software. Not only do these programs save time, they increase grading accuracy and provide immediate feedback to students of their performance.

Sending a status report home to the parents at the end of the week keeping them informed of their child's progress is an easy task for schools using electronic grading [CSRK 8.21]. Grading software range from simple shareware programs, such as *GradeEase, Grading Assistant, Noble Gradebook,* to more complicated systems, such as *Integrade.*

Schedule Classes, Courses and Activities

No other concern provides as much concentrated effort as the school schedule. Hughes and Ubben comment, "If well done, the schedule will strongly support the instructional and curricular program of the school. On the other hand, if poorly designed, the schedule will be a roadblock to a balanced curriculum and instructional flexibility."[20]

Design the Elementary School Schedule

Elementary schools using self-contained traditional classrooms have a simple scheduling task. It involves assigning teachers to classrooms, then scheduling special classes (for example, art, music, physical education) throughout the week. Students are assigned to grade level classes within each grade. Most curriculum guides, such as those published by Bob Jones University and A Beka, provide detailed daily schedules. A typical elementary daily schedule follows:

8:15	Preclass Activities/Prayer/Pledge
9:00	Bible
10:00	Math
11:00	Reading
12:00	Lunch
1:00	Social Studies
2:00	Science
3:00	Prepare for dismissal

Consider scheduling Bible, math and reading as the first three subjects in the morning while the students are most attentive. Furthermore, scheduling math and reading in the same time block for all grades offers an opportunity to assign students to skill groups across grades.

For example, given a 10:00 a.m. to 12:00 noon instructional block, teachers in grades first to third could create groups for reading instruction and math. Students progress along a continuum of instructional goals. Mastery of a pre-determined set of objectives leads the child to progress to the next unit and then to the next grouping.

The goal is to provide students with a wide variation in time and materials to learn the same minimum levels of achievement. The important part is that all students learn all of the objectives of their course.[21]

Implement a Junior High Schedule

At the junior high or middle school, try scheduling teachers in blocks where one teacher and a single group of students are together in one classroom for two or more subjects. For example, a single teacher could teach a math and science block while a second teacher instructs in history and language arts. Figure 8.8 shows an example of a two-teacher block.

Figure 8.8 Teacher Block

Period	Teacher A	Teacher B
1	Bible Group 1	Bible Group 2
2	Math Group 1	Language Arts Group 2
3	Science Group 1	Social Studies Group 2
4	Math Group 2	Language Arts Group 1
5	Science Group 2	Social Studies Group 1
6	Elective Group 1	Elective Group 2

Formulate the High School Schedule

The larger a school's enrollment becomes, the more complex will be the schedule. Most high schools use the mosaic method of scheduling. The mosaic method is a flexible scheduling plan. It involves placing individual class sections on a master schedule one at a time in those periods where there are fewest student conflicts. The mosaic method includes the following actions:

Schedule Students

Start with those classes for seniors, juniors, sophomores and then freshmen. First, place classes on your schedule that have only one section. Next, add classes with two sections, etc.

Conflict Chart

Construct a conflict chart for those courses that provide the greatest opportunity for conflict during the same period. Identify only single-section classes. Figure 8.9 shows a section of a conflict chart indicating the number of students with conflicts. Classes are then shifted on the schedule so those courses that are conflicting will be offered at different periods.

Figure 8.9 Schedule Conflict Matrix

	Algebra II	Chem.	Physics	Speech	Drama	Band
Algebra		2	4	1		
Chemistry					2	
Physics		3		4		
Speech			2			
Drama						1
Band				1		

Master Schedule Board

Display the schedule on a master schedule board. Make the board out of plywood or masonite, placed on a large 36 inch roll of paper, or drawn on a chalk board. The size of board will depend upon the number of teachers and the number of periods. A sample master schedule board is part of the Christian School Resource Kit [CSRK 8.22]. After scheduling a student in a class, place a tally mark on the board so others know the total enrollment of the class. These tally marks form the basis for adding or deleting a class. Place the room capacity under each room number. Classrooms assigned for specific subjects may be adjusted based on the number of students enrolled. The maximum capacity is the number of students permitted based on square footage requirements.

Schedule Form

Design a schedule form where students can indicate which classes they desire to take. These are then tallied on the master board. After the first year of operation, adding a pre-registration procedure will help the school better estimate the classes and number of sections needed for the upcoming year [CSRK 8.23].

Scheduling Timeline

The following scheduling steps are presented for your considera-tion.[22]

November – December
Identify Curriculum Needs

- Identify college or university entrance requirements.
- Establish graduation requirements using state standards as mini-mal requirements.
- Review proposals to add or delete courses.
- Analyze staff qualifications to teach courses.

January
Collect Preliminary Information

- Calculate anticipated enrollment data for each grade level by surveying present student body and adding the number of new students expected to enroll.
- Survey students to see which courses they desire to take.
- Review current staff requirements in view of anticipated enroll-ment changes.
- Evaluate facility needs.
- Ask for staff to identify which subjects they desire to teach.
- Prepare a list of courses to be offered next year.

February
Inform students and Parents

- Prepare a student/parent handbook listing curricular programs.
- Use homeroom classes to inform students of possible subject changes next year.

March
Preliminary Registration

- Distribute preliminary registration forms to students.
- Conduct individual conferences for students with special pro-gram challenges.
- Provide list of all courses to be offered to students.
- Have students complete preliminary registration forms and

obtain parent signature before turning the form in at the office.

- From the pre-registration forms, calculate the number of class sections needed for each subject.
- Review all class offerings in terms of reasonable class size.

April – May
Prepare Master Schedule

- Begin work on a master schedule immediately after the results of enrollments by subject are completed from the preliminary registration.
- Schedule subjects by teacher and period.
- Balance subjects by reasonable class size and appropriateness of period offerings.
- Identify single periods that do not conflict with other single period subjects.
- Place all required and double-period subjects next on the schedule. Give preference to subjects that appear in multiple sections.
- Place the remaining elective subjects that appear in multiple sections.
- Check room assignments for possible conflicts.
- Provide teachers with copies of a tentative master schedule for review. Have each teacher initial her schedule, indicating approval. Consider all staff assignments as tentative and subject to change due to the uncertainty of enrollment, staff resignations and new members with special instructional expertise.
- Allow flexibility in the schedule for late enrollees.
- Develop final draft of the schedule.
- Check for conflicts. Do not schedule in the same period those single-period subjects that show a large number of conflicts.

May – July
Schedule Students

- Assign each student by period and each teacher for the subject that he chose during preliminary registration.
- Prepare list of all students who signed for advanced classes and obtain approval of teachers who will teach these advanced classes.
- Schedule seniors and juniors first so they can complete their requirements.
- Keep tallies of each class to determine how fast they are filling

and prepare to open additional class sections.

- Send schedules home for student review and parent signature and request they be returned to the office [CSRK 8.24].

July – August
Finalize Schedule

- Send final schedule home to students. Retain a copy in the school office filed by A to Z within each grade level.
- Prepare for new student orientation/registration.
- Make final adjustments in master schedule.

September
First Day Procedures

- Have all students report to first period class and all students without schedules to report to a central location.
- Manually schedule new students.
- Have any returning students with schedule conflicts come to the office.
- Post the first week's schedule in hallways.
- Post master schedule in hallways.
- Delay for two weeks any requests for course changes. This delay prevents "shopping" for courses and teachers. Make all changes on a "change of schedule form" and require teacher and parent signatures [CSRK 8.25].

New schools should construct the master schedule with as much flexibility as possible. Offering basic courses that are available in public schools should be standard; for example, math, science, social studies, and language arts. Schedule as many single section courses as needed to accommodate your enrollment estimates of the number of students at each grade level. Prepare to offer double sections as needed as well as combining classes, should enrollment not meet expectations.

When there are not enough students to offer a full range of courses, consider offering upper-level courses on a rotating basis; for example, chemistry and physics, World History and U.S. History. However, offering alternate year courses may cause challenges for transfer students, that is, some students may need a specific course not offered but required for graduation or college entrance. If this becomes the case, consider offering the course through correspondence. In some communities, courses are available over satellite or educational television.

Construct Other Schedules

Two other schedules require careful attention. These are student activities and assemblies. Consider the following suggestions:

Student Activity Schedule

Since most Christian schools enroll students from various locations in and around the community, you will increase your student participation by designing one period for student activities. This action also frees teachers to act as advisors. For example, you may consider having all clubs meet on a Tuesday or every other Tuesday.

Schedule school athletic activities when they will not interfere with the classroom program and preferably scheduled on weekends. In addition, schedule "pep" rallies during the last period of the school day. (For more information on student activities, see Step 9.)

Assembly Schedule

Every school should have a master calendar with all important school events of the year. Place all assemblies on the master calendar. These might include assemblies to welcome new students, patriotic commemoration, Veteran's Day, special holiday programs, induction of members into the National Honor Society, special award assemblies, homecoming and election of student government. Consider music productions, panel discussions, forums, special films, guest speakers, school rallies, honoring of community ministers whose churches have students in your school, all boys and all girls assemblies, fine arts and assemblies for reviewing policies and procedures.

Computer Scheduling

Aided by the introduction of the microcomputer, many of the challenges in scheduling can be eliminated. In addition, what was once a long, laborious task can be accomplished in a matter of minutes.

Various parameters are loaded into the computer, such as staff, course structure, length of class periods, size of class, rooms, special periods and number of sections. Schedules can be printed and automatically addressed to be sent home to parents.

Pitfalls to Avoid

1. Constantly changing curriculum. Direct efforts toward stabilizing curriculum change. Many times curriculum innovation and enhancements are a direct result of teacher influence. Unless these changes are integrated into the curriculum structure, when teacher turnover occurs, the innovations and enhancements may be lost. A continual in-service program focused on curriculum innovations is a viable solution to the teacher turnover issue. Furthermore, convincing students, parents and teachers of the value of a curriculum innovation helps ensure its continuation in face of changes in leadership.

Often, curriculum innovations are made as a direct result of new funding sources. These sources may include donations from corporations, grants from foundations, state and federal agencies, or even special school fund-raising activities. Often, when the funding source dries up, so do the programs. Adjusting the school budget to accommodate these innovations will ensure that they continue when special funding is no longer available. Furthermore, the longevity of curriculum innovations requires linking these innovations to the school's long-term goals and course objectives.

Some schools also fall into the trap of making curriculum changes for the wrong reasons. Regardless of the curriculum chosen, at some point in time, there will be those (parents, teachers, church elders, special interest groups) who want to change what they expect children to learn, and "all too frequently curriculum improvement proposals are adopted and implemented without a valid assessment of the real need for improvement."[23]

Solve this challenge by basing curriculum changes on whether the school is achieving its established educational goals. Adequately determining if goals are achieved requires assessment and evaluation of several factors, such as student achievement, adequacy of instructional methods, activities, materials and equipment, time for learning and quality of the learning environment.

Each school should establish its own criteria for determining the adequacy of the curriculum. The following criteria have been adapted from Krajewski.[24] Mark those that are true of your school.

☐ Educational goals and objectives of the school are identified, clearly stated and prioritized.

☐ Subjects taught relate directly to instructional objectives of the school and help promote their attainment.

☐ The subject matter content meets the needs of all pupils.

☐ The school teaches those subjects expected by the community it serves.

☐ All subjects reflect the integrated Word of God.

☐ The curriculum is within the legal and regulatory framework of state requirements.

☐ The content of the curriculum provides for the learning of attitudes, values, knowledge and skills and character traits.

☐ Instructional methods and subject matter content are appropriate for the interests, abilities and developmental levels of pupils.

☐ Learning objectives are clearly stated and consistent with school goals.

☐ Pupils adequately learn what is taught.

☐ Subject matter is articulated between grade levels, correlates among subjects and is comprehensive in scope.

☐ Time periods during the school day are adequate to provide for teacher planning.

☐ Time schedules are consistent with development levels of pupils.

☐ The physical environment contributes to effective learning.

☐ Instructional resources and materials are adequate and available when needed.

☐ The school makes use of available human resources from within and outside the school.

2. Making curriculum decisions without consulting those involved in its implementation. Sometimes administrators and school boards consider curriculum development so important as not to involve staff in curriculum decisions. Failing to include staff in curriculum decisions that affect them is asking for resistance when it comes time for implementing the curriculum. Most teachers agree that they are more enthusiastic about the new curriculum when they have had an opportunity to participate in its selection or construction.

If the curriculum is to change, the teachers must change; the quality of change relates directly to how convinced teachers are of its worth. Therefore, schools can facilitate change by involving teachers in curriculum development. When the perceptions and motivations of the classroom teacher are considered, any curriculum decision will be successfully implemented [CSRK 8.26].

3. Failing to provide for quality time on learning. Keep instructional time inviolate. One of the frequently voiced complaints of teachers is interruption of instruction, such as PA announcements, changed schedules, unannounced visitors, last minutes activities, and so on. Effective school research correlates time spent on a particular subject or skill to academic achievement. A scheduled time for announcements is preferable. Eliminate all other interruptions.

When high school teachers were asked, "How much time do you feel you waste each period to non-instructional tasks?" most teachers answered, "Between three and seven minutes." When a high school teacher spends five minutes per class period on non-learning, as the result of interruptions, by the end of the year the students would have lost fifteen instructional days.

4. Failing to establish a homework policy. On an average, teachers assign about ten hours of homework each week—about two hours per day. High school seniors report they spend only four to five hours a week doing homework and 10 percent say they do none or have none assigned.

Most curriculum guides will specify the amount of homework. However, the actual amount of time each student spends doing homework varies from student to student and from household to household. For example, we have found that when students and parents are asked how much time is spent doing homework, parents overestimate the amount reported by their children by a two to one factor. That is to say, when Johnny's parents report he spends 50 minutes doing his English assignment, Johnny reports only 25 minutes. It appears that out of the 50 minutes the parents thought it took Johnny to complete his English homework, 25 minutes was wasted time. Schools might consider a parent-teacher workshop that focuses on helping parents reduce the homework hassle and training students how to maximize homework time..

Schools with no homework quantity policy run the risk of all six or seven high school teachers assigning 50 minutes of homework all on the same night. For this to be the pattern rather than the exception, is to ask for trouble.

Design a homework policy that reflects quality. Assigning homework for homework sake is not justified. Students are more willing to complete their homework when they perceive it as useful. To be useful, homework must receive as much attention by the teacher in planning as preparing for the lesson. Treat homework as importantly as you treat daily instruction. Consider requiring students to maintain an assignment notebook. (See *Student Study and Assignment Guide*).

NOTE: *Homework assignments should not only supplement the classroom lesson, they should teach students to be independent learners. Furthermore, homework is most useful when teachers give prompt feedback.*

5. Failing to properly group students. "Ability-grouping" or "multiple-tracking" is a common practice in public and private schools. The process involves identifying students who exhibit similar characteristics, such as learning style, skill level, ability level, achievement level and interest. The basic assumption is that students who are more alike (homogeneous) will learn more effectively because the teaching-learning situation will be more structured to their ability to learn.

Although ability grouping makes it easier for teachers to organize and prepare materials and to teach, research clearly indicates that such grouping "shows no consistent positive values for helping students generally, or particular groups of students, to achieve more scholastically or to experience more effective learning conditions."[25] In addition, homogeneous ability grouping has unfavorable affective results on those whose placement is in average and below average groups.

The best classroom grouping is a heterogeneous group created to represent a cross-section of all students available for a particular grade level. Attempt to balance classes according to number, gender, achievement level, student compatibility and parent requests.

The Christian School Resource Kit contains a process for balancing classes [CSRK 8.27]. Computer programs are also available to assist in this task. One program is *Elementary Class Assigner* by MacKinney Systems, Inc.

Group students within their heterogeneous classroom for instructional purposes; for example, reading. As students master objectives, reorganize the group. In fact, skill groups and achievement groups should be flexible enough to be reorganized daily if needed.

6. Failing to make provision for slow learners. As long as there are individual differences in learning, there will be students who will be unable to master the content within a standard amount of time; for example, nine months. These students are usually identified as below average or as the slow learning group. Similarly, students who learn at a faster rate are viewed as above average, advanced learners, even as gifted students.

How schools deal with this range of individual differences varies. Below average learners are given special helps classes, sent to resource rooms, or assigned to tutors and so forth. Some schools lower learning and graduation expectations and use multiple tracking. For example, a high school may offer a vocational track and a college preparatory track. The merits of each of these strategies is beyond the scope of this book.

NOTE: *We do believe that it should be the school's goal and the teachers' responsibility to manage curriculum options and learning opportunities so all students develop their God-given talents to the fullest extent.*

7. Failing to establish promotional and retention policies. One of the biggest challenges facing teachers and administrators is establishing an acceptable promotion and retention policy. As long as schools are organized as graded-schools, there will be those who do not qualify for advancement to the next grade.

Given the large body of educational research supporting the negative aspects of retention, schools are modifying their promotion policies to reduce the number of non-promotions. Think of retention this way. Suppose you need to drive from Tulsa, Oklahoma, to Dallas, Texas. Under normal conditions and with an adequate vehicle and plenty of gas, you should make Dallas in five hours. Let us say, after five hours, you only reach Oklahoma City just 100 miles from Tulsa, for whatever reason—car malfunction, detours in the road, accident, etc. Should you be sent all the way back to Tulsa and told to start all over?

Unless your car is repaired, the road fixed, more gas put in the tank or detours eliminated, there is no assurance you will make it to Dallas a second time. Retaining a student at a grade level for a second year without attempting to deal with the reasons affecting his rate of learning gives no assurance that the student will be any more successful on the second trip.

When a student fails to advance as expected, it is possible that the fault rests as much with the school and teacher as with the student. Dr. Bruce Wilkinson, author of *The 7 Laws of the Learner*, states, "It is the responsibility of the teacher to do everything in his power to cause the student to learn."[26] Consider the following strategies:

Assessment. Incorporate a system that accurately assesses individual and group progress towards achieving curriculum objectives (prescribed learner outcomes). As soon as it is evident that students are not making progress, look for reasons within the entire teaching-learning environment, not just the student [CSRK 8.28].

Class Periods. Consider extending the class period, school day, time allocated to a specific skill, or even the school year (summer classes) to accommodate individual differences in learning rate. If summer school in not an option, develop an individual study program for the student over the summer, where the student can work on mastering the objectives that were missed; then, re-evaluate the retention decision before the start of the new school year.

Instructional Adjustment. Permit teachers to adjust instructional programs, materials and methods to better meet the growth pattern of their pupils.

Reading Materials. Provide reading materials within each classroom that cover a wide range of difficulty over several "grade levels."

Class Size. Promote smaller class sizes for teachers. Encourage them to adjust their teaching methods and to focus on small group and individual skill development.

Communication. Keep parents regularly informed about the growth and progress of their children in all aspects of the school curriculum (daily or weekly if needed) and solicit their support and assistance in helping their child(ren) achieve specific learner outcomes.

Word of God. Bring the uncompromised Word of God to bear on academic challenges. Declare Ephesians 2:10 over your students, "**For** (your students) **are his workmanship, created in Christ Jesus unto good works....**" Part of the good works of students are good grades.

Help students to guard their words. Words can help create within them a conquering attitude thus stimulating faith rather then doubt. Their belief, coupled with God's promises, gives your students God's ability and power to overcome any homework assignment, special project, quiz, nine-week test, or any other school challenge.[27]

Training. Sponsor a school-wide in-service, conference or video series, such as *The 7 Laws of the Learner, The 7 Laws of the Teacher,* and *Teaching With Style,* to equip your teaching staff to meet the needs of their students.

Computerization. Investigate using computer-aided instruction in a wide variety of subjects. For example, tutorial software is designed to teach a subject as well as drill over it. Programs are intended to stand alone as an instructional entity in the curriculum. Thus, the computer is the teacher for a particular skill or area of information.

Use tutorial programs in the classroom under the direction of the teacher, or send them home with the student to be monitored by the parent. Some schools include a variety of tutorial programs in their school library, making them available for checkout by students and parents.

Other programs can assist with drill and practice. Incorporate these programs to supplement the regular instruction. For example, concepts which have been presented in the classroom by the teacher can be practiced and refined by the computer (a good example is *Skills Bank II*). For more information on computer-aided and computer-assisted instruction, see *Microcomputer Applications for Christian Educators.*

8. Failing to challenge students who are fast learners. Schools who are alert to individual differences will quickly identify students who learn faster than normal expectations. Planning for these students requires extra effort. Consider the following strategies:

Avoid busy work. When students have completed regularly assigned work, avoid assigning busy work. Rewarding working faster with more time consuming work results in productive time being wasted and the gifted students adapting to mediocrity.[28]

Prepare enrichment opportunities. Arranging rewarding enrichment opportunities requires careful preplanning on the part of a teacher. Assign a special teacher the responsibility of designing and supervising individual enrichment projects. This will help avoid using valuable time of the classroom teacher whose primary responsibility is toward 25 to 29 other students who have not yet mastered the content. When the budget does not allow for a special teacher, give a teacher's aide or team of volunteers this task.

Organize a peer-tutoring program. Enhance the success of a peer-tutoring program. Consider the following three simple principles.

- Identify the exact purpose of the program and clearly communicate the program to everyone involved—tutor, those tutored, teachers and parents.

- Before a tutor assumes tutoring responsibility, they should have mastered the basis of the subject to be taught.

- A reward system should be in place to acknowledge the tutor's work. At the high school level, academic credit is an appropriate reward.

In the final analysis, "the value of the experience to the tutor and the tutored student must be weighed against the cost of holding back the faster learner from proceeding at his or her own pace. Unless a benefit is being realized by both learners, peer-tutoring can become explosive."[29]

Provide accelerated courses. Accelerated courses allow advanced students to proceed through the same content at a faster speed. However, do not skip content steps, especially when the material skipped is prerequisite to subsequent work.

9. Not planning for curriculum development. Curriculum development includes evaluating current curriculum as it relates to established goals and objectives, developing new designs, implementing and evaluating curriculum. Although much of the content that is taught in the Christian school is the same year after year, various factors demand additions or modifications to the existing curricula. These include: shifts in student achievement levels, societal conditions, advancements in technology, curriculum innovations, expectations of accrediting associations and state mandated competency testing, to name a few.

For example, a few years ago most Christian schools had no need to include sex education, AIDS awareness and drug education as part of the curricula. Today, these programs are not only a requirement of many states but an absolute must to provide the knowledge students need to live free of these destructive devices.

Furthermore, students in Christian schools are being bombarded by a host of ungodly influences—feminism, materialism, homosexuality, unwholesome media, (television, movies, video), pornography, new age, for which the church, parents and Christian school need to combat. The Christian school curriculum needs to address these issues.

A final example of the need for curricula development centers around advancements in technology. One of these advancements is computer technology. As we point out in our book, *Microcomputer Applications for Christian Educators*,

> "Computer technology is becoming a very real part of everyone's life...today, computers are a vital ingredient in the learning experiences of any career. Those graduating from our Christian schools need to be computer literate so they will have the same opportunities as their public school counterparts: to be successful in a computer rich society, full of minicomputers, desktop computers, laptop PC's, notebook PC's and pocket computers."[30]

Computer literacy needs to be a vital part of the Christian school curricula. Without this literacy, Christian school students "will find themselves becoming more dependent, not just on computers, but other people—those who have access to computers and know how to use them."[31]

Father, I ask for Your wisdom in developing educational goals and measurable objectives. Let me clearly know the curricula plans You have for this school. Let any idea that would exalt itself above Your perfect will for this school be brought down. Provide the staff we need for every grade level and for every subject, in the name of Jesus. Amen.

The purpose of the Christian school curriculum is the fulfillment of 2 Timothy 3:17: "That the man of God may be perfect, thoroughly furnished unto all good works."

Christian School Resource Kit

8.1   Course/Subject Overview

8.2   Christian School Publishers Directory

8.3   Textbook Control Card

Endnotes

1　H. W. Byrne. *A Christian Approach to Education.* 2nd Edition. Milford, MI: Mott Media, 1977, p. 90.

2　International Christian Accreditation Association. *Accreditation Handbook Standards and Procedures: Elementary and Secondary Christian Schools.* Tulsa, OK: Oral Roberts University Educational Fellowship, 1991, p. 52.

3　Joe Mercier. "The Principle Approach." Paper presented at the Oral University Education Fellowship's annual administrative and teacher conference, July, 1987. At this time, Mr. Mercier was principal of Bethany Christian School, a school using the principle approach in several subjects and at different grade levels. For another example of an entire curriculum based on the principle approach, contact Dixie Thompson at Calvary Assembly School, 1199 Clay Street, Winter

Park, FL 32789; (407) 644-1199.

4   Eugene R. Howard. *School Discipline Desk Book.* West Nyack, NY: Parker Publishing Company, Inc., 1978, p. 144.

5   *Ibid.* p. 150-151.

6   Donald F. Weinstein. *Administrator's Guide to Curriculum Mapping.* Englewood Cliffs, NJ: Prentice-Hall, Inc., 1986, p. 108.

7   Ruth C. Haycock. *Bible Truths for School Subjects.* Whittier, CA: ACSI, 1981 p. x, Vol. III.

8   Robert M. Miller. "Implementing the Christian Philosophy in Textbook Selection and Curriculum Development" in Paul A. Kienel, ed. *The Philosophy of Christian School Education.* Whittier, CA: ACSI, 1978. p. 126.

9   Lee C. Reno. "Importance of Curriculum" in Claude E. Schindler, Jr. and Pacheco Pyle. *Sowing for Excellence.* Whittier, CA: ACSI, 1987, p. 162.

10   Donald F. Weinstein, *op. cit.*, p. 29.

11   A. A. Baker. *The Successful Christian School.* Pensacola, FL: A Beka Book Publications, 1979, p. 135.

12   Robert J. Krajewski, John S. Martin, and John C. Walden. *The Elementary School Principalship.* New York, NY: Holt, Rinehart, and Winston, 1983, p. 112.

13   International Christian Accreditation Association. *op. cit.*, p. 51.

14   Oklahoma State Department of Education. *School Laws of Oklahoma.* Oklahoma City, OK: Oklahoma State Department of Education, 1986, Section 11, p. 6.

15   *What Works: Research About Teaching and Learning.* Washington DC: U.S. Department of Education, 1986, p. 49.

16   Byron W. Hansford. *Guidebook for School Principals.* New York, NY: The Ronald Press Co., 1961, p. 74.

17   Michael A. Lorber and Walter D. Pierce. *Objectives, Methods and Evaluation for Secondary Teaching.* Englewood Cliffs, NJ: Prentice Hall, 1990, p. 129.

18   Don Petry. Teled International Ministries. P.O. Box 62442, Virginia Beach, VA 23462; (804) 420-4680.

19   Larry W. Hughes and Gerald C. Ubben. *The Elementary Principal's Handbook: A Guide to Effective Action.* 2nd. Edition. Boston, MA: Allyn and Bacon, Inc., 1984, p. 151.

20   *Ibid.*, p. 203.

21   Don Stewart. *Educational Malpractice: The Big Gamble in Our Schools.* Westminster, CA: Slate Services, Publishers, 1971, p. 172.

22   Stanley W. Williams. *Educational Administration in Secondary*

Schools. New York, NY: Holt, Rinehart and Winston, 1964, p. 36.

23 Stewart, *op. cit.*, p. 185.

24 Krajewski, Martin and Walden. *op. cit.*, p.116.

25 Hughes and Ubben, *op. cit.*, p. 102.

26 Bruce H. Wilkinson. *The 7 Laws of the Learner.* Textbook Edition. Sisters, OR: Multnomah Press, 1992, p. 30.

27 Dennis M. Demuth. *Student Study and Assignment Guide.* Tulsa, OK: Victory Christian School, 1982, p. 2.

28 David Pratt. *Curriculum Design and Development.* New York, NY: Harcourt, Brace, Jovanovich, Publishers, 1980, p. 348.

29 *Ibid.*, p. 351.

30 Dennis M. Demuth and Carol M. Demuth. *Microcomputer Applications for Christian Educators.* Tulsa, OK: DEL Publications, 1992, p. 51.

31 *Ibid.*

References

A Beka Book Publications, 125 Saint John Street, Box 18000, Pensacola, FL. 32523; (800) 874-BEKA.

Accelerated Christian Education (ACE), P.O. Box 1438, Garland, TX 75041.

Alpha Omega Publications, P.O. Box 3153, Tempe, Arizona 85281; (800) 821-4443.

American Christian History Institute, 1569 Mural Drive, Claremont, CA 91711.

Bob Jones University Press, Greenville, SC. 29614.

Demuth, Dennis M. and Demuth, Carol M. *Christian School Administration: Administrator and Teacher Guidelines.* Tulsa, OK: DEL Publications, 1993.

Demuth, Dennis M. and Demuth, Carol M. *Substitute Teacher: Standing in the Gap.* Tulsa, OK: DEL Publications, In preparation.

Educational Research Analysts, The Mel Gablers, P.O. Box 7518, Longview, TX 75601.

Foundation for American Christian Education, Box 27035, San Francisco, CA 94127.

Heritage Institute Ministries, P.O. Box 1353, Buzzards Bay, MA 92532.

Jehle, Paul W. Heritage Institute Ministries. P.O. Box 1353, Buzzards Bay, MA 92532.

Pilgrim Institute, 53549 Gumwood Road, Grander, IN 46530.

Sing, Spell, Read & Write. International Learning Systems, P.O. Box 16032, Chesapeake, VA 23328; (800) 321-8322.

Slater, Rosalie J. and Hall, Verna M. *Teaching and Learning America's Christian History.* American Christian History Institute, 1569 Mural Drive, Claremont, CA 91711.

Wagner, David. Abundant Life Christian School, 4901 E. Buckeye Rd., Madison, WI 53716; (608) 221-1520.

Walk Through the Bible Ministries. *Teaching With Style*; *The 7 Laws of the Learner*; *The 7 Laws of the Teacher* Video series. P.O. Box 80587, Atlanta, GA 30058; (404) 458-9300.

Ward, David. *Zoe Health Fitness.* Tulsa, OK: Victory Christian School, 7700 South Lewis Avenue, 1983; (918) 499-9199.

Computer Software

Calendar Creator Plus. Power Up Software, P.O. Box 7600, San Mateo, CA 94403.

Elementary Class Assigner. MacKinney Systems Inc., 2740 South Glenstone, Suite 103, Springfield, MO 65804; (417) 882-8012.

GradeEase by Softwarr in *PC-SIG Encyclopedia of Shareware.* 4th Edition. Sunnyvale, CA: PC-SIG, Inc., 1991, p. 528.

Grading Assistant by Jim Reid in *PC-SIG Encyclopedia of Shareware.* 4th Edition. Sunnyvale, CA: PC-SIG, Inc., 1991, p. 529.

Intergrade. The School System. McGraw-Hill School Systems, 20 Ryan Ranch Road, Monterey, CA 93940; (800) 663-0544.

Noble Gradebook by Noble Software Co. in *PC-SIG Encyclopedia of Shareware.* 4th Edition. Sunnyvale, CA: PC-SIG, Inc. 1991, p. 530.

Skills Bank II. Skills Bank Corporation, 15 Governors Court, Baltimore, MD 21207; (800) 451-5726.

Textbook Inventory by Barry Alpern in PC-SIG Encyclopedia of Shareware. 4th Edition. Sunnyvale, CA: PC-SIG, Inc., 1991.

The School System. McGraw-Hill School Systems, 20 Ryan Ranch Road, Monterey, CA 93940; (800) 663-0544.

STEP 9

ESTABLISH ANCILLARY PROGRAMS

Other areas of planning include athletics, food services, health services, library services, parent-teacher fellowship, pupil personnel services and transportation services. The degree to which these services function smoothly and operate efficiently will influence the degree to which the Christian school attracts and retains quality families.

Athletics

John Churdar, a contributing author in *Some Light on Christian Education*, writes,

> "The inclusion of athletics in the educational program of a Christian high school (and elementary school) is expected: parents expect it, students expect it, and most educators expect it. Athletics probably contribute more to 'school spirit' than any other single factor."[1]

In surveying 144 principals and approximately 7,000 students regarding extracurricular activities, the National Federation of State High School Associations found the following:

- 95 percent believe that the sports program contributed to the development of the school spirit among students.
- 99 percent felt that good citizenship was fostered by participation in such activities as sports, debate, drama, cheerleading, and music.
- 95 percent said that participation provides lessons that cannot be learned in the traditional classroom.[2]

There are two major options for athletic programs: intramural and interschool sports. The quality of these programs has a direct relationship to program philosophies, objectives, organization and administration, finances, parent support and facilities.

Identify Program Philosophy and Objectives

Claude Schindler, Pancheco Pyle and Steve Karnehm have written an excellent book for Christian schools titled, *The Role of Athletics in the Christian School*. Every school needs a copy of this valuable resource tool. They recommend the following philosophy of athletics:

257

"The Christian approach to athletics must stem directly from the school's Christian philosophy of education, since it is foundational to everything done in the school system. A brief philosophical statement of athletics could be to develop the spiritual part of the athlete so the Holy Spirit is in control and directing his mind and body"[3]

In addition, a school must establish a well-defined set of objectives. These objectives provide direction for planning, criteria for evaluation and a foundation for keeping the program in proper balance. Consider the following program objectives. The athletic program helps all students:

- Possess Christ-like character qualities and to express them through athletics;
- Develop habits, skills and attitudes that will allow for unlimited achievement;
- Learn rules and regulations governing a variety of sports;
- Learn the techniques and fitness required for exemplary performance in a particular sport;
- Develop a good self-image;
- Learn diligence in participation and practice;
- Develop positive attitudes and interests toward physical and mental well-being;
- Learn to set high goals and standards, not only in athletics, but for their personal lives as well;
- Learn sportsmanship and self-control; and
- Learn to share the "Good News" of Jesus Christ, both on and off the playing field and be a living epistle.

NOTE: *A well-designed athletic program will minister to the individual needs of the participants as well as spectators.*

Select Competition

The statement of philosophy and program objectives will determine the type of school to compete against. The options are Christian, secular private, or public. It is not unusual for a Christian school to limit its athletic participation to only Christian schools. One of the deciding factors is a "basic philosophical concern about becoming unequally yoked with unbelievers or unnecessarily exposing young people to unwholesome behavior or immoral influences."[4] Unfortunately, unless a Christian school can effectively control the total life experience of its athletes twenty-four hours a day, athletes will face these influences through their peers, radio, television, movies, video, books, magazines and music.

Further complicating school participation with only Christian schools is finding enough Christian schools for competition. This is especially the situation for schools in smaller-sized communities. If this is the case, investigate competitive outlets through club teams and community-wide programs, such as soccer, basketball, softball and volleyball.

Other schools choose to compete with private and public schools. The thinking behind this choice is a ministry outreach opportunity to the teams they play and their fans. Pre- and post-game entertainment and half-time programs provide excellent opportunities to share Christ. Furthermore, opportunities for athletes and coaches to share Christ on a one-to-one basis are abundant in most sports.

Schools with evangelism as an objective should provide several team training sessions focusing on personal evangelism to instill confidence in sharing their faith. Schindler writes,

> "In some sports, our athletes see certain opponents many times during the course of the season. This fact in itself gives a special opportunity to some. A relationship can be built over the season and the Christian gets many chances to present a consistent testimony. The opposing athlete sees Christianity in action many times. After several conversations, tracts and friendly encounters, our athlete gets a chance to present Christ in a different way. Again, our athletes are taught the value of a consistent testimony, personal involvement in others' lives and preparation for outreach. Look for opportunities to teach kids outreach. Strive to make them aware of these opportunities. Witnessing in athletics in just like anywhere else—once it catches on, people enjoy doing it. We have found that many of our kids, after some experience, place that at the top of the priority list for a game or meet. Many of our kids who we never would have thought to be evangelists, have had the repeated joy of asking, 'Would you like to ask Christ to come into your life right now?' What a joy!"[5]

In addition to providing a witness in secular school systems, participation in the secular arena offers the following advantages:

1   Increases exposure of the school to the local media.

2   Proves credibility among peers and the community.

3   Provides opportunity for play or recognition through all-star and all-conference teams.

4   Furthers recognition of the school among colleges and universities.

5   Provides additional motivation for the school to better itself. For example, programs, coaching, facilities, etc.

Provide for Organization and Administration

Effective organization and administration are essential to producing a quality athletic program. Regardless of the size of the school, finding competent coaches, creating a balanced schedule, providing adequate facilities and finances are continual challenges. Success in these three tasks has a direct influence on whether the athletic program will meet its objectives.

Selecting Coaches

Coaches have a profound influence upon the lives of young people. Selecting a coach is as important as selecting a classroom teacher. Not only should a coach meet the same standards for employment, they also need to exhibit the following specific competencies:

- Foster a coaching philosophy compatible with that of the school.
- Meet qualifications to coach the assigned sport.
- Be familiar with the risks involved in the sport.
- Be able to respond to a medical emergency.
- Be willing to investigate college scholarships and post-high school athletic opportunities for students.
- Use and maintain safe playing facilities and equipment.
- Be able to adequately match opponents according to age, weight and maturity.
- Be willing to work with athletes to maintain eligibility.
- Set a Christ-like example at all times.
- Build Christian character in the lives of athletes through personal demonstration of these attributes.

Scheduling

Scheduling should be the responsibility of the athletic director with final review by the administrator. Smaller schools can appoint the coach with the most experience to act as scheduling coordinator. In any case, scheduling should be the responsibility of one person. This action helps avoid duplication of effort and improves coordination with the total school program. Scheduling policies and procedures should be written down and communicated to all coaching staff.

Offering a particular sport during a particular season depends upon the athletic association or conference. Most have three seasons—fall, winter and spring. The conference also determines which sports it will offer. Figure 9.1 presents common sport seasons:

Figure 9.1 Sport Seasons

Fall	Gymnastics
Soccer	Swimming
Football	Cheerleading
Volleyball	**Spring**
Cross Country	Soccer
Cheerleading	Baseball/Softball
Tennis	Track
Winter	Tennis
Basketball	Golf
Wrestling	

Consider the following scheduling tips:

1 Schedule no more than two games in any week.

2 Travel during the week only if less than one hour from school.

3 Travel on weekends (Friday & Saturday) for longer trips. Provide sufficient time on Saturday to return at a decent hour so athletes are rested for Sunday.

4 Schedule games and scrimmages to minimize time spent out of class.

5 Require coaches to clear all scheduling of practices, games and scrimmages through the Athletic Director or administration.

6 Require at least a full day advance notice of games or scrimmages requiring students to be out of classes.

7 Provide students and parents with a written schedule and itinerary.

8 Use written athletic contracts when athletic contests involve many fans and have financial implications [CSRK 9.1].

Girls Sports

An ongoing challenge facing public and private schools is providing a quality girls program. The goal of every Christian school should be to maintain an acceptable balance between boys and girls sports in areas of coaching expertise, scheduling, use of facilities and adequacy of equipment. Of special concern are the legal ramifications of unequal pay for coaching.

Policies and Procedures

A carefully planned procedural guide facilitates administrating the athletic program. As a minimum include:

- The vision, philosophy and program objectives
- Coaching philosophy and responsibilities (job descriptions)
- A description of the program and sports offered
- Keeping of records and statistics
- Scheduling responsibilities
- Conduct at practices and games
- Transportation and travel
- Care and maintenance of facilities, equipment and uniforms
- Practices
- Participation fees
- Lettering and awards
- Pre-Post game clean up
- Coordination with other church programs (for example, church leagues)
- Teacher supervision at games
- Eligibility and probation
- Ticketing and concessions
- Promotional fund-raising
- Physical exams [CSRK 9.2]
- Insurance coverage and parent release [CSRK 9.3]
- Game Day procedures and early dismissal from school. Develop a "Before Game," "During Game" and "After Game" checklist [CSRK 9.4].
- Tournament organization
- Tryout procedures
- Posting of team rosters [CSRK 9.5]
- Athletic application process [CSRK 9.6]
- Transportation and travel [CSRK 9.7]

Arrange for Adequate Funding

Building a quality athletic program requires adequate financial resources. Sources of income include:

- **Participation fees.** Establish a per sport fee; for example, $25 and $100 maximum per family fee. Require the payment of fees before a student can play in a game.

- **Gate receipts.** Base game tickets at the going rate, such as $3 for adults, $1 to $2 for students. Admit children six and under free. Some schools use a student activities fee and a family pass system. For one fee, students and family members can attend all athletic events.

- **Concessions.** Popcorn, pop, hot dogs, chips and cookies are great winners. Purchase your own popcorn machine and get Pepsi or Coke to loan the pop dispensers. You pay for the beverage gas, pop and cups. Working with a single vendor, such as Pepsi, could result in significant donations for sports equipment as well as pop used for other special events.

- **Sales.** T-shirts, jackets, athletic bags, bleacher seats, refillable soft drink containers are good winners.

- **Special fund-raisers.** Jog-A-Thon, car washes and silent auctions can be systematically expanded over time, resulting in a substantial level of income. One private school raises over $150,000 annually on a city-wide auction.

- **Programs, advertisements and sponsorship.** Consider approaching parents and members of the sponsoring church for sponsorships before going into the community. Having several committed sponsors will increase the chances of others to become sponsors.

- **Hosting tournaments.** Begin scheduling one major tournament per year. Make plans well in advance of the event.

Every effort should be made to hold athletic costs to a minimum. Consider the following suggestions:

1   All elementary and junior high school sport programs should be self-supporting. Students pay one fee for each sport.

2   Negotiate all hotel rates as well as discounts on food.

3   Provide up to a specified dollar amount for meals to be paid by the athletic fund (for example, $2.00 per meal) with the athletes paying the balance.

4   Limit the size of travel teams. For instance, in basketball no more than 17 players for varsity and junior varsity games, 10 for varsity only games, 12 for out-of-town tournaments and 10 for cheerleaders.

5   Limit the amount of out-of-town travel.

6   Rotate uniform replacement in a three- to five-year cycle.

7   Obtain parent and business sponsors for equipment.

8   Issue contracts to officials for several games [CSRK 9.8].

Evaluate the Athletic Program

Provide a comprehensive evaluation of coaches and programs. Check those items that are true of your school.

☐ Program objectives are being accomplished.

☐ All coaches and assistants qualify to coach the assigned sport.

☐ Girls' sports have access to the same resources, proportionately, as boys' sports.

☐ The athletic policies and procedural handbook adequately reflects the way the program operates.

☐ Practice and game schedules do not interfere with the regular school program.

☐ Parents are informed of all road trips and financial expectations [CSRK 9.9]

☐ Efforts are made to promote the Christian philosophy of education through each sport.

☐ Accurate records and statistics are kept of all varsity games.

This list is not inclusive, but the idea is to create an evaluation instrument that will gather the necessary information to adequately evaluate the sports program. A specially designed evaluation instrument is available from the authors that will provide information schools need to strengthen their athletic program. The instrument uses information obtained from students, coaches, teachers and parents and translates this information into objectives for the next school year [CSRK 9.10].

Solicit Help of Parents

Parents are a valuable resource to any sports program. They can assist in almost any aspect of the program. For example, coaching, score keeping, taking tickets, organizing fund-raisers, securing equipment, transporting athletes, preparing facilities, getting scholarships and coordinating sport teams.

A well-organized sports booster club can provide an effective ministry of helps to the athletic director and school administrator. The Christian School Resource Kit contains an outline of a typical booster club, a sample of a booster club membership application and athletic information form [CSRK 9.11].

Provide Adequate Facilities and Equipment

Adequacy of athletic facilities gives to or detracts from a school's ability to provide a quality sports program.[6] As parents and students evaluate the academic program by the condition of the school facilities, they also evaluate the quality of the athletic program by the availability of facilities and of equipment.

A school does not have to spend hundreds of thousands of dollars providing facilities and equipment, but it does have to meet the needs required for the sports offered. Sometimes this requires a creative effort. A case in point is Victory Christian School. During the first five years, the school grew from 269 students to 525. A full-range of sports was available for elementary through high school, yet it had no athletic facilities of its own. The school met this need by renting and leasing facilities within the community, such as city parks, YMCA's and church gyms. When lacking a soccer, baseball and softball field and a place to hold gym class, the school trucked in donated top soil and sod and created a grass playing field over blacktop. Where there is a will to provide facilities, there is a way. And when there seems to be no way, God will help make a way.

Consider the following checklist items:

☐ All competition fields and courts are regulation size. See Figure 9.2.

☐ Expansion, alteration or remodeling of facilities are within building codes.

☐ Facilities and equipment are inspected regularly to ensure safety.

☐ Adequate custodial and volunteer services ensure proper care and maintenance of the facilities and equipment.

☐ Temperature and lighting for indoor playing areas is properly controlled.

☐ Indoor court surfaces provide for minimum injury (floor surfaces that might be appropriate for church auditorium may not be conducive to competitive sports).

☐ Equipment is purchased from vendors who provide the best value for the best money and provide the best service.

☐ All equipment is of good-quality [CSRK 9.12]. Poor quality equipment wears out quickly. As Jensen points out, "Its short life-span is uneconomical in terms of the time and money required for ordering, transporting, and handling. In certain instances, it is a good idea to investigate buying used equipment when investing in large and expensive items. Sometimes equipment used for demonstration pur-

Figure 9.2 Playing Areas by Grade Level

	Baseball Field Dimensions	
Grades	1-6	210 x 210'
Grades	7-9	300 x 300'
Grades	9-12	300 x 300'

	Softball	
Grades	1-6	150 x 150'
Grades	7-9	200 x 200'
Grades	9-12	275 x 275'

	Basketball Court Dimensions	
Grades	1-6	40 x 60'
Grades	7-9	50 x 84'
Grades	9-12	50 x 84'

	Football Playing Field Dimensions	
Grades	9-12	160 x 360' (12 Man)
	9-12	120 x 300' (6 Man)
Grades	7-9	120 x 300' (touch)

	Soccer	
Age	6 and under	40 - 50 yards long / 20 - 30 yards wide
Age	8 and under	50 - 70 yards long / 30 - 50 yards wide
Grades	4-6	70 - 80 yards long / 40 - 50 yards wide
Grades	7-8	80 - 100 yards long / 50 - 70 yards wide
Grades	9 +	100-130 yards long / 50 - 100 yards long

NOTE: *These figures reflect minimum field and court dimensions. Consideration must be given to additional square footage for buffer zones surrounding the fields and courts.*

poses or that has been repossessed can be purchased at a considerable discount."[7]

☐ All equipment is secured and carefully monitored when in use.

☐ Current and accurate inventory records are maintained on all equipment and uniforms [CSRK 9.13].

Initiate an Intramural Program

Most traditional athletic programs serve 10 to 15 percent of the student body. This number can increase to between 20 to 30 percent by instituting a no-cut policy and expanding the number of teams. For example, cheerleading and pompon squads can be "quickly and painlessly doubled to form two instead of one squad for each sport. Squads take turns cheering at games."[8]

Establish a no-cut policy for all athletic teams unless restricted by association rules. This increases the number involved, allows for further development of skills and causes students who are in starting positions to work harder to maintain these positions. Many students give up on any further involvement in a particular sport when cut from a team. Up through 10th grade, form new teams when the number of participants warrants more than one team in any sport, and games can be scheduled. Final decisions on team roosters should be the responsibility of the coaching staff, directly involved in the coaching of their perspective teams with the review of the athletic director or administrator.

Even with these types of changes as many as 70 to 90 percent of the student body may never participate in a sport. A good intramural program would change this situation. There is a place for intramurals in Christian schools at all levels, although the purposes, approaches and content at each level may differ. Jensen presents the following objectives for each level.

Elementary School

Some objectives of intramurals in the elementary school are:
1. To develop movement and basic sport skills.
2. To provide moderate competition in a game setting.
3. To provide opportunities for cooperative play.
4. To foster fun.
5. To provide involvement in democratic processes.
6. To introduce students to play opportunities in a variety of activities.

Junior High or Middle School

Following are some important objectives of junior high school intramural programs:
1. To provide team activities for the enhancement of esprit de corps and group closeness.
2. To present a wide range of activities to satisfy the various levels of ability and the broad range of interests.
3. To provide co-recreational opportunities to aid in socialization.
4. To offer vigorous activities to dissipate nervous energy and contribute to fitness.
5. To give opportunities for individual achievement and recognition.
6. To offer some interesting special events so students can have fun, meet new friends, and enjoy both competition and cooperation.

Senior High School

"The general objective of intramurals at the senior high level is to provide a wide variety of activities, to encourage regular participation in team and individual sports and special events. Skill development, a positive self-image, fun, friendly competition, and the development of interest in life-time sports are all valid reasons for a high school program."[9]

Expand the intramural program by adding activities such as two-person volleyball, six-person volleyball, table tennis, gymnastics, two-person basketball, and arm wrestling. Add singles, doubles, mixed-doubles tennis, horseshoes, bicycle racing, racquetball, handball, bowling and a mini-marathon.

Consider Computer Software

Regardless of the size of your athletic program, the task of coordinating events, scheduling, communication to parents, managing eligibility, inventorying equipment, keeping statistics, submitting rosters, providing programs and creating handbooks can be overwhelming. Consider using a microcomputer to facilitate these tasks. In addition to word processing, spreadsheet and database programs, specialty programs specifically designed for athletic management are available, ranging from inexpensive shareware to full-featured commercial software.

Coaches Secretary is a program that makes coaching easier. Features include: easy and fast entry of all personal, athletic and academic information, player data reports, player transcripts, team rosters, team eligibility reports, and team academic reports, such as G.P.A., SAT and ACT records.

Sports League Management is an excellent shareware program consisting of three modules: Team MgrM contains players; Team MgrC records performance comments on each player; and Team MgrD maintains league and team information. Statistical modules are available for baseball, softball, football and basketball.

PC-Sport is an excellent program for producing tournament and player charts, organizing team information, player data and statistics. It can help organize church leagues, team and individual sport activities.

Food Services

Since the majority of students attending Christian schools commute to school, the school food service program is a primary service. A good cafeteria is an important part of the day for students and staff. It is an opportunity to develop positive attitudes and behavior of children and staff. A well-managed lunchroom will lead to good behavior and high morale. It needs to be a happy, joyful and warm environment. The scope of operation of a food service program is found in answers to the following questions:

Hot Lunch Program

Is it necessary for a new school to have a hot lunch program? A hot lunch program is not necessary for a new school. You may have students bring their lunch and the school provides milk or juice for a beverage. However, if you have adequate facilities for a hot lunch program, your objective would be to provide nutritional and tasty food at the lowest possible cost. Good management and a good cook are essential. The key is to fix nutritional foods that the children like and will eat.

Health Department Approval

Do you have to have approval from the health department? Check with your city Health Department regarding regulations for preparing and serving food. They will visit your site, help determine what you can and cannot do, and what you will need to meet regulations. Most city health departments offer food preparation classes for your food service personnel and other participants, such as students and parents. Expect to pay a small fee for this training. Many junior college and vocational schools offer food preparation courses.

School Menu

If the school has a hot lunch program, should a' la carte menus be available, or should all children to expected to purchase a plate lunch? Schools should plan to serve a "type A" lunch, a meal consisting of lean meat or an alternative, two or more vegetables or fruit, whole grain or enriched bread or an alternative, and fluid milk. The "type A" lunch provides about one-third of the recommended daily allowance (RDA) established by the Food Nutrition Board of the National Research Council and the National Academy of Sciences. Offer a single plate lunch or a single sandwich item at different prices for elementary and secondary students along with soup and salad.

Prepared or Catered

Is food to be prepared in the building or should it be catered? Preparation of food in the building is determined by adequate facilities, as well as permits obtained from the City Health Department. When it is not possible to prepare food in the building, consider catering services. Check with your local health department to see if caters are approved and perform the services in a correct manner. Not everyone is set up properly to cater [CSRK 9.14; 9.15]. Obtain bids from several local vendors. Look for the best quality food, good delivery services and the best quantity prices. Consider ordering such items as chicken, hamburgers, tacos and pizza. Serve these items no more than three days per week, with sack lunches on the remaining two days. Consider installing a juice vending machine.

Open or Closed Lunch Periods

Should the school observe "open" or "closed" lunch periods? This decision may be based on the amount of space available and the location of the school to eating establishments. If you enroll 100-300 students, you need 1,000 to 3,000 square feet in the general eating area, 250-600 square feet in the kitchen area, and 60 to 80 square feet for storage. If space is an issue, consider staggered lunch periods with approximately 1/3 of the students fed at one setting. The key is to have unhurried lunch to allow students to properly eat their food. Consider using separate elementary and secondary lunch periods.

Permit students to go off campus only when adequate eating establishments are available within a reasonable driving distance. This is important so students do not have to speed in getting to a place to eat and then return to campus. If you permit students to go off campus, reserve this privilege for juniors and seniors [CSRK 9.16]. Require students to obtain written parental permission to leave campus, to ride with other students, or to transport other students [CSRK 9.17]. All student vehicles should be properly insured, and this should be attested to in writing. Issue off campus privilege card and require students to sign out each day when leaving campus and then sign back in when returning [CSRK 9.18; CSRK 9.19].

Staffing

How many staff are needed to prepare and serve? As stated earlier, good management and a good cook are essential. You also need healthy, happy personnel who love children and adults. Figure 9.3 shows the number of staff needed to serve students.

Figure 9.3 Staff Servers

Number of Students Served	Staff Needed	Volunteers
0 to 50	1	1
50 to 100	2	1
100 to 200	3	2

NOTE: *You must know the number of students you are serving lunch to and not the number of students in your school, since some bring their lunch and others will choose not to eat.*

Food Costs

How much should I charge students for the meal? The food service program should be on a non-profit, self-supporting basis. Include the following expenses in determining the real cost of the program to establish a fair price per meal:

- Amortization of capital expenditures
- Replacement of equipment
- Utilization costs
- Custodial costs
- Overhead

A typical breakdown in food service operations includes: 60 to 70 percent food costs, 20 to 30 percent personnel costs, and 5 to 15 percent miscellaneous food [CSRK 9.20]. Consider providing both a daily ticket, as well as a weekly ticket. Offer the weekly ticket at a reduced price. It is much easier to use weekly tickets purchased through the school office than having students purchase tickets on a daily basis. Teachers in grades kindergarten through third grade should keep the tickets for the students.

Student Workers

Can a school use student workers? Students may be employed in the cafeteria provided they meet the city health department requirements and labor law requirements. Such work may be paid on an hourly basis or provision made for "free meals" [CSRK 9.21].

State and Federal Assistance

Should a Christian school participate in state and federal surplus food programs? Review state and federal programs with caution. Acceptance of state and federal food surplus may result in opening your school to state and federal audits and to hiring of workers that would not be acceptable to the school philosophy.

NOTE: *Check all regulations before committing to accepting federal or state funding.*

Supplies

Where should you purchase supplies? Develop a bid procedure with volume purchasing. If volume is a challenge, consider establishing a co-op with other Christian schools in the area. Avoid fancy labeled canned goods; these are usually premium priced and not essential to high-quality food services. Decisions to purchase fresh or canned foods, or frozen foods involves availability of cold storage (freezer and refrigerator) and dry storage. Schedule deliveries to ensure a consistent flow of supplies. Give careful attention to purchasing perishable foods (milk products, baked goods, etc.). Establish a good working relationship with one or two supplies. During times when you experience a shortage, they will go out of their way to obtain additional supplies.

Reporting Procedures

What kind of reporting is essential? Since the food service program intends to be self-supporting, record keeping is crucial to its success. A school should check with local and state officials to get manuals for the food service operation. Utilize a financial management system that:

- Establishes daily income accounting procedures; for example, each teacher collects monies for snacks and lunches, then files a daily accounting report with the school office;
- Keeps records showing number of meals served, income received, food and usable supplies consumed, labor involved, percentage of student participation [CSRK 9.22];
- Uses cash registers with tapes to collect money;
- Provides for a double check of all receipts;
- Makes deposits daily to the bank (all persons handling school food service monies should be bonded);
- Does not permit charge accounts; and

- Compiles daily, weekly and monthly cost analysis data [CSRK 9.23].

Continued Improvement

The following suggestions will help improve existing food service programs:

1   **Adjust the lunchroom physically.** Paint wall murals. Involve the Parent-Teacher Fellowship in a project to purchase some drapes and new furniture. Replace long gang tables with smaller ones. Create an outside eating area for use in good weather. Install sound-deadening acoustical panels to lower the noise level in the cafeteria.

2   **Formulate a noon-hour activity program.** Following the lunch time, consider providing an opportunity for a different activity each week for students in the gym. Schedule club meetings and other activities over the noon hour.

3   **Eat together.** Provide opportunities for teachers and students to eat together in a special area of the building for a special occasion.

4   **Enlist student assistance.** Recruit from various school groups to keep the lunchroom clean, such as the student government and service groups.

5   **Decrease length of lines.** Every effort should be made to decrease length of lines and other delays in the cafeteria.

6   **Provide adequate supervision.** See that the lunchroom and its facilities are properly supervised during lunch periods. The school lunchroom should not be a problem-creating situation.

7   **Change the schedule.** Modify the school lunch schedule so the lowest possible number of students are in the lunchroom at one time.

8   **Form a menu-planning team.** Involve the students in planning [CSRK 9.24]. Provide menus to students, parents and staff one month in advance [CSRK 9.25].

9   **Institute new programs.** Consider starting a breakfast program and encourage parents and teachers to eat together.

10 **Evaluate lunchroom rules.** Eliminate all unenforceable lunchroom rules and devise ways to enforce those remaining in an unobtrusive, routine manner.

11 **Evaluate the total lunch program.** Periodically ask for student and staff attitudes and opinions about the school's food service program. Develop a student and staff rating instrument to evaluate the food service program in your school [CSRK 9.26].

12 **Promote the cafeteria.** Begin a "We're Proud of Our Cafeteria" publicity campaign with posters, school paper articles, class meetings and assemblies. [10]

13 **Expand cafeteria services**. If the school is part of a local church, consider ways through which the school food service operation can be integrated as part of a ministry-wide food service program. For instance, provide banquets for senior citizens, volunteers, singles, an after-service youth snack bar, stewardship banquets, fund-raising dinners, mother/daughter, and father/son dinners, etc. [CSRK 9.27].

14 **Visit other school sites**. Arrange for visits to other food service programs, both public and private.

15 **Use a computer**. There are numerous computer programs to assist in the managing of the food service program. For example, *Master Meal Planner* allows you to plan up to 14 days worth of meals automatically by picking the recipes for each dish for each meal according to the dish and meal type codes entered into each recipe. The program automatically creates a shopping list of all ingredients used in each recipe in the meal schedule and you can even print the shopping list.

Health Services

School health services are an important adjunct to the school program. Christian schools want their students to be whole in there bodies, minds and spirits. Walking in divine health is a way of living designed to help students achieve well-being in four areas: nutrition, physical awareness, stress reduction and self-responsibility. Furthermore, to be an effective witness and do God's will, students need sound, healthy bodies. The Bible says that God's highest wish is that Christians may prosper and be in health, even as their soul prospers (3 John 2).

Each state sets health requirements for schools. States can require and provide such health regulations and services as they deem necessary to protect the "health and safety" of those who reside in the state.

Each Christian school needs to be familiar with its state health requirements. The primary concerns of the state include: ensuring adequate immunization, inoculation and vaccination; maintaining health records; reducing or eliminating communicable diseases; providing for a healthy environment; and offering health screening.

In addition to these key issues, Christian school health programs should focus on:

1 Assisting student physical, social, spiritual and emotional growth;

2 Ensuring adequate health facilities, supplies, and equipment;

3 Training other staff to administer first aid;

4 Providing drug, alcohol and substance abuse education programs;

5 Encouraging good health habits and healthy living; and

6 Training students and staff to walk in divine health.

Meet Immunization Laws

Immunization laws exist in several states. These laws require attendance in school dependent on immunization. The immunization record of each entering student must be checked and in some states this information must be sent to the state department of health. The immunization records of students already enrolled must be keep current.

The most common vaccinations and inoculations required are small pox, diphtheria and polio. However, some states include all existing preventive vaccines available: influenza, whooping cough, measles, etc. While parents who refuse to immunize their children may do so on religious and constitutional grounds, the courts have held that this refusal, because it is tied to school attendance, places the parents in violation of compulsory education statutes, and the parents' cases have not been upheld. (See Step 3 for more information on immunization laws.)

Maintain Accurate Health Records

Keep up-to-date health records on each student so school personnel have easy and immediate access to the information they contain. These records should contain current information on student height, weight, dental care, immunizations, childhood diseases, psychological test results, serious physical disorders, and vision/hearing screening results. The Christian School Resource Kit contains a Student Health Record [CSRK 9.28]. Using the same health record of your local public school will help avoid challenges when students transfer to other schools [CSRK 9.29].

Train Staff in First Aid

An important role of the school health service is rendering emergency aid for injuries. Unless trained to do so, school personnel are not expected to go beyond first aid. Having a signed permission form granting authorization to treat a student is usually required by most hospitals [CSRK 9.30]. Take these forms on all out-of-town field trips and athletic team events.

Prepare for Communicable Diseases

State statutes prohibit any child afflicted with a contagious disease or head lice from attending any school until he is free from the condition. Schools need to have written policies and procedures on dealing with these conditions.

One of the greatest concerns facing schools is the HIV virus that causes AIDS and the HBV virus that causes hepatitis B. The Occupational Safety and Health Administration now requires schools to develop a written plan focusing on the prevention of blood-borne pathogens. The guidelines require schools to determine the amount of exposure for each job classification, procedures for assessing the circumstances surrounding an exposure incident and the schedule and methods of compliance. Guidelines must consider first-aid reporting procedures, hepatitis B vaccinations, vaccination follow-up, and post-exposure follow-up, communication of hazards to employees through in-service training and record keeping.

A sample policy and plan is found in the Christian School Resource Kit [CSRK 9.31]. For recommendations on policies and procedures dealing with AIDS, see *Legal Requirements for Christian Schools*, 2nd Edition and ACSI's "Legal and Legislative Update," June, 1992.

Create a Healthy Environment

The health service department should monitor the sanitary conditions in school rest rooms, showers, swimming pool, cafeteria and kitchen. Give attention to the thermal climate of the school (heating, ventilation, and air-conditioning), as well as school safety (broken glass, pointed sticks, wet floors, unsafe furniture, equipment and play center) [CSRK 9.32].

Offer Health Screening

The school health service should see that each student participates in hearing and vision screening. Coordinate these services through the local county health department. Many times, private health clinics may conduct free screening services. Regardless of who provides this service, obtain parent permission before administering hearing, vision or speech screening [CSRK 9.33].

Select Health Service Staff

Whenever possible, employ a school nurse. If this is not financially possible, consider contacting other private schools in the area and arranging to share a contracted health service professional. Don't overlook the use of parent volunteers to staff the school clinic. Volunteers can complete an eighteen-hour first aid course taught by the Red Cross.

Ensure that the school's liability insurance covers these key volunteers. Staff the clinic daily to ensure adequate care in case of emergency. The great advantage of operating a school clinic with trained volunteer staff is that it reduces the time required by school clerical staff and administrators to supervise sick and injured students.

Obtain Basic Equipment

Outfit a school health service clinic with proper equipment. For example:

- Two small beds, preferably with curtains or dividers to make them semi-private
- Chairs for students to sit on
- A desk and chair for nurse or staff assigned to the health service
- Shelving or storage unit
- A lockable medical cabinet
- A refrigerator for storage of medicine and ice
- First aid supplies and linens
- Telephone

Establish a Health Referral System

All schools should keep a daily report of referrals to the school clinic, stating the name of the pupil, the symptoms, the first aid administered, any contact with parents, the final disposition of the referral and the person handling it. The Christian School Resource Kit contains a sample report [CSRK 9.34].

Consider the following procedures:

1   Follow up on all accidents with a completed accident report [CSRK 9.35].
2   Report all injuries immediately to the parents.
3   Report any injury to the head, neck, back, or bones to a medical doctor "on-call."
4   Maintain an accurate log of the administration of all medication [CSRK 9.36].

Complete a School Health Services Checklist

Complete the following school health services checklist. Place a check mark in the box if the statement is true of your school.

- ☐ The school health services (SHS) are based upon specific measurable objectives.
- ☐ Faculty and administrators understand SHS objectives.
- ☐ Students and parents understand SHS objectives.
- ☐ School health personnel have written job descriptions of their job and expectations.

☐ There is periodic supervision and evaluation of SHS staff throughout the school year.

☐ School health personnel are accessible to faculty, students and administrators.

☐ The SHS meets the needs of the students and faculty.

☐ The results of periodic evaluations provide information for planning improvements.

☐ Faculty and parents view the services as a valuable adjunct to the total school program.

☐ The organizational structure of the SHS provides a way that the potential for achieving objectives is great.

☐ An annual report identifies SHS achievements, failures and activities.

☐ SHS encourages students to participate in health and safety clubs.[11]

NOTE: *Carefully plan the health services from the start because of the litigious society we live in. Someone must oversee this area carefully and in the event of an emergency, assigned personnel must know what to do* (See CSRK 9.37 for a checklist of medical emergency procedures).

Library Services

The purpose in establishing a library is to glorify the Lord Jesus Christ and consequently support and complement the courses taught in the school's curriculum and to facilitate reading skills. The library provides the opportunity for quality Christian recreational reading and for introducing the students to the rich heritage of edifying Christian literature. Finally, it helps the development of skills in using library and reference materials.

Every school can have a quality library. All it takes is a little planning. Consider the following guidelines and suggestions.

Organize the Library

Prior to school opening, purchase the services of a trained school librarian to help in organizing your library—consider contacting other Christian and public schools for the names of librarians. Once school begins, if enrollment is less than 200 students, employ a teacher with some training in library science, or a part-time professional librarian. Schools enrolling 200 to 500 students should employ a full-time librarian.

Schools with grades K-12 need to plan for two library sections—a junior collection for elementary grades and a senior section for grades 7-12. As a minimum, the collection should include the following:

Junior Collection

- Junior Fiction (adventure, history, nature, mystery, sports, short stories, etc.)
- Junior Non-fiction (biographies, science, etc.)

Senior Collection

- References (encyclopedias, dictionaries, almanacs, etc.)
- Senior Fiction (novels, poetry, essays, etc.)
- Senior Non-fiction (creative writings in religion, biography, literature, social science, etc.)
- Periodicals
- Pamphlets
- College handbooks, indexes of colleges, ACT and SAT study books and career information.

Arrange for a Centralized Library

Under a centralized library, anybody in the school can check out all library materials. To increase your library holdings, contact the public library and public schools. Periodically, libraries take old books off the shelves to make room for new books. These books are either sold to the public at substantial savings or given away to other educational institutions. Some cities have a book depository that receives used and surplus books from several sources. These books are usually free to non-profit organizations.

Many times, publishers will have books returned that are slightly damaged in shipment. These books can usually be obtained free for the asking.

Other methods of building a library include: organizing a special library booster club, seeking donations, writing library grants and holding book fairs. For example, David C. Cook Publishing Company has a program called Chariot Book Fair. They send the school a preselected package of best selling books that retail for about $135. For participating, a school may receive up to $65 worth of books free (1-800-323-7543).

If space for a central library is not available, consider placing books on carts and moving them among the rooms, or establish small collections of books in each classroom. It is important to establish a regular rotation system to ensure adequate circulation of all books.

Provide for Classroom Books

In addition to books in the library, teachers should be able to purchase new books for the classroom that would augment the instructional program and provide opportunity for recreational reading by students during spare moments. A budget of $50 to $100 per year per classroom would be a goal.

Plan for a Well-Balanced Collection

Your goal should be to establish a well-balanced book supply in sufficient variety and number. Unfortunately, the libraries in many Christian schools have the same old books, most of which are ragged, torn, soiled and unattractive. They stay on the shelves for years. Usually, they are collections of worn-out textbooks, out-of-date encyclopedias and reference books—unsuitable to the active needs of students. Furthermore, it is not unusual to find Christian school libraries with 90 percent of its collection, religious books.

Stock the library with up-to-date encyclopedias, dictionaries of words, people, and places, almanacs, current magazines and periodicals. Figure 9.4 shows volume and title recommendations as presented by the American Library Association.

Figure 9.4 Library Titles and Volumes

Enrollment	Number of Titles	Number of Volumes
Up to 200	1700	2000
500	3500	5000
1000	5000	7000

You can obtain a list of suggested references from most Christian school accrediting associations, such as the International Christian Accrediting Association (ICAA). Schools that are seeking accreditation usually have to devote a specified dollar amount from each year's budget for the purchase of books. For example, Figure 9.5 shows annual expenditures published by The Association of Christian Schools International (ACSI).

Figure 9.5 Library Expenditures

Enrollment	Expenditure
Less than 500	$450
500-999	$1,050
1000 or more	$1,800

NOTE: *It is important to review all library books for content that is contrary to the values of the school. Teachers, librarian or a committee of concerned parents can perform this task. Review each volume thoroughly, since the title may not reflect the content.* [CSRK 9.38]

Create Library Handbook

Schools can increase their library resources by effectively communicating library policies and procedures through a library handbook. Include topics such as:

- Statement of philosophy
- General Policies (Circulation, when books can be checked out, loss and damage, hours the library will be open, overdue books, fines, conduct of students, etc.)
- Procedures (Checking out a book, returning a book, classification process, book repair, use of audio/visual equipment and materials, library use by classes, acquisition of new materials, shelving of books, etc.)
- Librarian and teacher responsibilities (Include the teaching of library and research skills)
- Book review guidelines

Plan the Environment

Develop a warm, caring environment that is conducive to learning with frequent access. A smooth-functioning library could become a hub of the school program. Publish a library usage schedule to ensure that each class has an opportunity to visit the library no less than twice each week.

Arrange for Adequate Space

There should be space enough to seat the largest class in the school plus around twenty more students. Locate the library centrally so it is accessible to the largest number of students. Disconcerting noises should be at a minimum.

Provide for Adequate Equipment

Every library should be equipped to meet the needs of staff and students. Use the following list as a guide:

- 1 Cabinet, card catalogue, 15 trays
- 8 Chairs, 14 inch
- 30 Chairs, 16 inch
- 2 chairs, 18 inch
- 1 Teacher's desk and chair
- 1 Filing cabinet, 2-drawer
- 1 Globe
- 1 Stand for unabridged dictionary
- 2 Round tables
- 5 Work tables (6 per table)
- 1 Book cart

Book shelving should be adjustable with five feet as the standard and sections partitioned for picture books and bulletin boards.

Expand the Library

Plan to expand the library into an instructional materials center that would eventually benefit the entire ministry. Start a collection of pamphlets, bulletin clippings, travel folders, pictures, maps, charts, etc.

Minimum audio-visual materials might include: 16 mm projector, overhead projector, filmstrip and slide projector, record player and cassette record player. Add an opaque projector at a later date. Establish an effective checkout system for all AV equipment [CSRK 9.39].

Computerize the Library

Modern computer technology automates the mechanics of checking materials in and out (seeking loan types, calculating due dates and fines, recording hold, etc.). It maintains daily transaction summaries, prints notices (overdues, holds, waiting for pickup, etc.), transaction reports and inventory lists. One of the best commercial products available is *The Columbia Library System.*

Using database programs, libraries can maintain library community resource directories, telephone and address directories, film catalogs and bookings and teacher resource listings. In addition, the library can be the center for online information searches and community electronic bulletin boards. With the addition of CD-ROM technology, students and staff have access to volumes of information. One of the most favorite is *SIRS* published by SIRS, Inc.

NOTE: *The two main advantages in computerizing the library are the library can be run by trained parents and the librarian is freed up to teach classes on library usage and research skills.*

Parent Participation

Ultimately, every Christian parent will be held accountable for the education their children receive (Deut. 6:7; Eph. 6:4). By sending a child to a Christian school, the school functions in *loco parentis* (in the place of the parents).

Since the Christian school and the parents share for the welfare of a child, it is understandable that they should develop a cooperative partnership. Formulating such a partnership is the purpose of the parent involvement program.

This partnership may include a formally organized parent-teacher association or fellowship, parent action groups, parent board advisors, parent-school task forces, volunteer programs, booster clubs, parent training seminars and much more.

Create Opportunities for Service

Many parents want to be actively involved in the school. They see the school as an opportunity to utilize specific skills, or to have something to do. Some parents volunteer because they enjoy new experiences, others because they firmly believe in the purpose of the school.

Historically, parent involvement has been restricted to room mothering, chaperoning field trips and Parent-Teacher Fellowships. Today's parents can still find usefulness in these areas; however, expanding the opportunities for service fosters a greater chance to win parent support.

Parents can function in almost any aspect of the school program. They can share their career, hobbies and artistic or technical expertise in the classroom. Leading workshops, sponsoring parent classes, listening to students read, serving as tutors, overseeing clubs and hobby days, running a copy service, making teaching aids, helping in the publication of the school newsletter, newspaper, or yearbook are but a few non-traditional areas of service. Consider the following strategies for enhancing parent involvement.

Parent Survey

Conduct a parent volunteer service survey; find out what parents want to do [CSRK 9.40]. Ask parents to complete this survey during registration. Place information of each area of involvement on a three by five volunteer card system, or computer database program. Plan to involve every parent who signs up. Establish a goal of 100 percent participation.

Involvement Strategies

Enhance parent participation by effectively addressing reasons for non-involvement. Consider the following reasons and strategies for dealing with these reasons.

1 **Parents are apprehensive of the school.** Reassure parents of your concern and support. Draw attention to the concern shared for the student.

2 **Parents feel that educating their children is the job of the school to which they pay tuition.** Stress the benefits of parent involvement; urge communication and observation to bring about new understanding.

3 **Parents have preschool children to care for.** Encourage parents to share babysitting chores with other volunteers or provide a free nursery in an unused classroom.

4 **Parents have no transportation.** Appoint a parent to help coordinate transportation.

5 **Parents do not have the time because they work 40 hours a week.** Encourage participation of activities scheduled for the evening and on weekends. Some parents who feel they are too busy should be asked to spend short periods on an irregular basis. In this way, their absence will not disrupt the school's schedule, and they may find that they really do have the time to be part of such a beneficial program.[12]

6 **Parents have no opportunity for advancement.** Allow parent volunteers to advance through a series of steps leading to higher levels of responsibility, skill learning and influence.[13]

7 **Parents do not know how to do certain tasks.** Provide a description and objective for each area of involvement with a written criteria for success and acceptable standards of performance. Before parents participate in the activity, provide necessary skills and knowledge to be successful in their assignment. Relate training to age level served. Remember, training builds confidence.

8 **The school doesn't know whether or not parents show up.** Keep a record of volunteer activities. Expect all volunteers to check in with the school office and sign in when arriving and sign out when leaving the building. This provides information for the school to record the number of total hours each parent contributes to his assigned task and to acknowledge his involvement [CSRK 9.41].

Volunteer Director

It is important to identify a parent who can serve as director of the volunteer program. This will take much of the coordination work off the school administration who already have plenty to do. The director will work closely with the administration to fulfill the purpose of the parent volunteer program. The director will:

- Assist in recruiting and training of key volunteers;
- Assign volunteers to classrooms;
- Let classroom teachers know when volunteers are absent;
- Be available at the school on a regular basis;
- Keep administrators informed of the program's progress and needs; and
- Assist the administration in evaluating the effectiveness of the program.

Show Appreciation

Express appreciation to all who serve. Appreciation requires admiration, discernment, sensibility, taste, gratitude and esteem. There is no substitute for a face-to-face "well done" declaration to the parent.

Parents (and others who volunteer) need to know you believe in their efforts and sacrifices of time and energy. Assure them their presence is having an eternal effect upon the lives of the students.

In addition to a one-on-one meeting with the parent, consider the following gestures of appreciation:

1 Encouraging students to send special cards (in addition to birthday) to volunteers.
2 Greeting them at the front door.
3 Holding a special parent appreciation assembly.
4 Honoring them on their birthday.
5 Inviting them out to lunch or to a special coffee or tea.
6 Invitation to return next year for further service.
7 Remembering their anniversary.
8 Special name badge.

Give Special Recognition

Showing recognition is important. Be consistent and include all parents, regardless of how small their involvement. Maintaining accurate records is vital to this recognition process. Some suggestions for special recognition might include the following:

1   Scholarships to special seminars.

2   Cafeteria discount cards.

3   Certificates of appreciation.

4   Discounts at bookstore.

5   Set up a special parent bulletin board featuring different families each month.

6   Establishing a Parent of the Month and Parent of the Year program.

7   Pins, gifts, or symbols of achievement.

8   Plaques for years of service, for example, 3, 5, 7, and 10 years.

9   Community interest story to local newspaper and television station.

Form a Parent-Teacher Fellowship

Any school can have an active, strong Parent-Teacher Fellowship (PTF); all it requires is a little planning. One of the easiest ways of ensuring participation of parents in the PTF is to make attendance a requirement, whereby at least one parent must be present at all meetings. Add a statement of commitment to your enrollment form, such as "I agree to faithfully attend all Parent-Teacher Fellowship meetings and to serve in those areas indicated on my Parent Survey." Pass out attendance cards at each meeting and send an absentee follow-up letter or make a personal phone call to all who were absent [CSRK 9.42]. In formulating a parent support group, consider the following:

1   **Identify the group's purpose and set goals.** Focus the group on improving the school and tackling problems.

2   **Provide a definite structure.** Publish an agenda; start and stop on time. As a minimum, the PTF should meet once each quarter, while the executive board meets monthly. Schedule meetings to avoid the least number of conflicts with school, church and community activities. Present a specific program followed by opportunities for small group interaction. A very successful program held early during the first quarter is a Back-to-School Night, where parents actually attend classes and do schoolwork—a mini-school day.

3   **Obtain enthusiastic leadership.** Appoint to leadership positions those parents who can keep members encouraged and inspired. Identify a president, vice-president, treasurer and secretary. Appoint chairpersons of standing committees, such as membership, hospitality, safety and welfare, program and budget. Allow these persons to serve on the executive board. Provide each board member with a notebook containing the by-laws, current budget, names of the school staff, names, addresses and phone numbers of all board officers, minutes of each meeting, agendas of all meetings and the current parent handbook.

4   **Foster teamwork.** Teamwork between parents and teachers, home and school pays handsome dividends; parents are delighted when they know everyone is focusing on what is best for their child(ren).

Provide Training Resources

Schools can have an effective parent program by providing essential training resources. [14] Administrators and teachers have found a valuable tool in the book entitled, *Grandees: A School-Based Volunteer Program.* This publication is a handbook and training manual containing techniques and methodology for establishing a parent volunteer program. It contains information on volunteer recruiting, screening and interviewing, placements, orientation and training. Suggestions and samples of curriculum and resource materials abound, along with a recognition system, and sample agreement forms, parent letters, record keeping forms and evaluation instruments. Obtain additional information on parent/teacher associations by writing the National Parent Teacher Association.

Set Up a Parent-Action Team

Some schools have parents serve on a Parent-Action Team (PAT). Two team members at each grade level are appointed by the administrator or school board. The goal is to form a study group to research problems and bring recommendations to the administration and the school board. As the name denotes, "action" is taken to resolve conflicts and solve problems.

The school administrator is part of the PAT that is chaired by a parent. The administrator's role is to provide information and advice and to present the school's point of view. Meetings are held monthly at the school. Place chairs in a circle or around a group of tables to enhance a cooperative atmosphere. Serving coffee and refreshments at mid-point provide opportunity for casual conversation and for personal response to an issue.

Identify members of the PAT before the start of school and conduct your first meeting no less than two weeks before school begins. Consider the following:

1   Provide a notebook similar to the one developed for the Parent-Teacher Fellowship officers.

2   Provide each PAT member with a list of current enrollees for his or her respective grades, identifying returning and new students.

3   Have PAT members make a personal phone call to all new families to see how the PAT might facilitate a smooth transfer to the school. Field any questions new parents might have. If answers are not available, find the answers and call parents back immediately.

4   Use PAT members to conduct a parent needs assessment and to tabulate the results at mid-point of the first quarter and again during the fourth quarter [CSRK 9.43].

5   Involve PAT members in your new parent/student orientation at the beginning of the school term.

Use Parents as Task Force Members

One of the key ingredients in the school improvement process is obtaining representative input from those who have a stake in the success of the students. This representative group should include teachers, administrators, students and parents. The primary focus of the School Improvement Task Force is to improve the effectiveness of the Christian school.

Rather than creating a school improvement process from scratch, consider adopting a program that has already proven useful, such as Bill Rauhauser's *Design for Implementing Effective Schools Research.*

Parents participate with other members of the task force in:

1   Defining a clear and focused school mission;

2   Establishing a safe and orderly environment conducive to teaching and learning;

3   Supporting the instructional leadership of the administrator;

4   Identifying the types of climates that foster high expectations, leading students to achieve at the highest possible level;

5   Suggesting ways to maximize opportunities to learn and the amount of time on learning;

6   Formulating ideas for frequent monitoring and reporting of student progress; and

7   Strengthening home/school partnerships so that parents understand and support the vision of the school and are given the opportunity to participate in helping the school accomplish this vision. [15]

Pupil Personnel Services

Helping students deal with physical, emotional, personal, social, spiritual, educational and vocational needs is the focus of pupil personnel services. Unfortunately, most Christian schools are financially unable to provide a cadre of special services, psychologists, social workers; few employ trained school counselors. Yet, if a Christian school is to be successful, these needs must be met, regardless of the size of the school.

Consider Staffing

We commend Christian school administrators for recognizing students' needs for guidance and counsel and for performing guidance functions in addition to all their other duties. However, to meet student service needs, administrators must be creative in their efforts. For example, arrange qualified teaching staff to coordinate release time for pupil personnel services until the school can employ the services of a trained guidance counselor.

There is no standard formula as to how large of an enrollment a school should have before it employs a school counselor. Some schools are able to employ a counselor for as few as 250 students. However, when enrollment reaches 500 to 600 students, a trained guidance counselor is an absolute necessity.

Offer Grade-Level Services

Meeting the needs of students involves all staff members. No school should be without pupil personnel services for all age levels. Consider the following grade-level services: [16]

Elementary School

1   Training teachers to assist with planning and implementing guidance interventions for children to increase self-esteem, personal relationships and positive school attitudes.

2   Building a healthy classroom environment.

3   Assisting parents in understanding normal child growth and development; improving family communication skills; and understanding their role in encouraging their children to learn.

4   Providing early identification, remediation, or referral of children with special needs.

5   Encouraging students in developing a strong relationship with the Lord and in walking in Christian maturity.

Junior High

1   Smoothing the transition for students from the more confining environment of the elementary school and self-contained classrooms to the junior high school where students are expected to assume greater responsibility for their own learning and personal development.

2   Continuing to build self-esteem and positive attitudes through group guidance, teacher in-service training, etc.

3   Organizing a career guidance program.

4   Providing direction in developing Christian life attributes and spiritual maturity.

High School

1   Helping students with life issues, such as career choices, social relationships, self-identity, planning for the future, etc.

2   Assisting students with assessment of personal characteristics (for example, competencies, interests, aptitudes, needs) for personal use in such areas as course selection, post-high school planning and career choices.

3   Providing systems (print, computer-based, audio-visual) for educational-vocational planning and decision making.

4   Furnishing remedial interventions and alternative programs for those experiencing adjustment problems.

5   Fostering a total commitment by the students to be a doer of the Word of God and not a hearer only, and to be a disciple maker.

Provide Effective Guidance

The task of meeting the needs of students requires creative strategies: strategies that can be implemented regardless of the size of enrollment, or availability of professional guidance staff. Consider the following:

Homeroom Concept

The homeroom concept, originally used for administrative chores, provides a good situation for imparting information, discussing common problems and providing opportunity for individual assistance. A homeroom concept can have a major impact when the homeroom program follows a coordinated effort with uniform lessons rather than each teacher doing his own thing. [17]

Accomplish this by creating a planning team to identify themes and locate resources. Select themes that will provide answers to student concerns, such as social amenities with the opposite sex, relations with parents and siblings, and more. Topics will vary depending upon the age–level served. Employ activities that get the kids involved, such as brief groups, role playing, drama, debate, panel discussion, etc.

Curriculum Offerings

Consider adding self-esteem, life skills, study skills, personal relationships and other essential topics as developmental units in curriculum areas, such as English, social studies and math. For example, *Study Power* is a program for high school students to help improve study skills. It is not a remedial program intended for students with low grades; it is a program for all students, because all students can improve their school work, their employment options, and even their quality of life by learning how to learn. The series consists of six units: managing time and environment, reading textbooks, taking class notes, using resources, preparing for tests and taking tests.

Another excellent curriculum resource is free loan films and videos dealing with sexuality, substance abuse, relationships and historical and contemporary issues, such as suicide, abortion, infanticide, euthanasia, physical injury and rehabilitation, media and self-image. Gospel Films, Inc. makes these available, free to Christian schools.

Billy Zeoli, President of Gospel Films, Inc. writes,

"Your students are growing up on media. A good deal of what they learn comes from television, film and video. But much of what they watch leaves them without moral direction, confused about values, and often cynical...We're aware that you need quality film and video to assist you in your teaching task and we are honored to help you solve this predicament."[18]

Teacher Advisor

This concept pairs students with teacher advisors. Minimize the adviser-advisee ratio by including non-teaching staff, such as office staff, custodians, church staff, etc. Provide students with a list of advisors along with a biographical sketch, their hobbies, and other items of interest. Allow students to select three advisors they would like to have. Final pairings are made by a selection team.

Design the program to take place during normal school hours. Given 20 to 25 advisees and a 30- to 45-minute advisement period each day, a teacher could meet with two or three students each day, over a two-week period. The advisement plan may operate though the year, or at specified times, such as at the beginning of the first quarter, and again just before each semester ends.

Guidance Council

Another guidance strategy is a guidance council comprised of representatives from various groups within the school and church. For instance: teachers, parents, students, youth pastor, etc. The council is kept to a workable number (seven to ten people). The functions of the guidance council may include coordinating, policy making and assisting in program evaluation.[19]

Extra Class Activities

A full range of student activities are important aspects of the guidance program. They help students to understand themselves better and improve their social adjustment.[20] Activities, especially those that involve different grades, provide opportunity for establishing new relationships. (See section on student activities in Step 10.)

Provide for College Placement

There are few events as rewarding as the school's first graduating class and the pleasure of knowing that the school was instrumental in preparing its graduates for opportunities for education beyond high school. Given careful planning, the task of preparing for and selecting a college should be hassle free. Parents and students should not "find themselves lost in the thicket of admissions and financial aid procedures."[21] Consider the following strategies:

1 **Course Selections.** Plan to offer a full-range of courses designed to help students meet post-high school curricular requirements. For example, four years of English, three years of math, etc. Schedule these required courses to minimize scheduling conflicts.

2 **Course Plan Sheet.** Provide all beginning freshman a four-year course plan sheet (see CSRK 8.13). At the end of each semester, provide high school students with a graduation status report [CSRK 9.44]. Require parents and students to review these two documents before scheduling classes. Encourage students to select courses carefully, accurately, constantly. Keep in mind their capabilities, interests, vocation and post-high school education ambitions and the leading by God's Word and Holy Spirit.

3 **Chapels/Bible Classes.** Focus chapel presentations and include in the Bible curriculum opportunities for students to determine the call of God upon their lives. Although they can receive advice and suggestions from many sources, it is important to have God's direction. Proverbs 3: 5,6 instructs, **"Trust in the Lord with all thine heart; and lean not unto thine own understanding. In all thy ways acknowledge him and he shall direct thy paths."** Through chapels and Bible classes, students can learn how to tune into the voice of the Spirit of God and the Word of God and tune out the confusing impulses from any other source. They can know the perfect will of God for their life and the joy, and the reality and fullness of divine guidance.[22]

4 **Resource Center.** Establish an educational, vocational planning resource center. Locate it in the library, counselor's office, or classroom. Supply the center with college guides, such as *The Barron's Profiles of American Colleges*, *Peterson's Guide to Four-Year Colleges*, *Selection Guide to College*, and *The Access Guide to Paying for College*. Request colleges to furnish copies of their catalogs. Contact your State Department of Higher Education for additional resources.

5   **College Guide**. Publish or purchase a college planning guide (A sample is available from DEL Publications). Include within the guide the following topics:

- A listing of educational opportunities.
- Preparatory expectations for each grade level, 9th-12th.
- Planning guidelines for eleventh and twelfth grades.
- Admission test dates.
- An overview of types of tests and an eligibility index of grade point averages and corresponding required test scores.
- Curriculum requirements for institutions of higher education most attended by students in your region. Include the full range of opportunities including Bible schools and career schools.
- Sample letters for college admissions.
- College costs and financial aid, scholarship and loan opportunities.
- Activities record.
- On campus interview expectations.
- Advanced placement opportunities.
- Housing opportunities.
- Personal financial management.

6   **College Fairs/Representatives**. Participate in college fairs in your area. Coordinate your own fair in cooperation with other Christian schools. Arrange for a college recruiting officer to visit your campus. Better yet, invite alumni attending various institutions to share their experiences and recommendations.

7   **Scholarship File**. Establish a scholarship file. The best source of future scholarships are from institutions who have already granted scholarships to your graduates. Ask students and parents to provide a copy of all applications they receive for inclusion in your scholarship file. Furnish the file with financial aid reference materials, such as *College Grants from Uncle Sam, College Loan from Uncle Sam, Financial Aids for Higher Education, Peterson's College Money Handbook,* and *Scholarships, Fellowships, and Loans.*

8   **Use Computer Resources**. Computer software is available to foster college selection, scholarship searches and financial aid planning. Some of these packages include, "College Planning," "Financial Planning," and "Essay Writing." Contact college and request college selection and financial aid information on computer disk.

9   **College Aptitude Testing**. Two commonly used college aptitude tests are the American College Test (ACT) and Scholastic Aptitude

Test (SAT). Most institutions of higher learning require either the ACT or SAT for admission as well as for determining eligibility for scholarships. Consider the following suggestions:

- Register your school with the American College Testing Program testing service. Your school will receive a registration number and a schedule of test dates.

- Contact local, regional and state institutions of higher learning and request minimum ACT/SAT scores for admissions and scholarship requirements.

- Require all seniors to take either the SAT or ACT. Tracking these scores provides a good measure of your students' college preparation.

- Obtain free descriptive test booklets from the testing services for distribution to students. Make available other test preparation resources, such as practice books and computer programs.

- Include ACT/SAT test preparation materials as part of each subject. Many states and colleges offer teacher in-service training, or special short courses on how to prepare students for ACT/SAT testing. Contact these institutions for course and in-service offerings.

- Consider including a special ACT/SAT preparation course as part of your course offerings in the fall. If you do not have staff available to teach such a course, consider using a professional test preparation service, such as Stanley H. Kaplan Educational Center, Ltd. Often, special discounts are available when ten or more students attend.

- Encourage students to take the test more than once. Colleges will use the highest score. We have seen students improve their test results by seven points on the ACT and 50 points on the SAT from more than one testing.

Offer Vocational Awareness and Placement

Career planning begins in high school. God has a specific plan for each student. "**For I know the plans I have for you, declares the Lord, plans to prosper you and not to harm you, plans to give you hope and a future**" (Jeremiah 29:11, NIV). He also says: "**I will instruct you and teach you in the way you should go; I will counsel you and watch over you**" (Psalm 32:8, NIV).

We believe every Christian young person needs to determine God's plan and purpose for his life at the earliest possible time. James W. Deuink states:

"We must be primarily concerned with directing the student in finding God's will, with helping him discern his God-given abilities and with encouraging him to use these talents for Christ. There is no need for a Christian school graduate to be undecided as to God's direction for his/her life. Part of the responsibility of the Christian school is to help students understand the options available to them."[23]

Interest Inventories

The most commonly used interest inventories are the *Strong-Campbell Interest Inventories,* the *Kuder Preference Record,* and the *Ohio Vocational Interest Survey.* Often, these inventories are provided free of charge within the community. Check with your local public library, university or college extension, junior colleges and vocational centers. Call the public school service bureau or local high school for the names of regional test representatives and testing dates.

Computer Software

Several of the more well-known career assistance programs make the vocational counseling task much easier. For instance, *Career Information Systems* (CIS) and *Guidance Information Systems* (GIS) by Houghton-Mifflin. These two systems are available in many states and are accessible to residents of the state. CIS emphasizes local and regional information, whereas GIS provides access to various kinds of national data regarding careers, educational opportunities, and the armed services.

Other systems include: The *System of Interactive Guidance and Information* (SIGF) by Educational Testing Service; *Discovery Systems* by Discover, Inc.; and *C LECT* marketed by Chronicle Guidance Publications, Inc. Contact your public library, area colleges, and State Employment Agency for access to these programs. In many cases, these programs are made available as part of grants provided by government agencies and are free to the public.

Published Resources

There are many resource materials that are available to Christian schools. F.E. Burtnett cites five additional resources:[24]

- **National trade and professional associations.** *The Directory of the National Trade and Professional Associations of the United States* lists addresses for approximately one thousand trade and professional associations in this country. Virtually all of them welcome requests for information, and some respond with elaborate materials.

- **Governmental agencies**. Various federal, state and local agencies produce useful information that is free or relatively inexpensive. At the federal level, for example, there are the Department of Labor materials (*Occupational Outlook Handbook, Occupational Outlook Quarterly, Dictionary of Occupational Titles,* the labor statistics reports and the Women's Bureau materials). At the state level, useful information is available from the state labor and education departments or agencies.

- **Commercial publishers and producers**. As was stated earlier, private enterprise is involved with information services because there is a market. Most commercially produced information is aimed at early and middle adolescents. Commercial materials for children in kindergarten through sixth grade and for older adolescents are presently scarce.

- **Business and industry**. Potential employers, wanting to inform young persons about opportunities within their companies, publish useful information that is free to schools. These publications provide quality information on business and industrial organizations.

- **Educational institutions or training programs**. Information about their offerings is available from public and private educational or training programs. These sources are often able to supply information about related career opportunities.

NOTE: *When a student has this kind of information at his disposal, he can seek direction and confirmation from the Holy Spirit and begin to move toward the fulfillment of God's plan before he graduates from high school.*

Skills Training

Develop a skills training program with the help of interested parents, staff and community resources. According to Baker, "Skills training affords students an opportunity to present themselves in the best possible light and also helps them to understand the complexities of placement."[25]

Baker advocates the following intervention strategies:

- Complete a job application.
- Learn how to respond to announcements of job openings.
- Participate appropriately in job interviews.
- Develop resume and placement credentials.
- Use various resources to locate information about job openings.

- Understand the variables involved in holding a job—satisfactory appearance, attitudes, work ethics, honesty, etc.

Planned Activities

There are a number of special activities to expand students' knowledge and awareness of the world of work, such as career days, career shadowing, junior partners, and field trips. Combine the activities with audio-visual resources, such as *Vocational Visions* by Guidance Associates for junior and senior high, and *Charlie Brown's Career Education Program* by Random House for elementary students to experience.

One of the easiest activities to plan is a career conference or career week. Follow these steps:

- Establish a planning committee composed of staff, pupils, community business leaders, parents and others interested in assisting. Plan the first meeting no later than three months before the conference.

- Determine the vocational interests of the students using a simple questionnaire. Have students select three choices from a list of forty to fifty.

- Tabulate the results of the questionnaire and determine which occupations will attract most students.

- Establish the schedule for the conference using 30- to 40-minute presentation modules. Repeat each module at least twice throughout the conference. Allow ample time for questions and answers. Consider the size of the anticipated modules in assigning individual rooms.

- Invite all consultants. Use as many parents as possible. Provide a list of suggestions to help consultants plan their presentation. Include such points as time parameters and ages of students. Ask consultants to address issues of interest, such as facts concerning the field of work, importance of this vocation, kinds of tasks involved, tools, materials, processes, personal qualifications, special training, income ranges, pensions, benefits, promotions, and so forth.

- Identify students to serve as host and hostesses or guides. Use teachers whose rooms are being used to give the introduction, take attendance and to provide general supervision.

- Publish a schedule of all activities, participants, room numbers, class periods, student hosts/hostesses, teacher monitors.

- Provide schedules and conference packets to all consultants and guest speakers.

- Brief all students and staff on the conference activities. Allow students to sign up for as many modules as the schedule provides. Students usually need some assistance in the proper utilization of any consultant.

- At the close of the conference some type of evaluation would be helpful for future planning.[26]

Placement Records

Establish a system for keeping placement records up to date. Send letters to prospective employers addressing the merits of employing students from your school and request job opportunities and applications. Keep records of job opportunities, training opportunities, potential employers, lists of full- or part-time jobs, contact persons and successful placements. Providing a list of past employers of your students may be the tool to an open employment opportunity.

Develop a Referral System

Central to any pupil personnel services program is a well-developed referral system. This system includes referrals made to the pupil personnel services (school referral) and referrals made by the public personnel services (community referral).

School Referral

Include in your staff handbook: criteria for those who should be referred; when a referral should be considered; which referral resource is appropriate (for example, disciplinary vs. developmental); how to make a referral; and follow-up procedures. The CSRK provides an example of a disciplinary referral form [CSRK 9.45]. Print this form on three-part carbonless paper. The person making the referral keeps one copy, two copies are sent to the office. After the referral has been processed, a copy is placed in the student's file and a copy is sent to the parent. The copy must be signed and returned by the parent.

Community Referral

Schools need to be aware of the services available within the community. There will always be cases demanding time and expertise beyond what the school is able to provide. Awareness of these services includes identification of the sources, a working knowledge of their services and knowledge of ways to use the services.[27] Some of these services include:

- Job Placement Service
- Rape Crises Center
- County Board of Assistance
- County Health Services
- Foster Home Care
- State Department of Health

- American Cancer Society
- American Red Cross
- Chamber of Commerce
- Easter Seal Society
- YMCA

Start a Testing Program

No other topic has generated as much controversy over the past 50 years as has standardized testing. Although the critics of standardized testing abound, standardized testing continues to be an important ingredient in educational evaluation both of students and institutions. For the Christian school, test results become part of a schools "good works." In several states, producing "good test results" is a method of determining instructional equivalency.[28]

Standardized testing is one method of determining whether or not a school achieves its objectives. Galatians 6:4 says,

"But let every man prove his own work, and then shall he have rejoicing in himself alone, and not in another."

The two most commonly used standardized tests in Christian schools are aptitude and achievement. Some schools use group intelligence testing, such as the Henmon-Nelson tests of Mental Ability. Since intelligence testing is subject to numerous problems—reliability, validity, cultural bias, misuse, misinterpretation, they should be used with extreme caution, if in fact they are to be used at all. Most states have strict legal guidelines covering procedures and policies for use of psychological (intelligence) tests.[29] We do not recommend their use.

Unlike intelligence tests that measure general ability, aptitude tests attempt to assess multiple or specific abilities, such as scholastic aptitude. The two most popular scholastic aptitude tests are the ACT and SAT, discussed earlier in this chapter.

Achievement testing is an area of standardized testing that is used by most Christian schools and "measures the degree of student learning in specific curriculum areas common to most schools."[30] The most popular are:

- CAT California Achievement Test—McGraw-Hill
- ITBS Iowa Test of Basic Skills—Houghton Mifflin
- MAT Metropolitan Achievement Test—Psychological Corporation

- SAT Stanford Achievement Test—Harcourt Brace Jovanovich

Testing Schedule and Scoring

Testing all students at the beginning of school and then again at the end of school is an ideal, yet costly situation. Some schools test all grades in the spring while others limit testing to several grades, such as first, fourth, eighth and eleventh. Following the testing schedule of the local public schools will facilitate the transfer of students and their test scores.

Consider machine scoring of all achievement tests. Not only will your teachers be blessed because they don't have to score the test, you will obtain more accurate and a wider variety of scores; for instance, standard scores, grade equivalent scores, national percentile ranks, normal curve equivalent scores, stanines, and much more. In addition, the school will obtain individual student, classroom, grade level and school district composites. Scoring costs range from $1.50 to $3.50 per student.

State Required Testing

Several states require Christian schools to participate in state sponsored testing programs. For example, schools in New York must administer tests that are part of the Pupil Evaluation Program (PEP) and Program Evaluation Tests (PET). Third and sixth graders are tested in reading and mathematics and fifth graders in writing. Sixth and eighth graders are tested in social studies. In addition, Regents Competency tests or their equivalent must be administered in reading, writing, science, U.S. History and government at the high school level. Christian schools may contact their State Office of Education, the Division of Educational Testing for more details on state testing and reporting.

Test Purchases

Some Christian school service organizations, such as ORUEF (Oral Roberts University Educational Fellowship) and ACSI (Association of Christian Schools International), provide a centralized purchasing and scoring service. By pooling test orders, schools are able to obtain discounted prices. They are also able to receive national norms as well as Christian school norms.

Evaluate the Program

Evaluation of the pupil personnel services should be an ongoing process that takes into consideration input from staff, students and parents. According to DeRoche,

"A principal's roles and responsibilities for organizing, administrating, and supervising pupil personnel services and staff will vary in direct proportion to the number of students and teachers, the kinds and extent of existing services, and the availability of administrative assistance. But size does not detract from the principal's responsibility to see to it that the program is one of quality and that, personnel effectively provide services approved by the school board."[31]

The student survey found in the Christian School Resource Kit contains questions used to assess counseling and guidance services [CSRK 9.46]. Specific questions should be added to reflect areas unique to your particular school. Begin by administering the survey to seniors before graduation.

Transportation

Since most Christian schools are commuter schools, the need for transporting students to school is very real. There are four major avenues for transporting students.

School Ownership and Operation

Buses may be purchased with cash, bank financed or leased. When possible, purchase with cash. However, operating one or two buses may represent a tremendous financial drain upon the school because buses require a high capital investment as well as ongoing costs for maintenance, fuel, insurance and drivers. One major advantage of school-owned and operated transportation services is the ability to provide them on an actual cost basis.

The school also may be eligible for certain tax exemptions in purchasing vehicles, minimum cost for vehicle licenses and reduced insurance rates. Another advantage in owning your buses is the availability for multiple use by other areas of the ministry, such as youth groups, Sunday school, singles, street ministry teams, etc.

Private Ownership and School Operated

Some schools, to provide a more favorable cash flow, lease buses from private companies and operate the buses by using school employees. School ownership and private ownership provide the following advantages to the school when the operation is controlled by the school:

- The school can be selective in employing capable, Christian drivers who are responsive to the desires and concerns of the school.

- Vehicles can be easily scheduled for educational and co-curricular field trips.
- It is easier to route buses when you own them.
- The supervision of drivers and children is facilitated because the school has control.
- A direct line of communication can be established between parents and the school.

Schools interested in leasing should call their local leasing companies and obtain price quotes. Consider leasing a vehicle over a three- to five-year period and then purchasing the vehicles using a buy-out clause.

The number of buses to purchase or lease depends upon the number of children needing transportation. This should be determined as soon as it is possible. A simple statement, "Does your child need transportation?" added to the student application will help collect the data needed to make a decision.

Contracted Services

Contracting for transportation services requires no capital investment. Also, the cost of maintenance for vehicles, storage facilities and insurance can be avoided. However, most contracted services result in the school losing most of the control over the transportation program.

Parent Ownership and Parent Operated

Most administrators will agree that this is the best arrangement. Parents may transport any individual child to school in their own vehicle, or join another with a group of families from the same area and car or van pool. The school works with the parents by providing a list of families by zip code grouping. Parents needing transportation can be given the name of a parent coordinator in the zip code area in which they live.

Map the Routes

The best single instrument for mapping routes is a map of the community, prepared and kept up to date. The mapping process begins as requests for transportation are received.

1   Affix each student's name, age, grade, and house number to a pin and plot it on the map.

2   Total the number of pupils to be transported. Do not base transportation needs by the total enrollment, but by the number needing to be transported.

3   Using the scale on the map, determine the total mileage of the shortest route by which all pupils can be reached.

4   Determine tentative routes, avoiding retraces.

5   Total the number of pupils on each route to see what the required capacity will be for each bus.

6   Check the route to mark "common" pick-up points that can be identified. The more common points the school has identified, rather than a lot of door-to-door pick-up, the less will be the cost and the time in transporting children. Neighborhood loading zones should be located away from hazards and busy corners. Where possible, establish pick-up points that are off the main highway. Students should not cross a busy street or highway. Furthermore, plan the route so students are not at the pick-up more than five minutes before the pick-up time; this will greatly reduce disciplinary challenges.

7   As a rule of thumb, no student should be picked up earlier than one hour before school starts. The scheduling of additional buses or larger buses will eliminate the need of students riding too long.

8   Distribute transportation schedules to parents and teachers, and include as a minimum, bus number, name of primary driver, location of bus stops, pick-up times, after school arrival time, and name and phone number of school transportation coordinator.

9   Place the transportation map in a conspicuous place and review the routes quarterly making changes as needed.

Use Computer Technology

Application of computer technology in the area of transportation can reduce inefficiency and provide better control. Some of these applications include: vehicle inventory, bus routing, computer generated driving instructions, bus scheduling, budgeting, purchasing, accident reporting and insurance and ridership. Use computers for disciplinary referral tracking, driver evaluations, vehicle maintenance and pre-trip inspections.

One such program is a shareware program called *Schedule Magic*. Don't allow the word "Magic" to cause you to prejudge this excellent program. Use the program to optimize transportation services, buses, vans, even car pools. Operating buses and vans represents a tremendous financial drain upon the school because they require a high capital investment as well as ongoing costs for maintenance, fuel, insurance and drivers. *Schedule Magic* shows you how to maximize routes and minimize the number of vehicles. Using *Schedule Magic*, you can identify straight line distances from grid coordinates and then calculate travel times.

Calculate Transportation Costs

It is important to identify all costs to establish a standard unit cost. Include the following in cost calculations:

- Cost of vehicles depreciated over three years (cost purchased, leased or financed)
- Insurance
- Maintenance and repair

- Wage of drivers
- Benefits of drivers
- Fuel consumption
- Tag and inspection fees

Once this information is obtained, determine the following cost units: cost per mile, cost per rider and cost per fiscal year. To secure comparable data, contact your state transportation office, public school, or Christian schools that have been operating buses for some time.

Select Drivers

The key to an effective transportation program is the driver. Deuink and Herbster comment,

"Good drivers can be valuable assets in a public relations program; a bad driver can destroy the efforts of an army of public relations experts. A bus driver is much more than the operator of the vehicle. He spends time with the students in an atmosphere that affords the opportunity to enhance or destroy the effectiveness of the entire school program. Bus drivers must be born again, sold out on Christian education in general and their school in particular, and good with children. Their attitude toward the school and its program is as important as their ability to drive a school bus."[32]

All bus drivers should attend a bus driver's training program and become certified by the state. Contact your public school district for time and location of training schools. Most schools are free of charge. Usually, the only cost is for a physical. Request a copy of the prospective driver's driving record from the State Motor Vehicle Department [CSRK 9.47]. And finally, make sure the driver reads and understands the information contained on all school policies, and the information contained in your bus drivers manual.[33] Include in your manual, the topics found in Figure 9.6.

Monitor Bus Behavior

It is important that the school establish an effective system of discipline to ensure the orderly and safe transportation of students to and

Figure 9.6 Transportation Manual

- Requirements for Drivers
- Personal Habits for Drivers
- Drivers' Responsibilities
- Daily Responsibilities
- Fueling Information
- Activity Trips
- Selection of Drivers
- School Bus Regulations
- Speed Limits
- Railroad Crossings
- Loading and Unloading
- Students' Requirements
- Discipline
- Incident Report (Discipline) [CSRK 9.48]
- Emergency Evacuations
- Motor Vehicle Accidents [CSRK 9.49]
- Vehicle Inspection Report [CSRK 9.50]
- Economic Driving
- Payroll Information
- Salary Schedule
- Dismissal Reasons
- Vehicle Request [CSRK 9.51]

from school. The final responsibility for student behavior on buses belongs to the school principal. Develop policies with the cooperative effort of bus drivers, teachers, students and parents. Once the guidelines have been agreed upon, they must be understood by students, parents and drivers.

The responsibility for the safety of the bus and discipline on the bus rests primarily with the driver. The Christian School Resource Kit contains a copy of a transportation agreement between the Christian school, bus riders and their parents [CSRK 9.52].

Pitfalls to Avoid

1. Failing to maintain a reasonable athletic competition schedule. An overly aggressive athletic schedule will affect the academic well-being of most athletes as well as place extra hardships on families supportive of their student athletes. Some coaches fall into the trap of thinking that as long as time is spent in practice why not play a game. However, a two-hour athletic competition is longer than a two-hour practice when one considers transportation to and from the game, preparation for the game, etc.

The number of games should not exceed the average expectation for each particular sport at various grade levels. A good policy is to play no more games than public school counterparts. Participation in a city, state, or regional conference may dictate the number of games allowed.

2. Having no agreed upon policy for adding new sport teams. Having a clearly written set of criteria for adding sport teams will help address the many requests coming from students and their parents. The following four criteria have been effective in helping Victory Christian School in Tulsa, Oklahoma, set up over 50 different sports teams serving 835 students in elementary through high school.

- There are enough students to field a team.
- There are necessary facilities for practice and games.
- A qualified coach is available.
- There are sufficient financial resources to set up and sustain the sport.

3. Over-emphasizing health foods in the cafeteria. Those parents who are health food advocates should be encouraged to send sack lunches with their children and to concentrate on serving health foods for their own children at breakfast time and for their evening meal. Let the school concentrate on providing a meal that most of the students will eat.

Experience has shown that "lunch" type meals, like tacos, hamburgers, pizza, spaghetti, hot dogs and sloppy joes served with chips are favorites that the children will eat. Fruit and vegetables are a great hit when added to the favorites listed above. The key is to serve the favorites along with foods that are low in fat, cholesterol and sodium, and high in fiber.

4. Misinterpretation of test results, grade equivalents, and comunication of test results. Assist staff in properly interpreting test data to avoid drawing the wrong conclusions. For example, a sixth grader with a ninth grade equivalent score does not possess the skills of a ninth grader. The most accurate statement that can be made in this example is that the sixth grader did exceptionally well on 6th grade material. For more information, see *The Proper Use of Standardized Tests* published by Bob Jones University Press.

Another challenge with using test results is the confusion over grade equivalents. Be cautious of publishing the "fact" that a certain grade of students are half a grade above the national norms. It may be that your students' mean ability level suggests that they ought to be at least that much, if not more, above the average.[34]

Along with grade equivalent cautions, be careful in assuming the average performance for all students. Stating your fifth grade students scored two grades above the national norms leads to the assumption that this in true of all fifth graders, when in fact, some may have performed below the national norm.

Failure to properly communicate test results also causes challenges. Whenever a test is taken, students and parents want to know the results. When addressing students and parents, consider the following: Construct a student profile and explain the purpose of the profile; and point to the child's strengths and the meaning of their strengths. Focus on areas needing improvement and suggest constructive strategies leading toward improvement.

See that each parent receives a copy of the testing results along with a carefully constructed letter of explanation. Address those points that need to be called to the attention of parents and translate the testing terms so parents can understand them. Most test publishers provide narrative reports that describe a child's results in layman's terminology.

A parent-teacher conference is an excellent avenue for reporting achievement results. In a conference setting, parents can ask questions and teachers can:

- Provide test data from quizzes, unit tests, etc.;
- Correlate testing performance with daily classwork;
- Provide samples of the child's successes and difficulties;
- Discuss strategies for improvement and enrichment;
- Explore parent, student, teacher expectation in comparison to the student's abilities and interests; and
- Come into agreement in prayer for the continual success. "...**If two of you shall agree on earth as touching any thing that they shall ask, it shall be done for them of my Father which is in heaven**" (Matt. 18:19). For more information on putting together an in-service program for teachers, see D. M. Dougherty, "An In-service for Training Teachers to Interpret Tests for Parents." *School Counselor*, 1979, 26:317-324.

5. Overlooking other important uses of achievement test results. The primary use of achievement test results for evaluation purposes overshadows other important uses, such as diagnosis. By using achievement test profiles, schools can pinpoint pupil weaknesses and strengths and determine remedial work, or the need for revising methods of teaching. They can also be used as a basis for specifying objectives for teacher training.

Many times administrators fail to consider other achievement measures when making educational decisions. One of these alternative testing measures is criterion-referenced testing. Whereas norm-referenced achievement testing compares the performance of one child with his peers, criterion-reference testing compares the performance of a child on a set of specific acceptable goals, skills, or objectives.

Criterion-referenced tests also can provide a measure of how well the individual has done by comparison with themselves. They also enable the teachers to check on student progress at regular intervals. This enables the teacher to use the results to more readily adjust curriculum and individualize instruction. Schools can use criterion-referenced tests as minimal competency assessments.

Dear Heavenly Father, we set ourselves in agreement for a full-range of ancillary programs. We ask for quality programs in every area and the necessary finances as well as qualified and experienced staff. We ask for parent involvement in every aspect of the total school program along with effective parent leaders. Amen.

> **The degree to which ancillary programs function smoothly and operate efficiently will influence the degree to which the Christian school attracts and retains quality families.**

Christian School Resource Kit

9.1   Athletic Event Contract
9.2   Physicians and Parent Certificate
9.3   Insurance and Athletic Release
9.4   Game Checklists
9.5   Team Rosters
9.6   Athletic Application
9.7   Travel Checklist
9.8   Officials Contract
9.9   Athletic Itinerary
9.10   Athletic Program Evaluation
9.11   Booster Club Outline and Athletic Information Form
9.12   Equipment Issue
9.13   Athletic Inventory

9.52   Bus Rider Agreement

Endnotes

1   John B. Churdar. "Athletics in the Christian School." John W. Deuink, ed., *Some Light on Christian Education*. Greenville, SC: Bob Jones University Press, 1984. p. 157.

2   National Federation of State High School Associations, 11724 Plaza Circle, P.O. Box 20626, Kansas City, MO 64195, 1985.

3   Claude E. Schindler, Jr., Pacheco Pyle, and Steve Karnehm. *The Role of Athletics in the Christian School*. Whittier, CA: ACSI, 1981. p. 4.

4   James W. Deuink, and Carl D. Herbster. *Effective Christian School Management*. 2nd Edition. Greenville, SC: Bob Jones University Press, 1986. p. 123.

5   Schindler, Pyle, and Karnehm, *op. cit.*, p. 34.

6   Dennis M. Demuth and Carol M. Demuth. *Recruiting Strategies for Christian Schools*. Tulsa, OK: DEL Publications, 1993, p. 131.

7   Clayne R. Jensen. *Administrative Management of Physical Education and Athletic Programs*. 2nd Edition. Philadelphia, PA: Lea and Febiger, 1988, p. 355.

8   Eugene R. Howard. *School Discipline Desk Book*. West Nyack, NY: Parker Publishing Company Inc., 1978, p. 134.

9   Jensen, *op. cit.*, p. 286.

10   Adapted from Howard, *op. cit.*, p. 51.

11   Adapted from Edward F. DeRoche. *An Administrator's Guide for Evaluating Programs and Personnel*. Boston, MA: Allyn and Bacon, Inc., 1987, p. 231.

12   Adapted from G. John Berclay. *Parent Involvement in the Schools*, NEA, 1977.

13   Paul Ilsley and John A. Niemi. *Recruiting and Training Volunteers*. New York, NY: McGraw-Hill, 1981, p. 89.

14   Dennis M. Demuth, Mary Martha Black and Carol M. Demuth. *Grandees: A School-Based Volunteer Program*. Tulsa, OK: DEL Publications, 1990, p. 1.

15   Bill Rauhauser. *Design for Implementing Effective Schools Research*. Lewisville, TX: School Improvement Specialists, 1992.

16   Adapted from Robert L. Gibson and Marianne L. Mitchell. *Introduction to Counseling and Guidance*. MacMillian Publishing Company, New York, NY: 1990, p. 471.

17 Mauritz Johnson, Jr., William E. Busacher and Fred Q. Bowman, Jr. *Junior High School Guidance*. New York, NY: Harper and Brothers, 1961, p. 66.

18 Billy Zeoli. *Free Loan Film and Video Program Catalog*. Muskegon, MI: Gospel Films, Inc., 1994.

19 Robert J. Krajewski, John S. Martin and John C. Walden. *The Elementary School Principalship*. New York, NY: Holt, Rinehart and Winston, 1983, p. 135.

20 Johnson, Busacker and Bowman, *op. cit.*, p. 94.

21 Jeff Blyskal and Marie Hodge. "College Guide." *Readers Digest*, Pleasantville, NY, 1988.

22 Dennis M. Demuth. *College Preparation*. Tulsa, OK: DEL Publications, 1990, p. 2.

23 James W. Deuink. *The Ministry of the Christian School Guidance Counselor*. Greenville, SC: Bob Jones University Press, 1985, p. 99.

24 F. E. Burtnett in Stanley B. Baker. *School Counselor's Handbook: A Guide for Professional Growth and Development*. Boston, MA: Allyn and Bacon, Inc., 1981, p. 143.

25 Baker, *Ibid.* p. 168.

26 Adapted from Edward C. Raeber, Glen E. Smith and Clifford E. Erickson. *Organization and Administration of Guidance Services*. New York, NY: McGraw-Hill Book Co., Inc., 1955, p. 189.

27 Baker, *op. cit.*, p. 118.

28 Dennis M. Demuth and Carol M. Demuth. *Legal Requirements for Christian Schools*. 2nd Edition. Tulsa, OK: DEL Publications, 1993.

29 *Ibid.* p. 83.

30 C. Sax. *Principles of Educational and Psychological Measurement and Evaluation*, 2nd Edition. New York, NY, The Ronald Press, 1980, p. 438.

31 DeRoche, *op. cit.*, p. 193.

32 Deuink and Herbster. *op. cit.*, p.118.

33 Dennis M. Demuth. *A Comprehensive Manual For The Christian School Bus Driver*. Tulsa, OK: DEL Publications, 1983.

34 Johnson, Busacker and Bowman. *op. cit.* p. 163.

References

Association of Christian Schools International, P.O. Box 4097, Whittier, CA 90607; (213) 694-4791.

Association of Christian Schools International. Whittier, CA: ACSI. *Legal and Legislative Update.* June, 1992.

Association of Christian Schools International (ACSI). *Legal and Legislative Update.* February, 1994.

American College Testing Program, P.O. Box 168, Iowa City, IA 52243 (ACT).

College Entrance Examination Board, College Board ATP (Admissions Testing Program), P.O. Box 6200, Princeton, NJ 08541 (SAT).

College Grants from Uncle Sam: Am I Eligible and for How Much? Octameron Associates, P.O. Box 3437, Alexandria, VA 22302.

College Loans from Uncle Sam: The Borrower's Guide That Explains it All. Octameron Associates, P.O. Box 3437, Alexandria, VA 22302.

Demuth, Dennis M. *College Preparation for Christian School Students.* Tulsa, OK: DEL Publications, 1990.

Demuth, Dennis M. *Resource Center Handbook.* Tulsa, OK: Victory Christian School, 1982.

Demuth, Dennis M., Black, Mary Martha, and Demuth, Carol M. *Grandees: A School-Based Volunteer Program.* Tulsa, OK: DEL Publications, 1990.

Demuth, Dennis M. and Demuth, Carol M. *Legal Requirements for Christian Schools.* 2nd Edition. DEL Publications, Tulsa, OK, 1993.

Demuth, Dennis M. and Demuth, Carol M. *Microcomputer Applications for Christian Educators.* Tulsa, OK: DEL Publications, 1992.

Demuth, Dennis M. and Demuth, Carol M. *Recruiting Strategies For Christian Schools.* Tulsa, OK: DEL Publications, 1992.

Department of Labor, 200 Constitution Avenue N.W., Washington, DC, 20210; (202) 219-6411.

Deuink, James W. *The Proper Use of Standardized Tests.* Greenville, SC: Bob Jones University Press, 1986.

Fiske, Edward. *Fiske Guide to Colleges.* New York, NY: Times Books, Random House, Inc., 1994.

Free Loan Film and Video Program Catalog. Gospel Films, Inc., P.O. Box 455, Muskegon, MI 49443.

Gabler Foundation, P.O. Box 7518, Longview, TX 75601.

Harcourt Brace Jovanovich, Inc., 757 Third Avenue, New York, NY 10017.

Houghton Mifflin Co., One Beacon Street, Boston, MA 02107.

International Christian Accreditation Association. 7777 South Lewis Avenue, Tulsa, OK 74171; (918) 495-7054.

Kalman, A. Chany and Martz, Geoff. *The Access Guide to Paying for College.* New York, NY: Villard Books, 1992.

Kesslar, O. *Financial Aids for Higher Education: A Catalog for Undergraduates.* Dubuque, IA: Wm C. Brown, 1990.

Kuder Preference Record. CTB MacMillian/McGraw-Hill, Delmonte Research Park, 2500 Garden Road, Monterey, CA 93940; (408) 649-8400.

Ohio Vocational Interest Survey (OVIS). Psychological Corporation, 555 Academic Court, San Antonio, TX 78204.

Oral Roberts Educational Fellowship, 7777 South Lewis, Tulsa, OK 74171; (918) 495-7054.

Peterson's College Money Handbook, 7th Edition. Princeton, NJ: Peterson's Guides, 1991.

Peterson's Guide to Four-Year Colleges, Peterson's Guide, Princeton, NJ: Peterson's Guides, 1994.

Scholarships, Fellowships and Loans (vol. 8). S & M. Feingold. Arlington, MA: Bellman Publishing, 1987.

Stanley H. Kaplan Educational Center, Ltd. 810 7th Avenue, 22nd Floor, New York, New York 10019; (800) 527-8378.

Strong-Campbell Interest Inventories (SCII). Consulting Psychologists Press, Inc., 577 College Avenue, Palo Alto, CA. 94306; (800) 624-1765.

Study Power. Iowa City, IA: American College Testing Program (ACT), 1987.

The Barron's Profiles of American Colleges, Hauppauge, NY: Barron's Educational Series, Inc., 1992.

The Directory of The National Trade and Professional Associations of the United States. Washington, DC: Columbia Books, 1994.

The National Parent Teacher Association, 700 North Rush Street, Chicago, Illinois 60611; (312) 787-0977.

The Psychological Corporation, 757 Third Avenue, New York, NY 10017.

Computer Software

The Columbia Library System. McGraw-Hill School Systems, 20 Ryan Ranch Road, Monterey, CA 93940; (800) 663-0544.

C LECT. Marketed by Chronicle Guidance Publications, Inc., P.O. Box 1190, Moravia, NY 13118; (800) 899-0460. The system includes three modules: an occupational module, an educational module, and a financial aid-apprenticeship module.

Career Information Systems (CIS) and *Guidance Information Systems* (GIS) by Houghton Mifflin Co., One Beacon Street, Boston, MA 02107.

Coaches Secretary. Software Associates of North East, P.O. Box 70, North East, PA 16428; (814) 725-9279.

Discovery Systems by Discover, Inc. Marketed by American College Testing Program (ACT), P.O. Box 168, Iowa City, IA 52240.

Master Meal Planner. Thomas C. Johnson. 9920 S Palmer Rd., New Carlisle, OH 45344.

PC-Sport. Geoffrey Celic Monkley listed in *The PC-SIG Encyclopedia of Shareware.* 4th Edition. Sunnyvale, CA: PC-SIG, Inc. 1991.

Schedule Magic. Murray Spitzer Associates listed in *The PC-SIG Encyclopedia of Shareware.* 4th Edition. Sunnyvale, CA: PC-SIG, Inc. 1991.

SIRS. Social Issues Resources Series, Inc. P.O. Box 2348, Boca Raton, FL 33427; (800) 232-SIRS.

Sports League Management. Sports League Management Association listed in *The PC-SIG Encyclopedia of Shareware.* 4th Edition. Sunnyvale, CA: PC-SIG, Inc. 1991.

System of Interactive Guidance and Information (SIGF) by Educational Testing Service (ETS), Rosedale Road, Princeton, NJ 08540.

STEP 10

MAKE FINAL PREPARATIONS

M aking the final preparations for the opening of school is a critical time. Edward DeRoche offered these thoughts:

"The problems of and procedures for opening the school for a new school year will vary depending upon the size of the school, the level of the school (elementary, middle, senior high), and the experience of the school principal. However, the one task that every principal faces is that of proper planning. There is no excuse for the confusion and chaos that sometimes occur during the first few days of school. Certainly, proper planning will not take care of every problem and emergency, but it will help you and your staff handle problems more effectively."[1]

Complete Final Preparations Checklist

Having read the material and completed the checklists found in steps one through nine, you should be well on your way to being ready to open your new Christian school. Only a few more details need your attention. Consider the following six different categories—staff, office, instruction, facilities, finances and students.

Complete Final Checklist

Review each category and check those items that are complete. Transfer each incomplete item to the action plan found in appendix C. Indicate the task objective and identify a completion date along with the name of the person responsible for completing each item.

Staff

☐ Complete teacher hiring.

☐ Assign teachers based on enrollment.

☐ Finalize teacher/staff handbook.

☐ Prepare teacher orientation.

☐ Assign staff to unit leaders.

☐ Complete teacher checklist of tasks to do.

☐ Complete substitute teacher list and procedures.

☐ Prepare staff employment packets.

☐ Send out formal welcome letter to staff.

☐ Invite new teachers to the school to acquaint them with the school's facilities, resources and services. Answer questions about school routine, school activities, development and evaluation, supervision responsibilities and other school procedures.

Office

☐ Assign staff mailboxes.

☐ Complete school directory.

☐ Finalize school calendar.

☐ Prepare lunch schedules.

☐ Prepare first month's lunch menu.

☐ Prepare pupil attendance tracking system.

☐ Publish student handbook with last-minute changes.

☐ Produce school activities schedule.

☐ Prepare checklist of first-day tasks.

☐ Prepare registration materials and procedures.

☐ Issue school opening news release.

☐ Check on missing immunization records, birth certificates and transcripts.

☐ Prepare chapel seating charts.

☐ Finalize parent-teacher fellowship officers.

☐ Plan first staff meeting.

☐ Write pre-opening staff newsletter.

☐ Design a staff directory, complete with pictures.

☐ Appoint a school historian.

☐ Arrange for taking pictures, especially of the very first day.

Instruction

☐ Place order for additional textbooks based on late enrollments.

☐ Place supplies in classrooms. Hicks and Jameson exhort, "The principal and his office staff should leave no chalk box unturned in their effort to have in each teacher's room those tools she has ordered and the equipment she needs."[2]

☐ Prepare special subject schedules.

☐ Produce secondary student schedules.

☐ Finalize field trip procedures.

☐ Prepare textbook distribution procedures.

☐ Finalize all instructional scopes and sequences.

☐ Check all AV equipment.

☐ Double check classlists.

Facilities

☐ Make final classroom furniture placements.

☐ Set clocks, bells and intercom.

☐ Complete lunchroom facilities.

☐ Check all heating and cooling systems.

☐ Prepare bus schedules.

☐ Prepare locker assignments.

☐ Check fire alarm system and fire drill procedures.

☐ Formulate traffic regulations and determine traffic flow.

☐ Add desks and chairs for late enrolling students.

Finances

☐ Inventory late arriving books and supply orders.

☐ Prepare student insurance packets.

☐ Finalize all scholarships and work-study programs.

☐ Prepare lunch ticket procedure.

☐ Finalize all accounting procedures.

Students

☐ Plan new student orientation.

☐ Formulate policies for student council, clubs and safety patrol.

☐ Schedule assembly programs.

☐ Finalize athletic eligibility rules.

Prepare First-Day Procedures

The first day of school is important. It sets the stage for the entire school year. It is the one school day that every parent will ask their children about, teachers will over-plan for, and administrators will look to put behind them. Some friends of ours asked their daughter, who was starting kindergarten, "How was your first day of school?" The little girl gave the thumbs up sign and said, "Great."

The key to a successful "Day One" is preparation. Include the following in your planning.

Teacher Communications

Even though teachers, new and veterans, have been at school three to ten or more days before the students arrive, preparing their classrooms, developing lesson plans and attending orientation workshops, it is necessary to disseminate information in writing about first-day expectations. Consider the following items, keeping in mind that your list may vary depending upon your school's unique needs.

1   **Arrival times.** Expect teachers to arrive an extra 30 to 40 minutes early for devotions and last-minute instructions. Schools with K-12 programs can stagger the arrival times and start dates of elementary and secondary school. Starting elementary school students a day early has many advantages, the greatest of which is freeing up secondary staff to help manage first-day routines.

2   **Lesson Plans.** Require teachers to present a well-organized lesson plan for the first day. As the Chernows' encourage, "It is better to have too much material in the lesson plans for the first days than too little. Make the first day of school a 'real' day, complete with homework. This will tell pupils that you mean business."[3]

3   **Student Arrival.** Various arrangements are possible, depending upon the grade levels of the school and numbers of students enrolled. Smaller schools may have students come directly to classrooms. When this is the case, send a welcome letter to the parents notifying them of the room numbers and names of teachers. Have class lists available during registration and post class lists on the entrance doors and hallways. Providing the weather is acceptable, larger schools with more than one class per grade level may line children up outside by grade level. Classroom teachers then escort their class to the assigned classroom. Send students whose names do not appear on the class lists to the school office to check on enrollment information before going to class. Have plenty of parent volunteers ready to assist when students arrive.

4   **Student Schedules.** Secondary students with schedules can go directly to their first-hour class. If schedules have not already been distributed, instruct students to go to an assigned room number by grade level to pick up their schedule. Send all students without schedules to the school office.

5   **Supervision assignments.** All teachers need to be on duty for the first two weeks of school. Clearly identify play zones and supervi-

sion expectations. Pay close attention to supervision of student unloading zones.

6   **Lunch.** Review cafeteria procedures and off-campus procedures, dismissal times, lunch ticket purchases and lunch count.

7   **Attendance.** Although attendance systems will vary from school to school, consider the following ideas:

- Collect attendance at the end of the first hour of school.
- Compare attendance rosters against registration roster.
- Make arrangements to call all parents whose children were not in attendance. This process will help determine whether or not the student is absent due to illness or to a decision not to attend your school. This is especially critical for schools with students waiting for a class opening. Contact these parents as soon as space is evident.

8   **Other teacher tasks.** Other first-day tasks include:

- Assigning lockers
- Distribution of textbooks
- Registering student vehicles
- Reviewing bell schedules
- Establishing classroom routines
- Conducting student tours of the building and grounds
- Monitoring hallway behavior
- Reviewing transportation issues

9   **Dismissal procedures.** Larger schools should consider a staggered dismissal of five to ten minutes between elementary and secondary school. Plan on having teachers escort all elementary students to either the bus loading zone or the vehicle pick-up area. Assign secondary teachers to traffic supervision. Escort all elementary students to any after-school program.

Office Tasks

The first day is generally one of the busiest days of the year. Here are some suggestions to make the day a success for office staff.

1   **Parent Volunteers.** Pre-train a few key parent volunteers to assist with receptionist duties, such as answering the phone and making parents and students feel welcome. Use them to collect attendance, to call absentees and to escort late arrivals to their classroom.

2   **Late Registration.** Be prepared to deal with late registration, having available all necessary information, forms and registration packets.

3   **Unexpected Challenges**. Anticipate everything that can come up. Be prepared to deal with a false fire alarm, sick students, lost lunch money, misplaced bus tickets, child-parent separations, absent teachers, high school pranks and much more.

Administrator Tasks

The first day of school finds administrators at two extremes. At the one end are those who are confined to their office, having to deal with multiple first-day parent issues. On the other extreme are administrators who are all over the building taking care of situations that should have been dealt with days, weeks, or months earlier. Ideally, the first day should be "a day of sitting back and enjoying the sweet fruits of your long hard hours of preparation. Oh, wonderful day!"[4]

The following administrative activities will ensure a smooth first day:

1   Check loading and unloading of buses.
2   Be at the entrance before the bell rings to greet students and parents. Have a teacher available to speak with parents who have concerns. However, don't allow a few parents to monopolize your entire day.
3   Visit each teacher in his or her classroom. There is something about the presence of the administrator that helps calm teacher butterflies and establishes the fact that everything is under control.
4   Visit special teachers and librarian.
5   Check lavatories during class changes.
6   Check on absent students.
7   Visit lunchroom during class changes.
8   Meet with new students and parents.
9   Be present at the main exit at dismissal.
10 Plan no less than a 15-minute staff briefing and planning session following dismissal for the remainder of the first week.[5]

Plan Student Activities

New schools often fall into the trap of waiting until after school starts to plan student activities. Since the student activities program is an important part of the total educational program, it should be part of your final preparations before school starts.

According to effective school research, "High school class rank and test scores are the best predictors of academic success in college, but involvement sustained over time in one or two extracurricular activities contributes to overall achievement in college. On the other hand, when these activities become ends in themselves, academic performance may suffer."[6]

Establish the Activities Program

Activities are going to happen in any school. They can be either planned or unplanned. It is to your advantage to plan for these activities. Only through creative planning and staff commitment will you develop a good student activities program.

The success of your program depends on establishing written goals. For example: the student activities program provides opportunities for recognition, personal success and broader experience to complement academic achievement; the chance to develop intellectual, social, cultural and physical talents; and to develop leadership skills and to foster Christlike behaviors and attitudes.

Range of Activities

In selecting activities, look for ones to enrich and reinforce the philosophy of the school. Offer a wide variety of activities one to three days a month, such as arts and crafts, in-depth academic activities, science exploration, model building, library club, stamp collecting and more.

Other effective activities are fun fairs, academic olympics, chess or checker tournaments, spirit week, spiritual life council, model building, treasure hunt, hobby day, science scavenger search, secret friend day, record breaking day, egg drop, paper chaining, mural painting, international dinner, school-wide talent show and frog racing.

Student Participation

Encourage maximum attendance by scheduling some activities during the school day. This allows students with out-of-school obligations and interests to attend. It also alleviates the challenge of students who want to participate, but must rely on a school or city bus, or others to transport them home.

Adding an extra period at the beginning or the end of the school day allows for scheduling of more activities with fewer conflicts. Modular scheduling allows students with unscheduled time and opportunity to reschedule in order to participate in activities.

Don't overlook elementary and middle schools as you plan; they should have activity programs as part of the total school program. Students who become involved in student activities are more likely to continue in those activities, therefore increasing a school's enrollment potential for the next year.

Activity Budget

Plan your student activities program as an integral part of your school budget. Parents and students prefer paying a one-time activities fee rather than being "nickeled and dimed" every time an activity takes place.

Establishing an activity fee and collecting it at the time of registration will reduce the number of special fund-raisers. The following guidelines will enhance accounting of activity funds:

- Assure that funds will be used for their intended purpose. Accomplish this by establishing a restricted account for each activity. Funnel deposits and withdrawals through the school office.
- Issue official receipts for all money deposits.
- Disperse all money through a purchase order, check request and petty cash fund system.
- Require supporting documents for all expenditures made; for example, sales slips.
- Provide for staff supervision to assure adequate control.
- Require monthly reconciliation by those in charge of each restricted fund.

Schedule All Activities Before School Starts

Require all major activities to be pre-scheduled prior to the start of school and placed on a master activities calendar. When scheduling events, consider other activities planned by the churches of your students and the community. Consider using a computer calendar program, such as *Creative Calendar Plus,* to help avoid scheduling conflicts.

Establish a Written Approval System

According to Hansford, "A well-designed, well-planned, and well-executed student activities program can aid in raising student morale and in accomplishing the objectives of the school."[7] For these factors to be present, you should establish a written approval system. Use a planning/approval form that clearly defines the following elements: time, place, and location of event or activity; staff and parent sponsors; staff/parent to pupil ratio (5:1 for elementary, 10:1 for junior high and 15:1 for senior high); telephone numbers to reach in case of an emergency; departure, arrival and return times; and costs [CSRK 10.1].

The approval system should include the following assurances:

- Approval no less than two weeks in advance of the event.
- Chaperons that are pre-approved by administration.

- Written parental release for all school-sponsored off-campus events [CSRK 10.2].
- Signed medical release/treatment permission forms from parents for any overnight event as well as those where there is a probability of injury, such as athletic teams, wilderness adventures, hiking, hayrides, camping, mission trips, and others.
- Completion of a post-event evaluation to be retained for future reference [CSRK 10.3].
- Registration of all bus drivers with the school's insurance provider.
- Completion of a student activities roster [CSRK 10.4].

Properly Communicate Activities

It is very rewarding for parents and students to know the who, what, when, where and why of student activities. They should also be able to call the school office and find someone who knows what is happening. Maintaining a master activity log at the receptionist desk would be a great benefit to all concerned. Require a daily posting of activities and updating of changes. Consider using a voice message machine giving the times and locations of all after-school activities.

Establish Key Activities

There are several student activities that are basic to any Christian school. These include:
- Chapels and Assemblies
- Student Council
- School Publications
- Clubs and Organizations
- Fairs
- Ministry Opportunities
- Fun and Fellowship

Chapels and Assemblies

The primary focus of chapels is to enhance the spiritual goals of the school. Chapel programs may consist of a number of elements, such as praise and worship, special music, guest speakers, etc. Many schools have chapels for subgroups within the student body, such as grades one to three, four through six, junior high, and senior high. Each group meets one or two times per week for forty to ninety minutes.

DeRoche notes, "Assemblies provide opportunities to expand the knowledge and content of the regular curriculum, to motivate students, to build interest, to promote acceptable group behavior, and to promote school spirit."[8] Schedule no more than one assembly per month (including pep rallies) and no fewer than one per quarter.

Enhance the success of chapels and assemblies by the following actions:

1   Form a student/teacher group to plan, organize, direct and evaluate chapels and assemblies so everyone in the school feels that the chapels and assemblies are theirs.

2   Keep as the primary focus of chapels the spiritual development of the student body.

3   Have education and entertainment as the primary goal of assemblies.

4   Avoid chapels as "just another chapel service." Add variety through the use of dramatizations, musical groups and programs, films, panels and other creative activities.

5   Consider outside groups for chapel and assembly presentations.

6   Plan chapels and assemblies well in advance of the date scheduled and include topics in the school's activity calendar.

7   Obtain approval from the administrator for all guest speakers [10.5].

8   Add variety to assembly programs with debates, panel discussion, student exhibits, honor society, awards, "pep" rallies, motion pictures, forums on current topic related to students, plays, patriotic themes, hobbies, and more.

9   Conclude chapel and assemblies on time.

Student Council

One of the most worthwhile student activities is student council. DeRoche comments, "The earlier we get children and young people involved in government of the school, the quicker they will learn their rights and more importantly their responsibilities. They may even come to appreciate the problems and processes of decision making in a democracy and the role of principals and teachers in operating a school."[9]

Elementary. Student governance at the elementary level should include several responsibilities, such as class officers (elected each month), hall monitoring, clean up, collection and distribution of homework, seatwork, attendance takers and lunch money collection. Students in grades five and six can serve on a principal's advisory council. They provide suggestions about regulations, rules, procedures, chapels and special projects. If a school is not comfortable with an elementary student council, establish a student advisory committee. Let them work with teachers and parent advisors on meaningful projects.

Junior and Senior High. Develop student leadership within the student body by establishing a Junior Council (grades seven and eight) and a Senior Council (grades nine to twelve). Under the supervision of the secondary administrator or faculty advisor, create a student constitution.

Establish and operate the council according to the constitution. Include in the constitution the name of the organization, membership, power vested, elections, duties of council members, impeachment, powers and duties of elected officers, meeting procedures, amendments and by-laws, election dates and procedures, terms of office, vacancies of office, standing committees, and operations. (A copy of a sample student constitution is available through DEL Publications.)

School Publications

Every Christian school needs to provide avenues for student self-expression and creative effort, such as school newspapers, magazines and yearbooks. A well-prepared publication can be a valuable asset to the school, both elementary and secondary. One primary benefit often overlooked by many is the value of these publications in documenting the history of the school, its students, staff and events. They also serve as excellent promotional tools and build school unity—bringing students, parents and staff closer in contact with one another.

Establish a good foundation for your school publications by implementing the following actions:

1   **Guidelines**. Provide written publication guidelines and procedures that support the school's vision and philosophy. This requires careful review of the contents of all publications, both written and pictorial. Information should be true, should not cause embarrassment and be in good taste. Points of view should be constructive. Exclude all nonsense. This does not mean that wholesome humor should be excluded. [10]

2   **Advisors**. Appoint journalism teachers or publication advisors who know the ethics of good journalism.

3   **Editing**. Arrange for competent editing. Publications that are attractive, well-written, free of misspelled words and contain proper sentence structure and correct punctuation, make a positive impression on all who read them.

4   **Students Participation**. Allow student participation on the publication staff only upon teacher and administrative recommendation. Place qualifications for students to serve on these publications in

writing (for example, grade point average, leadership and spiritual qualities, etc.).

5   **Curriculum.** Develop a curriculum for each publication that includes a balance between production tasks (picture taking, layout, printing) and learning skills of editorializing, reporting and writing.

6   **Special Features.** Include features on school life, hobbies and interests of students and staff. Provide written accounts of notable accomplishments of students and alumni. Use good cartoons on the lighter side of school life; all of these stimulate interest in the school.

7   **Preparation Time.** Provide ample time for students and advisors to prepare the publications during school time.

8   **Budget.** Establish a budget for each publication. Include along with expenses, sources of income, such as student fees, advertising and sponsorships.

9   **Training.** Send faculty advisors and publication staff to summer workshops (Contact public school advisors for workshops in your area).

10 **Evaluation.** Provide for ongoing evaluation [CSRK 10.6].

Clubs and Organizations

Student clubs and organizations add fun and excitement to the school program. They provide opportunities for students to use gifts, talents and abilities that would otherwise go unnoticed and unfulfilled and to develop new interests. Involving students, teachers and parents together in clubs and organizations builds school unity.

Consider the following suggestions:

1   Establish a process whereby any group of students may start a club or organization [CSRK 10.7].

2   Consider chartering all student clubs and organizations through the Student Council.

3   Require all clubs and organizations to be registered with the Student Council by mid-October.

4   Provide advisory directions and obtain leadership from a parent or staff sponsor.

5   Increase student participation by scheduling club and organization activities during the day.

6   Keep participation costs as minimal as possible.

The following is a partial grouping of clubs:

- Service—library, camera, radio
- Academic—foreign language, science, computer, creative writing, honor society

- Hobby—crafts, dramatics, dance, travel, woodworking
- Career—business, mechanics, medicine, science, education
- Ministry—puppets, music, drama, national and international missions

Fair

School fairs enrich the curriculum and provide opportunities for students to apply what they are learning. They provide an outlet for creativity, help develop problem-solving skills and are a great recruiting tool. Art, science and industrial arts are among the most popular.

Ministry

Many Christian schools provide opportunities for students to fulfill James 1:22, "**Be ye doers of the word, and not hearers only, deceiving you own selves.**" Ministry opportunities may include such activities as:

- Christian service, such as nursing homes, children's homes, hospitals, schools, for disadvantaged children, feeding the hungry,
- Missions trips,
- Evangelism,
- Music and drama ministry.

Participating in ministry opportunities will have a lasting influence upon the lives of those who participate. Consider the following suggestions:

1   Offer ministry opportunities for all grade levels not as an end in themselves, but as activities that help fulfill a specific school objective.

2   Plan activities well in advance to adequately prepare those involved for ministry.

3   Exercise caution in establishing criteria for ministry as not to exclude those students who could benefit the most by being involved. Over the years, we have found that some of the "less spiritual" students are the ones that have produced the most fruit from ministry opportunities.

4   Keep parents informed from the very beginning of ministry opportunities requiring students to miss school. Carefully plan all fund-raising and other financial assistance well in advance of the event. At the same time keep parents and students informed of the need and current status of monies available. Require all tuition accounts to be current before permission is given to participate in trips requiring significant funds.

5   Plan extended missions and ministry trips during days when students are not in school, such as during spring break or at the end of the school term.

6   Establish a working relationship with one or two mission organizations for all out-of-country mission trips so each year's activities can build upon the previous year. Also, as plans are refined from year to year, cost effectiveness is increased, and the amount of planning and preparation is greatly reduced.

7   Obtain consent for medical treatment/illness and hold harmless documentation for all foreign travel [10.8].

Fun and Fellowship

What would school be like if it were all work and no play? Offer a variety of activities for students to promote fun and fellowship. This contributes to high student morale, adds vitality to school life and enhances the overall school climate. Activities such as a pizza party, ice cream social, picnic, record breaking day, bonfire spirit week, fun fair, banquet, scavenger hunt, wilderness adventure, international dinner, talent show, bowling and skating are big winners.

In addition to the suggestions found in the first few pages of this section, consider the following:

1   Establish a system of approval and scheduling of all activities. If possible, use the same approval process for all activities.

2   Approve only those activities that are consistent with the school's statement of purpose and social goals.

3   Avoid competition with the church-sponsored youth program.

4   Limit the number of class-sponsored activities to no more than two per year, especially when the school is already planning school-wide events.

5   Enlist the leadership of only those teachers and parents who are interested and enthusiastic about the activity.

NOTE: *Quality fun and fellowship activities will be directly related to the quality of planning and supervision provided.*

Nurture School Spirit

Very closely associated with school activities is school spirit. Every activity that is well-planned, directed and enthusiastically nurtured contributes to building school spirit. Furthermore, a school song, colors and mascot all enhance school spirit.

School Song

An inspired school song embedded in the hearts of the students will be a song remembered years following graduation. Therefore, it should be selected with much thought and care. Consider the following:

1   Compose original words and music; tap the creative resources of your parents, pupils and staff.

2   Do not settle for school-created words written to some existing tune. Expect the inspiration of the Holy Spirit in creating a song that is unique to your school.

3   Create a tune that is lively, with strong rhythm, easily sung by all children in all grades.

4   Choose words that express the character and embody the philosophy of the school. Avoid phrases such as "ours is the best school," and "We can beat em all," etc.

5   Avoid using a contest in selecting the words and music. The song that receives the most votes may not be the one that meets the requirements for dignity, "singability," and expression of the schools philosophy.

School Colors

Everyone remembers their school colors. Selecting the right combination requires careful thought, especially when colors are given meaning, such as red representing the blood of Jesus or the fire of evangelism. Some suggestions follow.

1   Involve as many people as possible in the selection process—students, parents and staff. When selecting colors for a kindergarten through twelfth grade program, obtain input from students, starting in fifth grade.

2   Display suggested color combinations throughout the school, to show color harmony and color clashes.

3   Focus attention on basic color combinations that are readily available. This will become even more important when it comes time for outfitting the athletic teams. Certain colors, such as UCLA's Columbia Blue and Gold, may be two or three times more expensive than royal blue or navy.

4   Take into account other school colors within the same athletic association and conference.

5   Select the final three color combinations and have school students, parents and staff vote on the color combination they like the best.

School Mascot

Almost everyone knows about the Dallas Cowboys, Washington Redskins, Detroit Lions, Wisconsin Badgers, or Indiana Hoosiers. A carefully selected school mascot is an important element in fostering school spirit. Consider the following:

1   Select a mascot that is easily understood and identifiable and can be incorporated into cheers, placed on pennants, decals, stickers, notebooks, pencil boxes, or seat cushions.

2   Select names that focus attention on biblical and Christian concepts such as Conquerors, Patriots, Golden Eagles, etc.

3   Select a mascot that will be appropriate for years to come and can be incorporated into school tradition and custom.

4   As with school colors, select a mascot that will not conflict with existing mascots from the same community or athletic conference.

Other School Spirit Ideas

Other ways to foster school spirit are through a school flag, crest, license plates, bumper stickers, etc. Some schools place their crest on school uniforms (sport coats and jackets). License plates and bumper stickers have the advantage of providing free advertising. If at all possible, offer these free to students and parents at the time of enrollment.

Institute a Year-Round Tickler

Hicks and Johnson share, "One of the administrator's most dependable servants is his filing cabinet. Be it a handsome steel one with smoothly sliding drawers, or an antiquated affair that constantly rebels, it is indispensable. Don't keep it across the room or over by the door. Have it by your desk, reachable."[11]

One of the first folders in this filing cabinet is marked SEPTEMBER, followed by a file for each of the remaining eleven months—known as a tickler file. Don't be surprised if you find yourself making numerous important entries on a weekly basis. At one time or another, every Christian educator will come to realize that things can be done better the next time around.

Computer Assistance

Administrators who have ready access to a computer can easily create a tickler file using a spreadsheet or database program. Others may purchase ready-made time and task management programs, such as *Personal Calendar* or *Tickler*. Samples of two commercial programs are *Top Priority* and *Priority Manager*.

The advantage of *Priority Manager* is its ability to delegate to others and monitor these activities, automatically tracking due dates, displaying the number of days remaining until each activity is due, and reminding you when it is time to follow up on delegated activities.

Prepare for Month-By-Month Tasks

The following is a list of monthly tasks taken from an experienced Christian school administrator's tickler file system. Reviewing these tasks as a first year school will provide an idea of what to expect during a typical school year. Established schools can review these tasks for ideas that would enhance their present programs.

September

- Schedule first meeting of clubs.
- Sponsor a social for workers in other departments of the church that use the same classrooms, such as Sunday School, Youth, etc.
- Readjust schedules of individuals where indicated.
- Plan first open house, use Back-to-School as theme.
- Make late registration assignments.
- Begin sale of student and family activity passes.
- Meet with all class activity and club sponsors.
- Order needed books and equipment (due to additional enrollment).
- Schedule fire drills—no less than one per quarter.
- Write letter of instruction to parents concerning the use of the *Student Study and Assignment Notebook.*
- Plan the Fall Spiritual Emphasis Week for early October.
- Plan pep assemblies.
- Begin planning for Spring Missions Week.
- Begin signing up students for annual Christian school competition.
- Post national ACT and SAT test dates.
- Submit yearly fund-raising strategies to finance board for approval.
- Appoint parents to School Improvement Task Force.
- Review and evaluate transcripts of grades and other data received through the mail pertaining to new students.
- Check on status of school newspaper.

- Meet with home schoolers association officers.

October

- Plan Spirit Week.
- Plan Columbus Day recognition.
- Evaluate the effectiveness of discipline policies.
- Schedule class visitations.
- Conduct student government elections.
- Enroll students in community Science Fair to be held in February.
- Review ACT/SAT test dates with students.
- Begin planning for Christian School Conference completion.
- Submit accreditation report.
- Meet with School Improvement Task Force.
- Secure commencement speaker.
- Improve the exit time for fire drills.
- Schedule Christmas outreach programs to shopping centers, children's homes, nursing homes, etc.
- Publish school student directory as fund-raiser.
- Order achievement tests.
- Make arrangements for participation in state spelling bee.

November

- Review report card failures with students and factors relating to underachievement.
- Begin budget for next year.
- Prepare article for New Year's edition of local newspaper.
- Plan appropriate recognition of Veteran's Day.
- Prepare for National Education Week (Christian).
- Remember Thanksgiving recess.
- Plan P.T.F. for middle of November.
- Begin definite plans for Christmas program.
- Start Christmas songs no later than November 7th.
- Conduct first formal teacher appraisals.
- Publish quarter-finals schedule.
- Arrange for the taking of school pictures.

December

- Plan the Adopt-A-Family program that collects food for needy families.
- Present Christmas program.
- Re-affirm snow call-list.
- Use Christmas art from the classrooms for local newspaper release.
- Schedule Christmas caroling at shopping centers, children's homes, nursing homes, etc.
- Establish uniform policy with regard to homework during Christmas break.
- Plan personal work for December vacation recess.
- Get teachers' holiday addresses and phone numbers.
- Prepare vacation schedules for office staff.
- Plan music for spring music festival.
- Meet with School Improvement Task Force.
- Plan program for P.T.F.
- Publish honor roll.
- Check on status of yearbook.

January

- Send sales tax rebate letter to parents encouraging them to donate their rebate to the school for science equipment.
- Hand out college scholarship applications.
- Evaluate effectiveness of Christian school in all areas.
- Work with faculty in the planning of subject offerings for the next school year.
- Prepare first outline of needed expenditures for next year.
- Review ACT/SAT tests dates.
- Publish finals schedule.
- Check on systematic progress through the texts to determine whether or not teachers are on target.
- Start list of new personnel needs.
- Plan changes for second semester.
- Gear up for second semester enrollment.
- Conduct second semester student survey; meet with all students who indicate they will not be returning.

- Plan college seminar.
- Began plans for eighth grade Wilderness Adventure.
- Plan exciting activity to overcome February blahs, such as student and staff socials (Valentine theme).
- Conduct administrative appraisal.
- Organize prom planning committee.

February

- Plan recognition of Lincoln's and Washington's birthdays.
- Prepare budget for the following school year in detail.
- Arrange for preparation of new student handbook.
- Begin plans for Easter program.
- Submit names for community-sponsored engineering day.
- Submit computer grant.
- Begin plans for summer school.
- Visit college campuses to interview prospective staff for upcoming school year.
- Conduct Science Fair.
- Begin plans for high school commencement.

March

- Begin re-enrollment for next year.
- Offer letters of intent to rehire teachers for next year.
- Hold math olympics.
- Make final commencement arrangements.
- Order graduation announcements, caps and gowns.
- Order diplomas.
- Confirm graduation speaker.
- Prepare newspaper release about graduates.
- Announce college scholarship; obtain written acceptance.
- Conduct first open house.
- Prepare spring vacation schedules for office staff.
- Prepare faculty and students for a new appreciation of Easter.
- Plan announcements concerning summer school.
- Conduct eighth grade Wilderness Adventure.
- Prepare to schedule high school students for next year's courses.

- Check test supplies and orders for spring achievement testing.
- Conduct eighth grade Parent's Night to explain ninth grade program.
- Hold open house for public.
- Begin rehearsing choirs for end-of-year program.
- Plan Church/School Emphasis Day.
- Notify juniors of summer pictures; invite area photographer to conduct presentation.
- Hold student activity–Record Day.
- Conduct tuition cost assessment for coming year.
- Send out re-enrollment letters.

April

- Conduct open house.
- Prepare for giving of achievement tests.
- Conduct achievement testing.
- Review with staff, challenges of individual students pertaining to retention or repetition of specific subjects or grades. Develop change strategies.
- Schedule all-school picture day.
- Get lists from teachers of equipment they would like to have for next year.
- Check on delivery date for yearbook.
- Finalize yearbook distribution.
- Conduct Christian radio-sponsored school day.
- Conduct college presented Health Fair.
- Go on Senior missions trip.
- Finalize next year's school calendar.
- Distribute end-of-year checklist.
- Complete new budget.

May and June

- Obtain summer school recommendations.
- Make curriculum and administrative changes.
- Remember Memorial Day.
- Hold awards assembly.
- Hold talent assemblies.

- Finalize Prom.
- Review athletic inventory.
- Post finals schedule.
- Develop summer Driver's Ed program.
- Request recommendations for class sponsors.
- Plan end-of-year teacher fellowship.
- Plan sports banquet.
- Hold report cards for past-due accounts.
- Process transcripts.
- Plan school picnic.
- Conduct New Horizons Day where elementary students visit a classroom in their next year grade level.
- Present Parent Action Team recommendations to school board.
- Register for PSAT.
- Renew subscriptions.
- Distribute Yearbook.
- Take school choir or tour.
- Organize a school-wide clean-up day.
- Place textbook order for next year.
- Plan Fun Fair for September.
- Conduct graduation.

July

- Ensure that all high school diplomas are sent.
- Post achievement labels on curriculum files.
- Install a program clock. Connect to bell or buzzer system.
- Revise teacher handbook.
- Revise student/parent handbook.
- Repair/replace student desks.
- Order supplies, especially bulletin board paper.
- Test and interview new students.
- Present Christian school to churches and community .
- Schedule radio programs that put the school before Christian parents daily.
- File Form 5578 with the state.

- Review job descriptions.
- Mail monthly newsletter to all former, returning, and prospective students, with emphasis on enrollment and re-enrollment.
- Plan student/teacher orientation.
- Review student insurance policy.

August

- Conduct teacher orientation.
- Set up equipment for hot lunch program.
- Conduct faculty dinner.
- Interview new teachers.
- Make room assignments based on enrollment.
- Finalize cleaning of facility.
- Revise kindergarten handbook.
- Plan kindergarten registration.
- Plan 1-12th grade registration.
- Set bell schedule.
- Assign faculty unit leaders.
- Revise policies for books and supplies.
- Establish goals for the new school year.
- Review cafeteria plan and food service program.
- Send faculty letter—formal announcement of school opening.
- Plan orientation assemblies for new students.
- Finalize school calendar.
- Acquaint staff with supplies and library.
- Revise first-day procedures.

Prepare for Weekly to Quarterly Tasks

There are a number of tasks that occur on a weekly, monthly and quarterly basis. Consider the following:

Weekly

- Conduct Administrative Team meeting.
- Sign teacher substitute payments.
- Sign purchase orders.
- Review cash reports.

- Publish eligibility lists.

Monthly

- Inspect grounds and facility.
- Prepare School Board agenda.
- Hold Parent Action Team Meeting.
- Hold department head meeting.
- Meet with School Improvement Task Force.
- Send out tuition statements.
- Write special promotions for church bulletin inserts.
- Conduct fire drill.
- Produce school calendar.
- Produce school menu.
- Produce school newsletter.

Quarterly

- Establish test schedules.
- Publish honor roll lists.
- Conduct parent/teacher fellowships.
- Review past-due accounts.
- Evaluate quarterly testing results.
- Review quarter Administrative Team task assignments.
- Review high school student attendance.
- Approve quarterly student activities for each grade level.
- Audit student activity accounts.
- Send out special tuition letter.
- Hold parent-teacher conferences following each grading period.
- Clear out the "Lost but Found" collection.

Plan End-of-Year Procedures

Closing school at the end of the school term begins weeks in advance of the closing day. There are three important time frames: the last week of classes; the week after school closes; and the weeks that follow.

Specific tasks within each of these time segments will vary from school to school. Accomplishing these tasks requires cooperation of faculty, staff, and yes, the students themselves.

Prepare for the Last Week of Classes

Some parents, students and teachers advocate ending school early and doing away with the last week because of how unprofitable it seems. Unfortunately, regardless of when school ends, there will always be a last week.

Preparing for a hassle free last week of school requires careful forethought without which "the school may unravel and simply fall apart."[12] Unless carefully planned and executed, faculty and staff will have their work cut out for them "just trying to hold the roof on." The following strategies may be just what the doctor ordered.

1   Prepare a detailed plan for the last week of school by using a team approach, including representative parents, teachers, support staff and students. Avoid all unnecessary details that are of negligible value. Using a computer-based calendar system, such as *Calendar Creator Plus*, will allow you to build as detailed a schedule as is deemed essential for the week.

2   Schedule classes right up to the time for final exams. Finals should be as close to the end of school as possible. Students usually conclude "once finals are taken, school for that class is over."

3   Arrange a finals schedule that would allow sufficient time to complete finals as well as checking books, final projects, equipment turn in, etc. Excuse students from attending school when they have no finals scheduled.

4   Issue a check-out form for each individual student that passes from class to class. This form is taken to each class period. Require period teachers to sign the form as verification that the student has been properly checked out. At the end of the week, the last period teacher collects the forms to see that they are complete. Once the check-out form is completed, the student is dismissed. Unless properly checked out, students will not receive any report card or be promoted to the next grade [CSRK 10.9].

5   Establish a writing policy to handle requests for early dismissal. Avoid any early dismissals. Once this door is opened, it is very difficult to shut without hurt feelings.

6   Prepare a comprehensive checklist for teachers and support staff, for example, secretaries, cafeteria workers, custodians, librarians, etc. Arrange the checklist by topics, such as: report cards and grades, curriculum, classroom tasks, etc. [CSRK 10.10].

7   Conduct the final awards assembly. Distribute awards, name honor rolls, scholarships, special achievements, etc. Issue student privilege cards to be used the next year. This provides an added incentive to re-enroll. Invite parents to the assembly. Hold it in the late afternoon so students can be dismissed following the close of the assembly. The

presence of parents usually will help maintain an orderly assembly. (See *Sowing in Excellence* for further ideas on awards programs.)

8   Organize next year's safety patrol.

9   Conduct class elections for the following year. Having the new officers available over the summer provides an opportunity for class planning. Use the officers throughout the summer to help follow-up on non-returning students as well as to welcome new students and conduct building tours.

10   Conduct PTF elections for new officers. Hold the first executive board meeting before school closes.

Plan for the Week After School Closes

It is not unusual for faculty to spend two to three days following the last day of school to complete their many closing tasks. For example:

1   Conduct a final inventory of books, curriculum guides and resource materials. Although many teachers may be returning, it is a good idea to collect these materials just in case there are changes in teaching assignments over the summer; teachers who were planning on returning may make other plans.

2   Require all requests for teacher room changes, teaching assignments and extra duty to be submitted in writing [CSRK 10.11]. If possible, make room changes before teachers leave for the summer.

3   Request all teachers to complete an end-of-year curriculum review. In the review request suggestions for improvement for the next year [CSRK 10.12].

4   Ask teachers to submit a final list of students recommended for summer school or make-up work [CSRK 10.13]. Elementary teachers should prepare a summer review calendar for each child. This will help lessen the loss of learning that occurs over the three months of summer vacation.

5   Make final preparations for summer school. Announce summer school no later than three weeks before school closes so that parents can plan their summer schedule.

6   Conduct special conferences with parents whose children are asked not to return next year [CSRK 10.14].

7   Once room assignments are finalized for next year, ask teachers to prepare first-day bulletin boards with displays and board materials. This saves valuable teacher time when school reconvenes in the fall. Also, select a few rooms (at least one room at each level–kindergarten, 1-3, 4-5, 7-8, 9-12) and prepare them for display to be shown during school tours conducted for prospective parents. A pleasant classroom, ready for students, will leave a very positive impression that will definitely boost enrollment.

8   Conduct a final staff meeting. Consider an early luncheon on the last day the teachers are present. Include the entire staff. This is a good time to reflect on a job well done, give staff opportunity to share high points of the year and summer plans. It is also a good time to recognize and appreciate those who have given of themselves and will not be returning next year. A positive farewell is good for everyone, even those who are not being asked to return.

Prepare for the Weeks that Follow

Most of the students and parents (and some staff) wonder what a school administrator does all summer once the teachers are gone: simple, prepare for next year. There are always parents to see, tours to conduct, curricula to review, policies to revise, professional course work to complete, handbooks to re-write, and the list goes on and on. In fact, the summer is one the busiest times for an administrator. Unlike most public schools, the Christian school is generally open year around. In addition to tasks already mentioned, consider the following:

1   Arrange vacation schedules for office staff. Since the school should be open all summer and when secretarial staff are not available, use trained parent volunteers, or recently graduated seniors to conduct tours, mail applications, answer phones, etc.

2   Complete a list of custodial and maintenance summer tasks—building repairs, renovations, equipment repairs, etc.

3   Work on student recruitment. The major focus during the summer is on building student enrollment. Some of these activities include:

- Sending out a special parent letter who have children at various grades encouraging enrollment.

- Telephoning families from the sponsoring church congregation who will have school age children.

- Conducting personal tours of the building

- Interviewing prospective students and their parents

- Following up on all possible contacts (See *Recruiting Strategies for Christian Schools* for more recruiting suggestions).

4   Interviewing prospective faculty and staff for the next year.

Pitfalls to Avoid

1. Failing to set reasonable termination times for all activities. It is a good idea to involve students, parents, teachers and administrators in establishing a "reasonable time." A general guide is the younger the child, the earlier the termination. No elementary activity should go beyond 10:00 p.m. and no junior high or high school activity beyond

11:30 p.m. Adjourn evening club meetings no later than 9:00 p.m. This will help increase participation and support of both teachers and parents.

2. Failing to properly train sponsors. Educate class sponsors to view student activities and sponsorships not as an extra, undesirable assignment, but an opportunity to minister to the needs of students. Time spent in formulating descriptions and expectations will help remove confusion and misperceptions of sponsor responsibilities.

3. Not having clearly defined guidelines for students who work. Over the years, an increasing number of high school students are holding outside jobs and many are working long hours each week. It is not unusual for some students to work in order to pay their own tuition. There are times when student jobs interfere with school attendance, homework, involvement in class activities, and in some cases, a student's health.

The following guidelines will help working teens keep their job and school in proper balance:

- Limit part-time jobs to 15 to 20 hours per week.
- Require students to complete an off-campus job agreement form. Include name, address and phone number of employer, work schedules, current grades and approval of parents and counselor or administrator [CSRK 10.15].
- Establish a standard of "all passing grades" prior to parent approval.
- Don't allow a student's job to interfere with school attendance.

Before you know it, the summer will be over and you will be awaiting the start of a new school year, wiser and better prepared than the year before, expecting God to make Himself strong on your behalf.

Father, we thank You for the opportunity to establish a Christian school ministry. Allow this school to be one that will bring forth a new generation of students who will move in and take over the schools, churches, universities and corporations and will effectively minister to hurting people. You said they would be for signs and wonders. We call these results forth, in the name of Jesus. Amen.

"For the eyes of the Lord run to and fro throughout the whole earth, to show himself strong in the behalf of them whose heart is perfect toward him..." 2 Chronicles 16:9.

Christian School Resource Kit

Endnotes

1   Edward F. DeRoche. *How School Administrators Solve Problems.* Englewood Cliffs, NJ: Prentice Hall, Inc., 1985, p. 79.

2   William V. Hicks and Marshall C. Jameson . *The Elementary School Principal at Work.* Englewood Cliffs, NJ: Prentice Hall, Inc. 1957, p. 18.

3   Fred B. Chernow and Carol Chernow. *Classroom Discipline And Control: 101 practical techniques.* West Nyack, NY: Parker Publishing Co., Inc., 1981, p. 18.

4   Hicks and Jameson, *op. cit.*, p. 2.

5   Adapted from DeRoche, *op. cit.*, p. 79.

6   *What Works: Research about Teaching and Learning.* Washington, DC: U.S. Department of Education, 1986, p. 61.

7   Byron W. Hansford. *Guidebook for School Principals.* New York, NY: The Ronald Press Company, 1961, p. 87.

8   DeRoche, *op. cit.* p. 273

9   Edward F. DeRoche. *An Administrator's Guide for Evaluating Programs and Personnel.* 2nd Edition. Boston, MA: Allyn and Bacon, Inc., 1981, p. 170.

10 Hansford, *op. cit.*, p. 85.

11 Hicks and Johnson, *op. cit.*, p. 6.

12   Robert D. Ramsey. *Secondary Principal's Survival Guide*. Englewood Cliffs, NJ: Prentice Hall, Inc. 1992.

References

Demuth, Dennis M. "Student Constitution." Tulsa, OK: DEL Publications, 1985; (918) 749-2157.

Schindler Jr., Claude E. *Sowing For Excellence*. Whittier, CA: Association of Christian Schools International, 1987.

Computer Software

Calendar Creator Plus. Power Up Software, P.O. Box 7600, San Mateo, CA 94403; (800) 851-1917.

Personal Calendar by Fun Stuff in *The PC SIG Encyclopedia of Shareware*. 4th Edition. Sunnyvale, CA: PC-SIG, Inc., 1991.

Priority Manager. Resource Associates, 19 West First Street, Edmond, OK 73034; (405) 348-7540.

Tickler. Olsen Outdoors, 68 Hartwell Avenue, Littleton, MA, 01460.

Top Priority. Power up Software, P.O. Box 7600, San Mateo, CA 94403; (800) 851-1917.

APPENDIX A

Starting A New Christian School Survey

The following is a review list for new Christian schools. Answer each of the following questions with a "Yes" or "No" by circling the appropriate letter. Your responses will give a measure of the amount of work needing to be accomplished in establishing your new school. An established school can use the review list to check to see that all items have been covered.

1. Y N Do you have a clear understanding of your philosophy of education?

2. Y N Have you checked the state laws concerning the establishment of private schools?

3. Y N Do you know what the county and state building and safety laws require for day schools?

4. Y N Has a survey been conducted to the availability of other Christian schools in your community?

5. Y N Have you visited other Christian schools who are known for their academic and spiritual leadership?

6. Y N Are you aware of the immunization requirements for school admission?

7. Y N If you intend on serving food in your day school, have you checked with the health department to see what the requirements are?

8. Y N Have you applied for incorporation and tax exemption as a nonprofit organization?

9. Y N Have you notified local and state officials of your intent to operate a day school?

10. Y N If you are establishing your school as a ministry of a local church, have you notified the church members of this new area of ministry?

11. Y N Has an organizational structure been identified for the school?

12. Y N Has a school study committee or a school board been appointed?

13. Y N Have you appointed the chief administrator of the school?

14. Y N Have other pastors and church congregations been notified of your intent to start a Christian day school?

15. Y N Have you assessed the level of community interest?

16. Y   N   Have you written to state and national Christian school associations for information on starting Christian schools?

17. Y   N   Do you know what you are going to be using as the major core of your curriculum?

18. Y   N   Do you have samples of the curriculum on hand and available for inspection by parents and teachers?

19. Y   N   Have you sent for your curriculum guides?

20. Y   N   Have you determined the major instructional approach that you will be employing; i.e., traditional, independent study, or combined?

21. Y   N   Has a financial feasibility study been conducted?

22. Y   N   Have you determined how many grades you will offer this first year?

23. Y   N   Do you have a plan for curriculum implementation over the next five years to take into account the adding of additional grades each year?

24. Y   N   Has a survey been conducted of teacher salaries for private and public school teachers?

25. Y   N   Do you know whether of not the church will underwrite your first year?

26. Y   N   Have you found out what other Christian schools have as their tuition base?

27. Y   N   Will you be able to order your curriculum materials by the end of April?

28. Y   N   Have you conducted an assessment of furniture needs?

29. Y   N   Is there a clear understanding of how the facilities will be used by various groups (e.g., school and church)?

30. Y   N   Have you prepared an information packet for new students and parents?

31. Y   N   Have you completed plans for advertising the school in the local paper and on radio?

32. Y   N   Is the student handbook completed?

33. Y   N   Will your teachers know what is expected of them because you have already completed a Teacher Policies & Procedure Handbook?

34. Y   N   Have you investigated insurance needs of the school; for example, student accident, liability, malpractice, theft, etc.?

35. Y N Have you considered whether or not there will be a need to provide transportation?

36. Y N Are you prepared to help parents with car pooling?

37. Y N Have you checked your state laws to see whether or not the state is required to pay the transportation of students to private schools?

38. Y N Have you established a salary and benefit schedule for teachers?

39. Y N Have you identified a tuition and fee schedule?

40. Y N Have admissions requirements been established?

41. Y N If you are operating at the high school level, have you established graduation requirements?

42. Y N Have you completed your student application forms?

43. Y N Are extracurricular activities planned, such as athletics, band, yearbook, newspaper, clubs, socials, special days, etc.?

44. Y N Have you published the school calendar?

45. Y N Has the Parent-Teacher Fellowship been organized?

46. Y N Has a decision been made on the number of classes that will be offered at each grade level?

47. Y N Have you developed a school brochure?

48. Y N Has a student record system been developed?

49. Y N Have you prepared a student and teacher orientation program?

50. Y N Have you truly committed this endeavor to the Lord?

_____ Yes Responses _____ No Responses

How well did you do? Count up the number of "Yes" responses. If you have 30 or more, you are well on your way to seeing your school open on time. If you counted between 20 and 30 "Yes" responses, you should be able to make it as long as you don't faint! However, if you have less than 20 "Yes" responses by the end of April of the year that you wish to open, your have a lot of work ahead of you.

APPENDIX B

New School Checklist

The following checklist contains key ingredients in starting a Christian school ministry. The items correspond to items found in each step and are identified by page number. Review each of the following checklist items. Place a mark in the box of every item that has already been completed. Transfer those items still needing to be completed to an action plan found in Appendix C. Include in the plan the task objective (checklist item), target date for completion of each item and the person responsible for completing the item.

Step 1
Identify Your Purpose

☐ Clarify Your Reasons for Starting a School 1
☐ Adopt God's Plan for Christian Education 5

Step 2
Determine the Organizational Structure

☐ Identify the Type of Sponsorship 17
☐ Select a Governing Board 18
☐ Determine School Board Functions 18
☐ Appoint a Christian School Steering Committee 23
☐ Select a School Administrator 25
☐ Identify Selection Criteria 25
☐ Determine the Involvement of the Pastor 28
☐ Organize the School Office 29
☐ Foster a Productive Office Climate 29
☐ Train Office Aides and Volunteers 32
☐ Set Up a School Records System 32
☐ Organize Staff Records 32
☐ Establish Student Records 33
☐ Set up a General Records System 35
☐ Create a School Forms System 36
☐ Create Handbooks 36

Step 3
Assess Legal Requirements

- [ ] Establish the School as a Legal Entity 45
- [ ] Incorporate the School 45
- [ ] Seek Tax-Exempt Status 48
- [ ] Notify State and Local Officials 48
- [ ] Comply with Federal Laws 48
- [ ] Check State Statutory Requirements 54
- [ ] Examine Local and Municipal Requirements 57
- [ ] Prepare for Other Legal Issues 57

Step 4
Obtain Adequate Facilities

- [ ] Investigate Federal and State Requirements 65
- [ ] Conduct a Facilities Self-Assessment 66
- [ ] Estimate Classroom Needs 77
- [ ] Allocate Classroom Space 77
- [ ] Determine the Number of Classrooms 78
- [ ] Consider the School Site 79
- [ ] Maximize the Use of the Present Building 81
- [ ] Develop a Strong Custodial/Maintenance Team 82
- [ ] Investigate the Use of Computer Technology 83

Step 5
Determine Size of Student Body

- [ ] Identify an Enrollment Philosophy 87
- [ ] Establish Grade Levels 88
- [ ] Determine Class Size 92
- [ ] Project School Enrollment 94
- [ ] Recruit Students 96
- [ ] Finalize the Application Process 97
- [ ] Determine Admission Standards 99
- [ ] Begin to Recruit Students 102
- [ ] Keep Good Records 103

Step 8
Plan the Curriculum

Step 9
Establish Ancillary Programs

Step 10
Make Final Preparations

APPENDIX C

Christian School Action Plan

This Christian School Action Plan provides an example on how to translate what is presented in each chapter (step) to a document that can simplify the planning and improvement process. The first page contains an example of one school's plan for recruiting students. Whereas, the second page contains a blank form. The authors grant permission to schools to reproduce and enlarge this form for use in their school.

Task Statement: Summer Student Recruitment
Step: 5   **Page :** 96
Date Assigned: March 1 **Completion Date:** Aug 15
Goal Statement: To spend no less than three hours per day on active recruitment of students. The goal is to enroll no less than 100 students for the new school term.
Person(s) Responsible: John Smith, Elementary Principal
Suggested Actions And Timeline: Recruitment will include the following activities.

1. Sending a letter of invitation to families of school age children who are members of the sponsoring church.
   Timeline: April 17

3. Telephoning families of school age children who attend the sponsoring church.
   Timeline: First call by June 15. Follow-up call by Aug 1.

4. Present a two to five minute presentation in each Sunday school class—children, youth and adults. Be prepared with information packets.
   Timeline: Each Sunday starting in May until all classes have been visited.

5. Sending out a letter to each preschool program director inviting them to provide information packets to prospective parents interested in a Christian day school.
   Timeline: May 15.

6. Setting up a contact log to effectively track each prospective student.
   Timeline: March 1.

7. Being available at the information table before and after church services.
   Timeline: Every Sunday starting in April.
   Reporting: Present a weekly report to the pastor and school board.

CHRISTIAN SCHOOL ACTION PLAN

Task Assignment: **Step:_____**   **Page: _____**

_____

_____

Date Assigned: _____ Completion Date: _____

Goal Statement:

_____

_____

Person Responsible:

_____

Suggested Actions and Timelines:

Action 1:

_____

_____
Timeline:

Action 2:

_____

_____
Timeline:

Action 3:

_____

_____
Timeline:

Action 4:

_____

_____
Timeline:

Action 5:

_____

_____
Timeline:

Reporting:

_____

INDEX

357